HANDLING

FEDERAL ESTATE

and

GIFT TAXES

LAW   PRACTICE   PROCEDURE

BY

HOMER I. HARRIS

1966 CUMULATIVE SUPPLEMENT

BY

JOSEPH RASCH

Of the
Publisher's Editorial Staff

Mount Kisco, N. Y.
BAKER, VOORHIS & CO., INC.
1966

TABLE OF STATUTES, REGULATIONS AND RULINGS

(References are to sections)

INTERNAL REVENUE CODE OF 1954

MISCELLANEOUS STATUTES PUBLIC LAWS AND REVENUE ACTS

ESTATE TAX REGULATIONS

(See Appendix B, this supplement, for text of regulations)

GIFT TAX REGULATIONS

(See Appendix C, this supplement, for text of regulations)

HANDLING FEDERAL ESTATE AND GIFT TAXES

6   [Harris Tax Supp]

TABLE OF STATUTES

TREASURY DECISIONS

TABLE OF CASES

(References are to sections)

TABLE OF CASES

CHAPTER 1

GENERAL PRINCIPLES

New sections added:
§ 9A. Rulings of the Internal Revenue Service.
§ 9B. Rulings And Determination Letters Available to Individual Taxpayer.

§ 2. Nature.

p. 3, n. 7. Vested contract rights to accumulated undeclared dividends on preferred stockholdings are properly to be considered in valuing for estate tax purposes stock in decedent's wholly owned corporation holding such preferred shares. However, the arrearages of dividends are not in themselves assets of decedent's estate, and when, after liquidation of the close corporation, and distribution of the preferred stock to the beneficiaries of decedent's estate, the preferred dividends are declared and paid, the recipients of such dividends may not treat the dividends as return of capital, but must treat them as income. Boyle v United States (1964) 232 F Supp 543 (DC NJ).

§ 5. Statutory Construction.

p. 7, n. 13. The Internal Revenue Code of 1954 was enacted as a statute, 68A Stat 1, and the division of sections of Title 26 USC is identical with the statute. The codification in Title 26 USC of earlier Revenue Acts was enacted into law by Act of Feb 10, 1939 c 2, 53 Stat 1. Prior codifications of earlier acts, as appearing in 26 USC, may establish prima facie the laws of the United States, by 1 USC § 204(a), which was itself enacted as positive law in 1947, 61 Stat 633.

18

Sec 6 of the Act of Feb 10, 1939 specifically provides that no inference is to be drawn of legislative intent from the classification and arrangement of the code sections, and outlines, cross references, or descriptive matter relating to the contents shall not have legal effect.

Renstrom v United States, 220 F Supp 688 (DC D Neb) where heading of subsection of the Internal Revenue Code of 1954, although as the court said, not technically part of the statute, was found to have some probative value in interpreting the statute.

§ 6. Law Applicable.

p. 8, n. 15. Where the state courts have not yet construed a provision affecting a spouse's allowance for maintenance the federal court should examine the best evidence and the most persuasive data, and in determining the intention of the legislature consider the type of non-judicial data that is considered by the state court itself. Bookwalter v Phelps (1963) 325 F2d 186 (CA 8).

Whited v United States (1963) 219 F Supp 947 (DC WD La), where in the absence of a state court decision determining the extent of a husband's statutory right to revoke gifts of various kinds of property to his wife, and of binding state court precedents applying the code provisions, the District Court itself interpreted the Louisiana Code.

Judgments held by decedent against his brother, who was administrator of the estate, are enforceable obligations to be included in determining the value of decedent's taxable estate though omitted from administrator's accounting and accepted by state court decree. The decree had been entered without a hearing, and on agreement of sister, who had excepted to the omission of the judgments, but withdrew her objections upon payment by brother representing her share of the judgments, plus interest and less the estate tax on the resulting increase in value of the estate. Hagenlocher v Comm (1964) 42 TC 1015, No. 80.

State court decision holding the partial release of a general power of appointment to be invalid was accepted as an authoritative exposition of state law, though the tax court refused to "say" that it was bound by the decision, on the basis of the cumulative effect of the following considerations: (1) the New York Supreme court has general jurisdiction and its decisions are precedents throughout the State; (2) such court had jurisdiction over the parties and the subject matter and its adjudication was binding on the parties; (3) the CIR was aware of the proceeding; (4) the opinion was a considered one, which the tax court could not with "confidence" call erroneous; (5) the result, while qualifying the appointive fund for the marital deduction in donor's estate, would also have tax consequences in estate of donee, and there were indication of her intent to exercise the general power. Bosch v Comm (1964) 43 TC 120, No. 11.

Decree of Connecticut probate court is not binding on a federal court in construing federal revenue laws. Second Nat. Bank of New Haven v United States (1965) 351 F2d 489 (CA 2).

p. 8, n. 2. Estate taxes will be apportioned and charged against remainders of inter-vivos trust with situs in Illinois, since the law of Illinois, the state of situs and of the forum, as found by the court, refers apportionment questions to the law of the domicile of decedent. Doetsch v Doetsch (1962) 312 F2d 323 (the court noted that New York and New Jersey refer to the law of decedents domicile, while Massachusetts and Minnesota apply the rules of the state of situs of trust).

Dauphin Deposit Trust Co. (McCormick) v McGinnis (1963) 324 F 2d 458 (CA 3) (terms of testamentary trust construed in light of Pennsylvania law in order to determine remaindermen).

Old Kent Bank & Trust Co. (Campbell) v United States (1964) 232 F Supp 970 (DC WD Mich), sustaining the decision of the fiduciaries of decedent's estate and of an inter vivos trust with respect to the apportionment of estate taxes to the trust assets and the exoneration of the share of the surviving spouse, where such decision, considerably increasing the value of the marital gift, was reflected in filed accountings, was consented to by beneficiaries with adverse interests, was approved by state probate court decree unappealed from, and was in accord with the terms of the testamentary gift of a percentage of the estate "before deduction of taxes". A testamentary provision directing payment of all estate taxes from the residue of the probate estate would not be given effect because in the events that occurred the residue was wholly insufficient, and the court, finding no governing Michigan statute or judicial precedent, applied the rule of equitable apportionment.

Absent statutory provision or conclusive judicial precedent directing the apportionment of federal estate taxes, the intestate share of a surviving spouse, qualifying in its entirety for the marital deduction, will be treated as excluded from the gross taxable estate and so will not be required to share the burden of the estate taxes. First National Bank of Topeka (Graham) v United States (1964) 233 F Supp 19 (DC Kan).

State court declaratory judgment holding decedent's interests under inter vivos trust indentures not vested, entered in proceedings brought after trustees had refused demand of executrix that assets be turned over to estate, as conclusive in determining that the interests were not taxable in decedent's estate, and not collusive in any sense, where all parties were represented, the position of the trustees and the special guardian for the infant beneficiaries was fully briefed, and the result was the continuance of the trusts for the benefit of decedent's children, instead of distribution of the assets to the widow.

Disposing of government arguments that the decree was collusive the court pointed out that although the Commissioner had not been advised of the state actions, the known policy of his office was against taking part in such state court cases, and there was evidence that the existence of the trusts was disclosed in the estate tax return. It was admitted that there were no Texas precedents, hence the court action was the only course open to the

trustees to determine the intentions of the settlor of the trusts. Since the court's opinion was duly considered, and the result reasonable, the failure of executrix to appeal was not significant; the action of her counsel at the trial where he in effect did little more than state the position of the widow-executrix was to be commanded as an effort to avoid the injection of bitterness into what might become a family dispute over property. Farish v United States (1964) 233 F Supp 220 (DC SD Tex).

Where testamentary trustees, on death of the life beneficiary (the decedent in the tax proceeding), bring an accounting proceeding in the state court having jurisdiction (New York Surrogate's Court) joining all necessary parties, and court decrees that a predeceased remainderman had (by general residuary clause in will) exercised a power to appoint his remainder in favor of one other than decedent, such decree, not shown to be erroneous under state law, is binding though uncontested and non-adversary. The trustees could not properly discharge their trust without such a will construction proceeding, and the decision of the local court would be given great weight. Stevens v Comm (1964) 23 TCM 921, TC Memo 1964-154.

§ 7. Domicile; Residence.

p. 9, n. 4. See §§ 185, 186, this supplement.

§ 8. Construction of Will.

p. 10, n. 10. Frazier v United States (1963) 322 F2d 221 (CA 5), where nature of interests created by decedent's father's will was determined under applicable state law.

§ 9. Authority for Proceedings.

p. 11, n. 16. Treasury Regulations consistently construed and applied by the courts, coupled with repeated reenactment of the legislation thus construed, "bespeaks congressional approval" of such Regulations. Senft v United States (1963) 319 F2d 642 (CA 3).

p. 11, n. 17. See § 168, this supplement.

§ 9A. (New) Rulings of the Internal Revenue Service.

The Secretary of the Treasury, or by delegation from him the Commissioner of Internal Revenue[18], issues various rulings[19], opinions and decisions. These may be of general application, or may apply to a specific fact situation, as where a ruling has been issued, perhaps by letter, to an individual taxpayer[20] and is then published, without identifying the taxpayer, as a matter of general interest.[1]

When these rulings are consistent with the Internal Revenue Code they have value as guides to the administrative interpretation placed on the Code by the Internal Revenue Service (abbreviated as IRS), the agency of the Treasury Department charged with the administration of the Tax Laws. These rulings also deal with IRS procedure, and are guides to the methods of obtaining review or reconsideration of a specific taxpayer's case.

Among the pronouncements of the Secretary of the Treasury or the IRS are the following:

Treasury Decisions[2] which are issued under the authority or with the approval of the Secretary of the Treasury[3]; like the Regulations they often promulgate or amend, they commit the IRS to the legal interpretation, unless inconsistent with the IRC.[4]

Revenue Rulings are official interpretations issued by the IRS, published for the information and guidance of taxpayers and Service officials.[5] They may be of a general nature or may be addressed to specific fact situations. These and other "rulings", including the unpublished ones issued to individual taxpayers, are indicative of IRS policy, and as such may be applied by the courts even though not directed to the actual facts of a specific case.[6]

In his concurring opinion in a leading case[7] Mr. Justice Frankenthaler cites and discusses a number of kinds of "rulings", including Office Decisions ("OD"); Solicitor's Opinions ("Sol Op"); General Counsel Memoranda ("GCM"); Revenue Rulings, and an unpublished Special Ruling, all as bearing on the administrative practice of the Service in applying a particular Code section.

In the absence of estoppel Rulings do not however generally bind the Commissioner. As products of his legal staff they are, per se, to be given no more effect than legal opinions in general.[8]

An unpublished ruling[9] does not commit the IRS, when relied on by a taxpayer unrelated to the one to whom issued[10], but a ruling conforming to the Code when issued, and relied on by the taxpayer it is addressed to, is binding on the IRC[11] at least as to the points covered.

Delegation Orders record the extent of authority delegated by the Secretary of the Treasury to specific officials. They may be of importance where a question is raised as to the right of an IRS employee to take a specific action, and as to binding effect on the Commissioner,[12] of the procedure adopted.

The *Rules on Administrative Procedure*[13] are issued by the Commissioner without hearing or the express approval of the Secretary.[14] Though they are "directory" as instructions to the Service, they are not binding on the government when disregarded by a Service official.[15] They may be amended by a

Revenue Procedure,[16] which may also deal with narrower procedural points.

The Commissioner also publishes from time to time in the Internal Revenue Bulletin announcements of his acquiescence or non-acquiescence[17] in Tax

Court and Federal Court decisions or parts thereof. While these are no more than valuable indications of Service policy, they may be honored by the Courts to the extent that their issuance may constitute an equitable estoppel preventing additional assessments against a taxpayer who has relied on them[18].

Under the Code[19] the Secretary or his delegate may prescribe the extent to which a regulation or ruling shall be applied without retroactive effect.

[18] As a practical matter the Secretary of the Treasury and the Commissioner act through their staffs, consisting mostly of lawyers. This is not unimportant, since in many cases the action taken is actually the issuance of a legal opinion, which is eventually passed on by other lawyers sitting as judges. Such rulings are treated in a different spirit from decisions of an elected official or acts of a legislative body.

[19] The authority to make rules and regulations is given by IRC § 7805 to the Secretary of the Treasury "or his delegate". The Regulations, § 301.7805-1, authorize the Commissioner to prescribe rules and regulations "with the approval of the Secretary". Whether or not a relevant regulation or ruling was issued by a properly delegated official with required Secretarial approval may therefore be important.

[20] Rules on Adm. Proc. § 601.201 prescribe methods by which an individual taxpayer may request and obtain rulings on a specific problem. See § 9B this supplement.

[1] Revenue Rulings are published by the IRS in its weekly Internal Revenue Bulletin (abbreviated as IRB).

22

Citations to the IRB are by year, a number representing the week of issue, and the page number. They may also be cited to the Cumulative Bulletin ("Cum Bull" or "CB"), the semi-annual reissue of IRB.

[2] Cited as "TD" followed by a serial number. These numbers run back to the first Decision, which antedated the Estate Tax Law. Treasury Decisions in recent years have been published in the IRB. TDs appear also in the Federal Register ("FR") and the Code of Federal Regulation ("CFR").

[3] IRC § 7805; Adm Reg § 301-.7805-1.

[4] Sims v United States (1958) 252 F2d 434 (CA 4), affd 359 US 108, 3 L ed 2d 667, 79 S Ct 641.

[5] *Revenue Rulings* are cited "Rev Rul", followed by an official number consisting of the year of issue (last two digits only) and an annual serial number, with reference to the Internal Revenue weekly or cumulative bulletin. They are generally also published in the Federal Register and the Code of Federal Regulations.

[6] Kaiser v United States (1958) 262 F2d 367 (CA 7), affd United States v Kaiser (1960) 363 US 299, 4 L ed 2d 1233, 80 S Ct 1204.

[7] United States v Kaiser (1960) 363 US 299, 305; 4 L ed 2d 1233, 1237; 80 S Ct 1204.

[8] Kaiser v United States (1958) 262 F2d 367 (CA 7) (an "OD"); Keystone Automobile Club v Comm (1950) 181 F2d 402 (CA 3), (a "GCM"); Miller v Comm (1964) 327 F2d 846 (CA 2), (an "IT").

[9] The method of obtaining such rulings, in estate tax cases, is discussed in § 9B, this supp, and in gift tax cases in § 415A, this supp.

[10] Pomeroy Cooperative Grain Co. v Comm (1961) 288 F2d 326 (CA 8). Minchin v Comm (1964) 335 F2d 30 (CA 2).

[Harris Tax Supp]

[11] Time Oil Co. v Comm (1958) 258 F2d 237 (CA 9); HSD Co. v Kavanagh (1951) 191 F2d 831 (CA 6), where a new Commissioner reversed the ruling of a prior incumbent, no new facts having been shown.

[12] Delegation Orders are cited as "Del O" and are published in the Federal Register and the IRB.

[13] Rules on Administrative Procedure may be cited as "Reg § 601" followed by a section number.

[14] The commissioner promulgated these rules under 5 USC § 22, not in IRC § 7805. They were originally published in 20 FR 4621 and appear in 26 CPR part 600 et seq.

[15] Luhring v Glotzbach (1960) 304 F2d 560 (CA 4).

[16] Revenue Procedures are cited "Rev Proc" by year (first two digits omitted) and annual serial number, and IRB reference.

[17] Acquiescences and non-acquiescences may be cited as "Acq" by year and number, with reference to the IRB.

[18] City Loan & Savings Co. v United States (1959) 177 F Supp 843 (DC ND Oh), affd 287 F2d 612 (CA 6). The Commissioner in the Cum Bulls customarily states, in listing acquiescences and non-acquiescences, that they are to be relied on by the IRS as precedents.

[19] IRC § 7805(b).

§ 9B. (New) Rulings and Determination Letters Available to Individual Taxpayer.

The Internal Revenue Service is authorized to issue rulings and determination letters in response to specific inquiries addressed to it by a taxpayer or his representative.[20] A ruling is a written statement issued by

23

the National Office in Washington, D. C. and is an expression of the official interpretation or policy of the Commissioner of Internal Revenue. It establishes principles and policies in the interpretation and application of substantive tax law to a taxpayer's specific problem or inquiry.

A determination letter is a written statement issued by a district director in response to an inquiry addressed to him which involves the application of clearly established rules as set forth in the statute, Treasury decisions or regulations, or rulings, opinions or court decisions published in the Internal Revenue Bulletin.[1]

Rulings and determinations will not issue on whether or not a transaction is in contemplation of death[2]; nor will they be issued after an estate tax return has been filed, and, ordinarily if a gift tax return has been filed and the period of limitation on assessment has not expired with respect thereto.[3]

[20] The procedure is set forth in Rules on Adm Proc § 601.201.

Requests for rulings made by an attorney should be accompanied by a copy of a power of attorney to him, and should be addressed to the Commissioner of Internal Revenue, Washington, D. C. 20224. If such request is not accompanied by copy of a power of attorney, and a copy is not furnished on request, the ruling will be mailed to taxpayer. Ann 63–110, IRB 1963–43 p. 29, summarizing

24

Rules Adm Proc 601.502, IRB 1963–43 p. 13.

The CIR has made provision for issuance of advance rulings on the basis of a "two part" request, where in addition to the usual complete statement of facts the taxpayer submits a summary of the facts he believes should control. The ruling may be based on these facts, if they are accepted, but the IRS reserves the right to seek further information or rule on the basis of a more complete statement of facts. Rev Proc 65–8, IRB 1965–12, p. 17.

[1] Decisions of the Supreme Court of the United States, and sometimes of other courts are published from time to time in the Bulletin.

[2] Rev Proc 64–31 Sec 3.01 subd 17; IRB 64–30, p. 14.

[3] Rev Proc 62–28, 1962 IRB 47 p 7.

§ 10. Applicable Statutes.

p. 12, n. 4. Shedd, 237 F2d 347, cited in the note to the text, upheld a deficiency assessment based on the value of a portion trust required by the 1939 Code to be included in the taxable estate; the additional estate tax paid was later refunded in accordance with the Technical Changes Act of 1958, and thus was no longer (after being refunded) a tax paid with respect to a prior transfer for purposes of credit in the transferee's estate. Shedd v Comm (1963) 320 F2d 638 (CA 9).

§ 11. Definitions; Gross Estate; Taxable Estate; Executor; Transferee.

p. 12, n. 5. IRC § 2031 was amended, effective October 16, 1962, to require the inclusion in the value of the gross estate of a decedent of all property, wherever situated, including real and tangible personal property. The amendment is effective in the case of decedents dying on or after July 1, 1964 as to all such property. As to decedents dying after October 16, 1962 and before July 1, 1964 it applies to property acquired by decedent (or by his donor, if acquired by gift) after January 1, 1962.

p. 13, n. 11. Effective October 23, 1963, Reg §§ 20.0–2(b), 20.2014–2, 20.2031–1, 20.2033–1 and 20.2053-7 were amended to reflect the removal of the exemption of real and tangible personal property situated outside the United States.

§ 12. Definitions; Citizens; Residents; Nonresidents Not Citizens.

p. 13, n. 13a. Reg. 20.0–1 was amended on Jan 18, 1961 to reflect changes made in taxation of residents of possessions by IRC §§ 2208 and 2209. See §§ 185, 186, this supplement.

p. 14, n. 16b. See IRC § 2209, Reg. 20.0–1, as amended, Regs. 20–.2208–1, 20.2209–1, and §§ 185, 186, this supplement.

§ 19. Preliminary Notice; Place of Filing.

p. 20, n. 2. "In exceptional cases, application may be made to the Commissioner for permission to file in any other internal revenue district." (1963-revision of instructions to Forms 704 and 705).

§ 22. Preliminary Notice; Penalties.

p. 22, n. 7. As of March 1963 the INSTRUCTIONS to Forms 704 and 705 were revised to call attention to the criminal penalties "for failure to file and for filing a false or fraud-

ulent notice" provided by §§ 7203, 7207 and 7269 of the Code; see text § 369.

§ 24. Preliminary Notice; Nonresident Not a Citizen.

p. 23, n. 18. Form 705 set forth in text under Form No. 2 was revised in November, 1958 so as to change the phraseology of paragraph 1(b) thereof as follows:

"(b) The undersigned, on the date of the decedent's death, had active or constructive possession of property situated within the United States, or of an interest in such property, which constituted part of the decedent's gross estate within the meaning of the Estate Tax Law; . . . (the balance of this subdivision remains the same as it appears in the text)."

The instructions accompanying this form have been revised to reflect Hawaii statehood.

Add note in paragraph (a) on page 25:

. . . personal property.[18a]

[18a] The instructions to Form 705 have been amended so as to provide: "(g) For a situs of works of art, owned by a nonresident alien, which were imported into the United States for exhibition purposes, see Estate Tax Regulations." The pertinent Estate Tax Regulation is § 20.2105–1 discussed in § 186 of the text.

§ 26. Return; Statute and General Instructions.

p. 27, n. 9. Form 706 may be reproduced. Rev Proc 64–39, IRB 1964–39, 22.

§ 28. Return; Time and Place for Filing.

p. 30, n. 6. The instructions to Form 706 indicate that in exceptional cases application may be made to the commissioner for permission to file the return in an internal revenue district other than that of decedent's domicile.

p. 30, n. 7. Reg. 20.6091–1, as amended, and 20.6091.2, adopted, May 28, 1962, Appendix B, this supplement.

§ 32. Return; General Information.

Add new note in sixth line on page 35:

. . . District Director.[1a]

[1a] The general instructions to revised Form 706, see § 26, this supplement, specify that the election of alternate valuation is not valid unless made on the return within the time prescribed by law and regulations. Prior to the issuance of the revised return it was ruled that whether an election to use the alternate method of valuation has been made is to be determined from all the facts disclosed in the estate tax return, and failure to designate an election in the box on the estate tax return would not preclude an election where the executor otherwise reported alternate valuations in the appropriate schedules and computed the tax by the alternate valuation method. Rev Rul 61–128, IRB 1961–28, p. 7. However, it would seem more prudent practice to fill in the box (Item 21, general information) as required by the instructions to the revised return.

FORM NO. 3 (as revised January 1966)

1. Address of decedent at time of death (Number, street, city, State and Postal ZIP code)

....

2. State in which domiciled at time of death

....

3. Year in which the domicile was established

....

4. Place of death

....

5. Cause of death

....

6. Length of last illness

....

7. Decedent's physicians

....

    NAMES   ADDRESSES (Number, street, city, State, and Postal ZIP code)

....

8. If decedent was confined in a hospital during his last illness or within 3 years prior to his death, give name and address of hospital

. . . .

9a. Date of birth

. . . .

9b. Place of birth (City and State or country, if other than United States)

. . . .

10a. Business or occupation.

. . . .

10b. If retired, state former business or occupation

. . . .

10c. Business name

. . . .

10d. Decedent's employer identification number, if any

. . . .

10e. Business address (Number, street, city, State, and Postal ZIP code)

. . . .

11. Marital status of decedent at date of death
Married.... Single.... Legally separated....
Widow or widower.... Divorced....

12a. Name of surviving husband or wife

. . . .

12b. Social security number of surviving husband or wife

. . . .

12c. Date of marriage to surviving husband or wife

. . . .

12d. Domicile at date of marriage to surviving husband or wife

. . . .

13a. If decedent was a widow or widower, give name of deceased husband or wife

. . . .

13b. Date of death of deceased husband or wife

. . . .

14. Individuals who receive benefits from the estate (do not include charitable beneficiaries shown in Schedule N or any heir receiving less than $1,000)

Name.—Enter the name of each individual who receives benefits from the estate directly as an heir, next-of-kin, devisee or legatee or indirectly (for example, as beneficiary of a trust, shareholder of a corporation or partner of a partnership which is an heir, etc.).

Social Security Number.—If the individual has no social security number, use his taxpayer account number.

Age.—On the date of the decedent's death.

Relationship.—Include relationships by blood, marriage, or adoption or indicate NONE.

Amount.—Value all interests on the date of death or the alternate valuation date, whichever is used for estate tax purposes. The interest of each beneficiary should be valued in the same manner as it would be valued for estate or gift tax purposes. Where precise values cannot readily be determined, a reasonable approximation should be entered. The sum of the values of the interests of all unborn or otherwise unascertainable beneficiaries should be shown on the last line (all unascertainable beneficiaries).

Name	Social security number	Age	Relationship to decedent	Amount

All unascertainable beneficiaries

....

15a. Did the decedent at date of death own property in any State or country other than that of his last domicile?

                                        Yes.... No....

If "Yes" state place of ancillary probate proceedings.

15b. Name of ancillary administrator or executor

....

15c. Address of ancillary administrator or executor (Number, street, city, State and Postal ZIP code)

....

16a. Did the decedent at the time of his death have a safe deposit box held either alone or in the joint names of himself and another? Yes.... No....

If "Yes", state location

....

16b. If held jointly, give the name of the joint depositor

....

16c. Relationship of joint depositor to decedent

....

16d. If the decedent had a safe deposit box at the time of his death, indicate by schedule and item number under what schedules in this return the contents are listed

....

16e. If any of the contents of the safe deposit box are omitted from the schedules, explain fully why omitted

....

17. Did the undersigned person or persons filing return make

28   [Harris Tax Supp]

diligent and careful search for property of every kind left by the decedent? Yes.... No....

....

18. Did the same undersigned make diligent and careful search for information as to any transfers (other than outright transfers not in trust) of the value of $5,000 or more made by the decedent during his lifetime without an adequate and full consideration in money or money's worth?
Yes.... No....

....

19. Did the same undersigned make diligent and careful search for the existence of any trusts created by the decedent during his lifetime or any trusts created by other persons under which the decedent possessed any power, beneficial interest, or trusteeship? Yes.... No....

....

20a. Name of attorney representing estate, if any

....

20b. Address (Number, street, city, State and Postal ZIP code)

....

20c. Telephone No.

....

ALTERNATIVE VALUATION*

(These instructions apply only if alternate valuation is elected. For further information on this subject, see General Instructions on page 4)

....

21. An election to have the gross estate of the decedent valued as of the alternate date or dates is made by entering a check mark in the box set forth below.
.... The executor elects to have the gross estate of this decedent valued in accordance with values as of a date or dates subsequent to the decedent's death as authorized by section 2032 of the Code.

....
....

ESTATE OF ....

§ 34. Return; Failure to File; Delinquency.

p. 36, n. 10. Effective May 14, 1960, IRC, § 6659(b) (1954 Code) was amended by P. L. 86–470, to provide that the additions to tax for the late filing of estate and gift tax returns are to be assessed and collected without the issuance of a 90-day letter with the exception that an addition to tax for late filing which is attributable to a deficiency in tax will be subject to the 90-day letter procedure. For discussion of the 90-day letter procedure, see § 337B.

Penalty provision of 1939 code applies regardless of reasonable cause where no return is filed. Kamm v Comm (1963) 23 TCM 1805, TC Memo 1963–344.

p. 37, n. 15. Illness of accountant was held not to be a reasonable cause for late filings where estate was apprised that accountant had suffered a second heart attack shortly after starting to prepare the es-

tate tax return material, and that whether he prepared the return on time depended upon his health. Lewis v Comm (1963) 23 TCM 1732, TC Memo 1963–331.

p. 37, n. 17. Late filing was not excused by reliance on attorney for estate, where executor was CPA familiar with income tax laws, had participated extensively in preparing the return, and had signed the preliminary notice which indicated due date for filing and penalty for late filing. Mayer v Comm (1964) 43 TC 403, No. 34, affd 351 F2d 617.

CHAPTER 2

GROSS ESTATE

§ 38. Property Subject to Tax.

p. 45, n. 2. Where one joint owner of E bonds during his lifetime makes a gift thereof by delivering the bonds to the person named as joint owner, and confirms such intention by letter, such bonds are not includible in his estate since he had effectively parted with his economic interest in the bonds prior to his death. Silverman v McGinnes (1960) 259 F2d 731 (CA 3).

p. 45, n. 4. Where all payments to exempt retirement pension plan, with provision for death benefits, were made by decedent's employer, where plan was subject to amendment or revocation by company, and where decedent never retired, but exercised his right to appoint wife as beneficiary of death benefits, decedent had no property interest in the death benefits at time of his death, under IRC 1939 § 811(a) (similar to IRC 1954 § 2033), and the commuted value thereof was not taxable to his estate. Charleston Nat. Bank v United States (1963) 221 F Supp 271 (DC SD W Va).

§ 39. Valuation; Fair Market Value.

p. 46, n. 7. Testimony of values of film rights and rights to produce musical based on events occurring some months after decedent's death, not in corroboration of facts known or foreseeable at date of death, does not avail to upset commissioner's valuation. Pascal v Comm, 23 TCM 1766, TC Memo 1963–336.

Reg § 20.2031 1(b) was am to provide further that the fair market value of an item of property is not to be determined by the sale price of the item in a market other than that in which such item is most commonly sold to the public, taking into account the location of the item wherever appropriate. Thus, in the case of an item which is generally obtained by the public in the retail market, the fair market value of such an item of property is the price at which the item or a comparable item would be sold at retail. For example, the fair market value of an automobile, generally obtained in the retail market, is the price for which a similar automobile can be purchased by the general public, and not the price which a used car dealer would pay. (See Appendix B, this supp.)

§ 40. Valuation; Alternate; Generally.

p. 48, n. 4. Election to value under the alternate valuation method is timely exercised if return in which election is made is postmarked on or before due date or expiration of any extension of time for filing. Rev Rul 64–105, IRB 1964–13, p. 18.

p. 48, n. 8. The general instructions to revised Form 706, see § 26, this supplement, specify that the election of alternate valuation is not valid unless made on the return within the time prescribed by law and regulations. Prior to the issuance of the revised return it was ruled that whether an election to use the alternate method of valuation has been made is to be determined from all the facts disclosed in the estate tax return, and failure to designate an election in the box on the estate tax return would not preclude an election where the executor otherwise reported alternate valuations in the appropriate schedules and computed the tax by the alternate valuation method. Rev Rul 61–128, IRB 1961–28, p. 7. However, it would seem more prudent practice to fill in the box (Item 21, general information) as required by the instructions to the revised return.

§ 41. Community Property; Generally.

p. 49, n. 10. Where testator designated certain property in his wife's name as community property and other evidence tended to prove that the parties so treated it, the mere assertion that a transmutation agreement had been executed transferring such property to the wife separately was insufficient proof to bar inclusion of such property in the decedent's gross estate. Vogel v Comm (1960) 278 F2d 548 (CA 9).

§ 43. Schedule A; Real Estate; What Included.

Add new note in sixth line on page 52:

. . . of the United States.[4a]

[4a] The exclusion of real property situated outside the U. S. was removed by PL 87–834, effective generally as to decedents dying on or after July 1, 1964. As to decedents dying after October 16, 1962 and before July 1, 1964 the exclusion continues for property acquired before February 1, 1962, for interests in property under Sections 2033, 2034, 2035 (a), 2038(a), 2040, and 2041(a) ac-

32

quired before that date; and for interests acquired by gift under Sec. 2511, or from a prior decedent (including by the exercise or non-exercise of a power of appointment) where the donor or prior decedent had acquired the property, or interest, or held a power of appointment before that date.

§ 49. Schedule A; Real Estate; Valuation.

p. 61, n. 3. The instructions to Schedule A, revised Form 706, see § 26, this supplement specify that if values are based on appraisals, copies of such appraisals, *together with an explanation of the basis of the appraisals,* should be attached to the return. This is a new requirement.

p. 61, n. 5. Expenses of selling realty sold within the alternate valuation period are to be disregarded when alternate valuation of real property is based upon sales price. Pridmore v Comm (1961) 20 TCM 47, TC Memo 1961–12.

p. 61, n. 19. Value of $157000 set by three probate appraisers and executors on some 400 acres of Ohio farm land suitable for development but subject to utilities' easements was raised to $240000 by the Tax Court, which accepted estate's experienced expert witness, and rejected commissioner's, who had little, and no recent, experience. Vinson (1963) 22 TCM 280.

§ 50. Schedule A; Real Estate; Valuation; Fractional Interests.

p. 63, n. 1. Value of fractional interest in realty owned by members of a syndicate was based upon an actual sale of a fractional interest by another member of the syndicate rather than upon previous estate tax valuation of the fractional interest of a deceased member, there being no

[Harris Tax Supp]

other market. Hancock v Comm, 19 TCM 1293, TC Memo 1960–230.

p. 63, n. 3. Drybrough v United States (1962) 208 F Supp 279 (WD Ky), allowing discount of fifteen percent.

§ 52. Schedule B; Stocks and Bonds; Generally.

p. 64, n. 12. Panama Canal bonds owned by decedent which were "exempt from all taxes or duties of the United States" under applicable federal law were held includible in decedent's gross estate and not exempt from estate taxes, since the bonds as property were not being taxed. Greene v U. S. 171 F Supp 459 (Ct Cl).

§ 54. Schedule B; Stocks and Bonds; Valuation; Generally.

Add text at end of section on page 69:

Where an estate has Treasury bonds which can be applied at par in payment of the estate tax, though the bonds are quoted at less than par on the date of decedent's death, their value for estate tax purposes has been held to be at least par, whether or not such bonds are actually applied by the executor in payment of the estate tax.[18a]

[18a] Bankers Trust Co. (Ellis) v United States (1960) 284 F2d 537 CA 2); Candler, Jr. v United States (ND Ga), 303 F2d 439 (CA 5).

§ 55. Schedule B; Stocks and Bonds; Valuation; Blockage.

p. 70, n. 3. See Bartol v McGinness (1960) 185 F Supp 659 (valuation on blockage theory sustained).

§ 56. Schedule B; Stocks and Bonds; Valuation; Bid and Asked Prices.

p. 71, n. 8. Where shares of open-end publicly offered mutual funds are to be valued in the estate of a decedent dying after October 10, 1963, the offering price at applicable valuation date is to be used, less any reduction publicly available in the case of the number of shares being valued. Reg § 20.2031–8. In the case of decedents dying before October 11, 1963, the Commissioner will not disturb valuations returned at redemption values, or at mean between redemption value and offering price, although a collateral agreement may be requested providing that values so determined will be used as a tax basis by interested parties. Rev Proc 64–18, IRB 1964–17, p. 31.

§ 58. Schedule B; Stocks and Bonds; Valuation; Sales Price Not Reflecting Value.

p. 72, n. 13. Where decedent's 25,000 shares in family controlled company represented about 19% of the stock, and about 1/3 of the stock was he in small lots mostly by relatives and employees, all from the Kouts, Indiana, area where the corporation ran the principal industry, sales of small lots to such persons at $10 a share did not determine the price; considering a book value of $7.71 per share with assets at appraised value, and of $4.81 per share with assets at depreciated values, a promised dividend rate of 40¢ a share, the size of decedent's block, and fact that some shares had been taken by creditors at $8.65, the court found $8 per share to be the fair market value of the stock. Heinold v Comm (1965) 24 TCM 26, TC Memo 1965–6.

§ 59. Schedule B; Stocks and Bonds; Valuation; Close Corporation.

p. 73, n. 1. Rev Rul 54–77, IRB 1954–1 CB 187 has been superseded by Rev Rul 59–60, IRB 1959–9, p. 8 which explains and restates the factors to be considered in evaluating closely held stock.

p. 73, n. 2. Valuation of closely-held grain elevator stock was arrived at by averaging the following factors: (1) book value; (2) future earning power; and (3) dividend paying capacity and discounting the resulting weighted average by 10% to reflect the unusual lack of marketability. Bader v United States, 172 F Supp 833 (SD Ill) (1959).

Central Trust Co. v United States (1962) 305 F2d 393 (Ct Cls).

p. 74, n. 6. Generally consideration is given to "earnings" in valuing operating companies, whereas in valuing securities underlying the holding type of company, primary consideration is given to "assets". Levenson v Comm (1960) 282 F2d 581 (CA 3).

p 74, n. 7. Comparison corporations must have same type of stock issued and outstanding. Levenson v Comm (1960) 282 F2d 581 (CA 3).

p. 74, n. 9. Gibbs v Comm, 18 TCM 178, TC Memo 1959–38.

p. 74, n. 14. Minority interest in real estate corporation valued at 35 percent of market value of assets. Drybrough v United States (1962) 208 F Supp 279 (WD Ky).

Obermer v United States (1964) 238 F Supp 29 (DC Hawaii) (investment company taxed as personal holding company, owned in equal shares by decedent and surviving spouse).

p. 74, n. 15. Obermer v United States (1964) 238 F Supp 29 (DC Hawaii) (investment company taxed as personal holding company with retirement of debt a charge on income and with large potential capital gains liability).

p. 74, n. 16. Tuck v United States (1959) 172 F Supp 890 (ND Cal), affd 282 F2d 405 (CA 9).

p. 74, n. 19. Stock in closely held corporation cannot be valued by any inflexible formula but by one tailored to the particular case based on a discriminating consideration of all information bearing upon an enlightened prediction of the future. Thus capitalization at ten times annual earnings was rejected as sole determinant of value in view of trend toward lower earnings. Snyder v United States (1961) 285 F2d 857 (CA 4).

p. 75, n. 5. See Levenson v Comm (1960) 282 F2d 581 (CA 3), holding that a ten-year period should be used since it would compensate for the undue increase in earnings resulting from the Korean war.

§ 62. Schedule B; Stocks and Bonds; Valuation; Subject to Option or Contract to Purchase.

p. 87, n. 13. Where family-owned corporation purchased decedent's stock during her lifetime with the price payable in installments or until her death, the Commissioner was unsuccessful in his attempt to tax the amount remaining unpaid as of decedent's death upon the theory that the purchase price had been transferred with a retained right to future enjoyment of that portion of the purchase price for the period beyond her death, there being no evidence of possession and control at any time of the entire purchase price by decedent or that corporation was able to pay the entire purchase price or that it had been set aside. Cain v Comm (1961) 37 TC 185, No. 24. Acquiescence, IRB 1962–41, p. 6.

p. 87, n. 14. Where partnership agreement provided that remaining partners had right to purchase an outgoing partner's interest at a one-third discount and a deceased partner's interest at full value, deceased partner's interest was valued for estate tax purposes at full value, since death terminated the option to sell at a reduced price, and sealed the fact that the estate's partnership interest would be purchased or redeemed at full market value. United States v Land (1962) 303 F2d 170 (CA 5).

Citizens Fidelity Bank & Trust Co. v United States (1962) 209 F Supp 254 (WD Ky), wherein option given to sons controlled valuation of stock.

p. 88, n. 20. Where decedent's stock in family owned corporation is not required to be offered for first refusal at book value unless to be transferred out of family, such value does not necessarily represent the maximum value for estate tax purposes, but agreements making such requirement must be considered in determining such value, as well as rights of 50% of stock to require liquidation, and the degree of control, or lack of it, inherent in decedent's 15% interest. Mathews v United States (1964) 226 F Supp 1003 (DC ED NY).

§ 63. Schedule B; Stocks and Bonds; Interest; Dividends.

p. 89, n. 5. Provident Trust Co. v United States, 170 F Supp 74 (ED Pa) (1959).

In the determination of the value of a decedent's gross estate, dividends declared before death, on stock includible in the gross estate, payable to stockholders of record after

the decedent's death, must be considered in making an adjustment in the ex-dividend quotation of the stock at the date of decedent's death. But such dividends are not included in the gross estate under the alternate method of valuing the gross estate either as a separate asset or as an adjustment of the ex-dividend quoted value of the stock as of one year or as of some intermediate date.

Under the alternate valuation method, stock includible in the gross estate and selling ex-dividend is to be valued at its ex-dividend quoted selling price as of one year after the date of the decedent's death or at any intermediate valuation date, increased by the amount of dividends declared on the stock during the alternate valuation period payable to stockholders of record subsequent to the date which is one year after the date of the decedent's death or such intermediate date. No part of the value determined is to be deemed excluded property in determining the value of the gross estate. Rev Rul 60–124, IRB 1960–14, p. 12.

p. 89, n. 6. Reg § 20.2031–2(j) was redesignated as § 20.2031–2(i), June 14, 1965, TD 6826.

§ 69. Schedule D; Insurance; Defined.

p. 96, n. 6. Comm v Noel (1965) 380 US 678, 14 L ed 2d 159, 85 S Ct 1238 (proceeds of flight insurance policies payable on the accidental death of insured).

p. 96, n. 7. Rev Rul 54–552 cited in the note to the text was modified by Rev Rul 65–69, IRB 1965–11, p. 21, to conform with the decision in Fidelity-Philadelphia Trust Co. (Haines) v Smith (1958) 356 US 274, 2 L ed 2d 765, 78 S Ct 730, which case decided that where decedent was divested of all interest in a single premium life insurance policy, bought in connection with an annuity, the policy proceeds were not includible in his estate, since the annuity payments were not conditioned on the continued existence of the contract of life insurance.

p. 96, n. 11. Gratuity Fund proceeds payable to beneficiaries designated by deceased security exchange member were deemed insurance proceeds. Moyer v Comm, 32 TC 515, No. 47 (1959).

§ 70. Schedule D; Insurance; Statutory Provisions.

Add note at end of paragraph 2 (a) on page 97:

. . . total premiums paid.[16a]

[16a] The application of "the payment of premiums test" to cases arising under the 1939 Code § 811(g)(2) (A) is not unconstitutional. United States v Manufacturers Nat. Bank of Detroit (1960) 363 US 194, 80 S Ct 1103, 4 L ed 2d 1158.

The fact that after the assignment, the beneficiaries, rather than the decedent, paid the premium was held not a basis for departing from the rule enunciated in the Manufacturers National Bank case, supra. Pritzlaff v United States (1961) 194 F Supp 548 (ED Wis).

§ 71. Schedule D; Insurance; Constitutionality.

p. 98, n. 4. The application of "the payment of premiums test" to cases arising under the 1939 Code § 811 (g)(2)(A) is not unconstitutional. United States v Manufacturers Nat. Bank of Detroit (1960) 363 US 194, 80 S Ct 1103, 4 L ed 2d 1158.

The fact that after the assignment, the beneficiaries, rather than the decedent, paid the premiums was held

36

not a basis for departing from the rule enunciated in the Manufacturers National Bank case, supra. Pritzlaff v United States (1961) 194 F Supp 548 (ED Wis).

§ 76. Schedule D; Insurance; Incidents of Ownership.

p. 104, n. 8. Where decedent had retained right to change beneficiary, proceeds of insurance on his life were taxable to his estate, though proceeds were paid to company controlled by his family and to SBA loan creditor, and company had paid all premiums. Piggott v Comm (1965) 340 F2d 829 (CA 6).

p. 104, n. 11. Right to obtain loans for payment of premiums without the consent of any beneficiary was held a sufficient incident of ownership to render insurance proceeds taxable. McCoy v Comm (1961) 20 TCM 224, TC Memo 1961-40.

§ 78. Schedule D; Insurance; Change of Beneficiary.

p. 108, n. 11. The right to change the beneficiary rendered proceeds of an airline accident insurance policy taxable, though as a practical matter the change could not be made during the flight. Rev Rul 61-123, IRB 1961-27, p. 14.

Proceeds of airline accident insurance policies covering a round trip and reserving to insured right to change beneficiary, were taxable to estate of insured who died on first part of the trip, even though such incident of ownership could not be exercised during flight. Comm v Noel (1965) 380 US 678, 14 L ed 2d 159, 85 S Ct 1238.

p. 108, n. 12. Hall v Wheeler, 174 F Supp 418 (D Maine) (1959).

§ 80. Schedule D; Insurance; Payment of Premiums.

p. 109, n. 15. The application of "the payment of premiums test" to cases arising under the 1939 Code § 811(g)(2)(A) is not unconstitutional. United States v Manufacturers Nat Bank of Detroit (1960) 363 US 194, 80 S Ct 1103, 4 L ed 2d 1158.

The fact that after the assignment, the beneficiaries, rather than the decedent, paid the premiums was held not a basis for departing from the rule enunciated in the Manufacturers National Bank case, supra. Pritzlaff v United States (1961) 194 F Supp 548 (ED Wis).

Under the 1939 Code as amended in 1941, payment of insurance premiums indirectly by means of a trust rendered insurance proceeds taxable. Carlton v Comm (1962) 298 F2d 415 (CA 2); Cahen v United States (1961) 292 F2d 33 (CA 7).

Where all incidents of ownership in a life policy had been given away the proceeds remained taxable to donor's estate in 1952 under IRC 811 (g)(2) to the extent of his premium contribution, though donee had applied the cash surrender value, as part of the rights transferred to him, to a conversion into a paid-up policy. The taxable transfer occurs when the beneficiary's benefits are enlarged on the occasion of donor's death, and he receives the increment as the result of donor's premium payments. Frohlich v United States (1962) 211 F Supp 775 (DC ED Mich).

§ 81. Schedule D; Insurance; Community Property.

p. 110, n. 1. The following cases, appearing in the text in Note 2, should also be added to Note 1: N Y Life Ins. Co. v Bank of Italy, 60 Cal App 602, 214 P 1 (1923); Travelers Ins. Co. v Fancher, 219 Cal 351, 26 P2d 482 (1933).

p. 111, n. 17. Where an insured husband had purchased several policies, including annuity policies, with community funds and had reserved the right to obtain the cash value and to change beneficiaries and his wife had, in respect of some of the policies, endorsed her consent to the designation of others as beneficiaries, it was held, upon the wife's predeceasing her husband, that, applying the California rule that the ownership of policies purchased from community funds is shared equally by both spouses unless the deceased spouse released her interests therein, the insured husband's right to the cash value of the policies was increased by his wife's death from a one-half community interest to an entire interest and that such increase constituted a taxable transfer from the deceased wife to the husband and was includible in the gross estate of the wife. The fact that the husband exclusively reserved the cash value under all policies and that the wife participated in the change of beneficiaries did not constitute a release of her community interest during her life. United States v Stewart, 270 F2d 894 (CA 5) (1959).

§ 84. Schedule D; Insurance; Return.

FORM NO. 15

Life Insurance Statement

The official form was revised (November 1965) in the following respects only:

[1–8, as appears in the main volume, unchanged]

9. Amount of accumulated dividends.
10. Amount of post-mortem dividends.
11. Amount of returned premium.
12. Amount of proceeds if payable in one sum.
13. Value of proceeds as of date of death (if not payable in in one sum).
14. Date of death of insured.
15. Date of issue of policy.
16. Amount of premium.
17A. Provisions of policy with respect to the deferred payments or the installments (Note: where marital deduction under Code section 2056 is involved, if other than lump sum settlement authorized, copy of insurance policy should be attached).
17B. Amount of installment.
17C. Date of birth and name of any person the duration of whose life may measure the number of dividends.
17D. Amount applied by the insurance company as a single premium representing the purchase of installment benefits.
17E. Basis (mortality table and rate of interest) used by insurer in valuing installment benefits.
18. Was the insured the annuitant or beneficiary of any annuity contract issued by the company. Yes.... No....
19. Names of companies with which decedent carried other policies and amount of such policies if this information is disclosed by your records.

The undersigned officer of the above-named insurance company hereby certifies that this statement sets forth correct and true information.

DATE OF CERTIFICATION   SIGNATURE   TITLE

INSTRUCTIONS

PURPOSE OF STATEMENT.—The information shown by this statement is required for the purpose of determining the statutory gross estate of the insured for Federal estate tax purposes.

[Harris Tax Supp]

STATEMENT OF INSURER.—This statement must be made, on behalf of the insurance company which issued the policy, by an officer of the company having access to the records of the company.

DUTY TO FILE.—It is the duty of the executor to procure this statement from the insurance company and file it with the return. However, if specifically requested, the insurance company should file this statement direct with the official of the Internal Revenue Service making the request.

SEPARATE STATEMENTS.—A separate statement must be filed for each policy listed on the return.

§ 88. Schedule E; Jointly Owned Property; Original Ownership.

p. 121 n. 15. Where H gave certain corporate shares to W, his wife, and on the same date a stock dividend thereon was declared which capitalized earnings of the corporation prior to the gift, the shares of stock issued as dividends as well as the shares so transferred, which subsequently became the jointly owned property of H and W, were includable in H's gross estate. Tuck v United States (1959) 172 F Supp 890 (ND Cal), affd 282 F2d 405 (CA 9).

English v United States (1959) 270 F2d 876 (CA 7).

p. 121, n. 17. Where bonds jointly owned by husband and wife were purchased from the wife's funds derived from the sale of stocks originally given to the wife by the husband, one-half the original value of the gift of stocks was includible in the husband's gross estate, representing the consideration attributable to the husband for purchase of the bonds. Swartz v United States (1960) 182 F Supp 540 (DC Mass).

First National Bank of Kansas City (Cline) v United States (1963)

223 F Supp 963 (DC WD Mo) (jointly owned property acquired through sale of stock given by husband to his wife).

§ 89. Schedule E; Jointly Owned Property; Consideration.

p. 122, n. 19. Where bonds jointly owned by husband and wife were purchased from the wife's funds derived from the sale of stocks originally given to the wife by the husband, one-half the original value of the gift of stocks was includible in the husband's gross estate, representing the consideration attributable to the husband for purchase of the bonds. Swartz v United States (1960) 182 F Supp 540 (DC Mass).

Add new note in seventh line on page 122:

. . . other owner.[19a]

[19a] Instructions to Schedule E, revised Form 706, see § 26, this supplement, amended to provide that unless it can be shown that any part of the property was acquired with consideration originally belonging to the surviving joint tenant or tenants, the joint property must be included in the gross estate.

§ 90. Schedule E; Jointly Owned Property; Tenancy by Entirety.

p. 124, n. 1. See related case, Hornor v Comm (1962) 305 F2d 769 (CA 3), involving taxability of same assets in survivor's estate.

§ 93. Schedule E; Jointly Owned Property; Bank Accounts.

p. 127, n. 15. Doyle v Comm, 32 TC 1209, No. 117.

§ 94. Schedule E; Jointly Owned Property; Evidence and Burden of Proof.

p. 128, n. 2. Where decedent and her brother, shown to have lived frugally, placed savings in joint accounts over many years, decedent had inherited property, and brother had held steady job, half of funds were found attributable to decedent's gross estate, though actual tracing of source of funds was not feasible. Harris v Comm (1964) 23 TCM 635, TC Memo 1964–109.

p. 128, n. 3. Shares of stock purchased with funds from a joint bank account were held includible in decedent's gross estate in the absence of proof that the same were wholly or partly purchased with the survivor's separate funds or were subsequently transferred to the survivor for an adequate consideration. English v United States, 270 F2d 876 (CA 7) (1959).

Where decedent had deposited cash in a savings account payable to himself "or" his son, the fact that the son had been given the passbook and had kept it in a place accessible to the decedent did not establish title in the son, and the entire amount was includible in the decedent's gross

40

estate. Doyle v Comm, 32 TC 1209, No. 117.

§ 95. Schedule E; Jointly Owned Property; Contemplation of Death.

p. 130, n. 6. Section 2040 of the 1954 Code has no application where property held by the entireties or in joint tenancy with right of survivorship is transferred before death, and commissioner's attempt to include the entire value of property formerly held by decedent and his wife as tenants by the entirety was overruled where before death they conveyed the property to their son retaining a life estate with survivorship, the court holding, as contended by plaintiff, that only decedent's one-half interest therein was taxable under Section 2036. Glaser v United States (1961) 196 F Supp 47 (ND Ind), affd 306 F2d 57 (CA 7), on the above point.

Add text at end of section on page 131:

The Commissioner has announced his nonacquiescence[8a] in the Brockway, Barner, and Carnall decisions, cited in the text in support of the principle that only one-half of jointly owned property transferred in contemplation of death is taxable, even though the decedent furnished the entire consideration. Thus, it would appear that the Commissioner will contend that such property is taxable to the extent that it was acquired with consideration furnished by the decedent. See similar test set forth in Reg.

20.2040–1 in Appendix A of the text, which, though not expressly made applicable to transfers in contemplation of death, seem pertinent in view of the nonacquiescence in the above decisions.

8a IRB 1962–20, 7.

§ 97. Schedule E; Jointly Owned Property; Interest in Partnership.

p. 132, n. 11. Where pursuant to a partnership agreement, a deceased partner's estate is to receive a share of the partnership profits for a definite period after the partner's death, such contractual right is property in which the decedent had an interest at the time of his death and the value of this right must be included in decedent's gross estate for Federal estate tax purposes. Rev Rul 66–20, IRB 1966–4, p. 13.

§ 100. Schedule F; Miscellaneous Property; Generally.

p. 134, n. 1. Where widow files joint federal income tax return for year of decedent's death, and obtains refund of overpayment as shown thereon, which consists only of amount of taxes withheld during tax year on decedent's wages, the amount of the refund is an asset of decedent's estate. Law v Comm (1964) 23 TCM 1554, TC Memo 1964–257.

§ 102. Schedule F; Miscellaneous Property; Interests in Business.

p. 135, n. 16. Britt, 9 TCM (1947), cited in the note to the text was reversed, sub nom Britt's Estate v Comm, 190 F2d 946 (CA 5) where

court found wife's interest in family partnership to have been bona fide, and evidenced by a formal recorded deed, so that even if evidence of her contribution in services were to be disregarded there was an outright gift, which was "bona fide, unconditional and final."

p. 135, n. 17. The partnership must be a valid one under Federal Law, and where widow performed no duties, exercised no control and received no salary or other monies, the value of her individual interest was taxable in husband's estate. Aldrich v Usry (1962) 211 F Supp 330 (DC ED La).

Add note in seventh from last line on page 136:
. . . future profits4a

4a Where decedent's interest in future income of his partnership, as determined by a formula set forth in the partnership agreement, was reduced by a compromise agreement entered into, within a year of death, between his estate and the former partners, the agreed valuation, under the circumstances, must be considered in arriving at the alternative valuation date, as such agreement does not make the interest one affected by mere lapse of time, required to be valued at date of death by IRC § 2032(a)(3). Such value may however be discounted to day of death, since the discount is occasioned by the delay in receiving the income, not by a change in valuation before the alternative valuation date. Hull v Comm, 38 TC 512 (1962). The commissioner has acquiesced in this decision IRB 1964–43 p. 6. For app on oth issue see Hull v Comm, 325 F2d 367 (CA 3), § 131, this supp.

p. 137, n. 6. Where pursuant to a partnership agreement, a deceased partner's estate is to receive a share of the partnership profits for a definite period after the partner's death, such contractual right is property in which the decedent had an interest at the time of his death and the value of this right must be included in decedent's gross estate for Federal estate tax purposes. Rev Rul 66–20, IRB 1966–4, p. 13.

p. 137, n. 8. Sum paid to estate of deceased partner in settlement of any claim the executor or beneficiaries might have in post-mortem profits of partnership was held not includible in gross estate of deceased partner. It is ordinary income accruing to estate. Mandel v Sturr, 266 F2d 321 (CA 2) (1959).

p. 137, n. 9. Payments made in settlement of interest due or to become due estate of deceased partner on his capital share remaining in partnership pending liquidation was not includible in gross estate of deceased partner. It is ordinary income accruing to estate. Mandel v Sturr, 266 F2d 321 (CA 2) (1959).

§ 104. Schedule F; Miscellaneous Property; Interests in Business; Valuation; Subject to Option or Contract to Purchase.

p. 139, n. 5. Where the surviving partners were given by a valid agreement an irrevocable option to purchase the deceased partner's share at book value and there were restrictions on any transfer of such share during the partner's life, it was held that the book value fixed the value for estate tax purposes. Fiorito v Comm, 32 TC 440, No. 51. Acquiescence, 1960–1 CB 4.

§ 105. Schedule F; Miscellaneous Property; Insurance on Life of Another.

p. 139, n. 7. Donaldson v Comm, 31 TC 729, No. 74 (1959).

Add new note in thirteenth line on page 140:
. . . Gift Tax return.[12a]

12a Form 938 revised May, 1961, to include provision that it may be filed with the Estate Tax Return where decedent owned insurance on life of another.

§ 106. Schedule F; Miscellaneous Property; Royalties; Pensions; Leaseholds; Judgments.

p. 140, n. 14. Where decedent had qualified for an early retirement allowance, and had the right to transfer it at his death by designating a beneficiary thereof, decedent was held to have a sufficient degree of control to render the commuted value of the death benefit paid to the beneficiary taxable under the 1939 Code. Garber v Comm (1959) 271 F2d 97 (CA 3); decedent had property rights under § 811(a), 1939 Code, in an exempt pension trust fund under a qualified plan to which his employer had been the sole contributor by reason of his employment, where he was receiving monthly payments in distribution, had had until the date of his retirement an indefeasible right to take down the entire cash value; and where the fund remaining at his death passed to his family or estate. Rosenberg v United States (1962) 309 F2d 724 (CA 7).

Where all payments to exempt retirement pension plan, with provision for death benefits, were made by decedent's employer, where plan

42

was subject to amendment or revocation by company, and where decedent never retired, but exercised his right to appoint wife as beneficiary of death benefits, decedent had no property interest in the death benefits at time of his death, under IRC 1939 § 811(a) (similar to IRC 1954 § 2033), and the commuted value thereof was not taxable to his estate. Charleston Nat. Bank (Small) v United States (1963) 221 F Supp 271 (DC SD W Va).

Employee's future services were held the consideration for which an agreement to pay his widow his annual basic salary after his death was made, and his entering into such agreement amounted in substance to a transfer to his wife, or whoever might be the ultimate beneficiary of the payment, rendering it includible in his estate under § 811(c)(3) of the 1939 Code, though decedent was held to have no property right therein so as to render it taxable under § 811 (a). The payment to the widow of a year-end bonus, which had been paid by company for the preceding ten years, and which was not included in the agreement because it was only an expectation was held not includible in decedent's estate, since decedent neither had a property right in it nor made any transfer of it. Worthen v United States (1961) 192 F Supp 727 (DC Mass) (following Lehman v Comm discussed in § 151 of text).

See § 181, as to exemptions of qualified plans under 1954 Code.

Compensation for services rendered, in the form of bonuses awarded to a decedent before his death but payable thereafter, and bonuses awarded after his death, are income in respect of a decedent subject to Federal income tax. However, only those unpaid bonuses awarded to a decedent before his

death are property includible in his gross estate subject to Federal estate tax. Rev Rul 65–217, IRB 1965–38, p. 5.

§ 112. Schedule F; Miscellaneous Property; Annuities; Life, Remainder, Reversionary Interests; Valuation; Generally.

p. 146, n. 9. Stillman v Comm (1965) 24 TCM 478, TC Memo 1965–94 (where tax court refused to apply hindsight and used mortality tables, though one of two persons whose lives measured a life estate died of cancer within 2 months after the gift).

§ 115. Schedule F; Miscellaneous Property; Remainders or Reversionary Interests; Valuation.

p. 151, n. 8. Where donee of power of appointment created in 1935 had a reversion in the appointive property, vested subject to being divested by the exercise of the power, and under state law could not validly agree to fail to exercise the power, or validly exercise it in favor of her estate or creditors, her interest was unsaleable during her lifetime and had no market value at her death which could be taxed to her estate. Maryland National Bank (Wilson) v United States, 236 F Supp 532 (DC Md 1964`.

Add new text at end of section on page 151:

A remainder interest, becoming operative upon the death without issue of a married woman, aged 44, though not susceptible of valuation under actuarial rules, should be included in the gross estate and evaluated in accordance with the general rules set forth in § 20.2031–1 of the regulations, and consideration should be given to all known circumstances relative to the particular life tenant, rather than to women aged 44 in general.[8a]

[8a] Rev Rul 61–88, IRB 1961–19, p. 12.

§ 118. Schedule G; Transfers During Life; The Problem.

p. 155. n. 1. Where family-owned corporation purchased decedent's stock during her lifetime with the price payable in installments or until her death, the Commissioner was unsuccessful in his attempt to tax the amount remaining unpaid as of decedent's death upon the theory that the purchase price had been transferred with a retained right to future enjoyment of that portion of the purchase price for the period beyond her death, there being no evidence of posssssion and control at any time of the entire purchase price by decedent or that corporation was able to pay the entire purchase price or that it had been set aside. Cain v Comm (1961) 37 TC 185, No. 24. Acquiescence, IRB 1962–41, p. 6.

§ 121. Schedule G; Transfer During Life; Transaction in Contemplation of Death; Generally.

p. 158, n. 5. Des Portes v United States, 171 F Supp 598 (ED S Car) (1959).

p. 159, n. 10. Gifts to grand-

children amounting to about 10% of donor's estate, effected at age 99, a year before donor's death were held not to have been made in contemplation of death where donor was in excellent health and was determined to and expected to live beyond 100, wished to assist his grandchildren, of whom he was fond, in their various needs; had recently acquired securities affording him a large increase in his already adequate income, and resulting in increases in income taxes which he violently objected to paying, and wished to reduce; and had in prior years made generous gifts. Kniskern v United States (1964) 232 F Supp 7 (DC SD Fla).

§ 122. Schedule G; Transfers During Life; Transactions in Contemplation of Death; Presumption.

p. 160, n. 14. See § 156, and Reg. 20.6018–3(c)(7).

§ 123. Schedule G; Transfers During Life; Transactions in Contemplation of Death; Motive.

p. 161, n. 9. Where mother operated business, inherited from deceased husband, in partnership with her son, and within three years of her death transferred her half-interest in the business to her son, and simultaneously therewith made her will distributing legacies to her other children equalling the value of the partnership interest, it was held that the transfer had been made in contemplation of death as one step in an integrated plan to dispose of her estate. Goodman v Comm, 19 TCM 927, TC Memo 1960–173.

§ 125. Schedule G; Transfers During Life; Transactions in Contemplation of Death; Health.

p. 163, n. 14. Gift made two years after diagnosis of heart disease, and 18 months before death of decedent, aged 57, from pneumonia, held not in contemplation of death where business reasons, income tax considerations, pattern of generosity to children, and decedent's continued activity in business primarily motivated the transfer. Beurman v Comm (1965) 24 TCM 599, TC Memo 1965–114.

p. 164, n. 3. Where decedent gave a home to each of his married daughters in 1951, taking back notes and mortgages without any consideration passing, his later releases of the mortgages made after he had knowledge of cancer and three months before his death in 1956, were held not made in contemplation of death. Lynch v Comm (1960) 35 TC 142, No. 18. Acquiescence, IRB 1961–38, p. 5.

§ 126. Schedule G; Transfers During Life; Transactions in Contemplation of Death; Activity; Longevity; Plans.

p. 164, n. 8. It has been held that the presumption that a gift was made in contemplation of death is not conclusively rebutted by evidence of a contemplated marriage; for marriage may be contemplated when death is imminent. Schneller v Comm, 18 TCM 654, TC Memo. 1959–152.

American Trust Co. v United States, 175 F Supp 185 (ND Cal) (1959).

§ 128. Schedule G; Transfers During Life; Transactions in Contemplation of Death; Tax Avoidance.

p. 166, n. 2. Butterworth v Usry (1959) 177 F Supp 197 (ED La).

Transfers to wife made within a month of death in 1958 from coronary arteriosclerosis of 59 year old husband then apparently in good health were taxable to his estate as having been made predominantly to avoid estate taxes, where evidence established that he had sought estate planning advice protection "Federal Estatewise," did not procure execution of wills prepared for him and wife, and transferred to her more property than planner had suggested. Speights v United States (1962) 214 F Supp 24 (DC D NJ).

p. 166, n. 8. Where the testator's motive was primarily income tax avoidance, the fact that he was in his late 80's, had recently been hospitalized, simultaneously executed a codicil to his will, made the disputed transfer to an object of his bounty and died within three years of the transfer, did not detract from his life-motive. Lockwood v United States, 181 F Supp 748 (SD NY) (1959).

§ 129. Schedule G; Transfers During Life; Transactions in Contemplation of Death; Business Transactions.

p. 167, n. 9. Eschen (1964) 43 Misc 2d 207, 250 NYS2d 761; citing text (presumption not rebutted).

§ 130. Schedule G; Transfers During Life; Transactions in Contemplation of Death; Consideration.

p. 167, n. 16. Transfer of remainder interest by surviving tenant by the entireties to stepchildren to compromise claims affecting title to the property, even though unliquidated, was for adequate and full consideration, and not includible in transferer's estate as in contemplation of death, even though made within 3 years of death. Friedman v Comm (1963) 40 TC 714. The Commissioner has announced acquiescence, IRB 1964–16 p. 7.

§ 131. Schedule G; Transfers During Life; Transactions in Contemplation of Death; Family Purposes.

p. 168, n. 7. Hull v Comm. (1963) 325 F2d 367 (CA 3) (gift of insurance policies to daughters, grantor aged 70).

p. 168, n. 8. Metzger v United States, 181 F Supp 830 (ND Ohio) (1960).

Gifts to children by an 86-year-old widow whose motive was to discharge an unfulfilled moral obligation of the husband who had often expressed an intention to make such gifts were held not in contemplation of death. Hoover v United States, 180 F Supp 601 (Ct Cl).

p. 168, n. 9. Eschen (1964) 43 Misc 2d 207, 250 NYS2d 761, citing text (presumption not rebutted by testimony only of family lawyer, son who benefitted not appearing).

p. 168, n. 13. Though made within three years of date of death, transfers made for purpose of helping children to purchase homes were held

46

not made in contemplation of death since the evidence established that the motivation for the transfers was decedent's desire to meet children's special needs. Boyd v United States (1961) 192 F Supp 242 (ED Ky).

Where decedent gave a home to each of his married daughters in 1951, taking back notes and mortgages without any consideration passing, his later releases of the mortgages made after he had knowledge of cancer and three months before his death in 1956, were held not made in contemplation of death. Lynch v Comm (1960) 35 TC 142, No. 18. Acquiescence, IRB 1961–38, p. 5.

p. 168, n. 15. Release of power to alter or amend a 1929 irrevocable trust was held not made in contemplation of death where grantor's predominant motive in originally creating the trust was to provide his wife with an independent income, and the release, executed upon advice of counsel in order to avoid estate tax due to a change in the regulations, was but a step in the integrated transaction. Wardwell v Comm, 20 TCM 1530, TC Memo 1961–295.

§ 132. Schedule G; Transfers During Life; Transactions in Contemplation of Death; Vesting.

p. 169, n. 18. Where a donor has made a completed gift of securities or money to a minor pursuant to the Model Gift of Securities to Minors Act or the Uniform Gifts to Minors Act and has died while serving in the capacity of custodian having paid a gift tax on the original transfers, his estate is entitled to a gift tax credit against the estate tax pursuant to IRC 2012 (1954 Code). Rev Rul 59–357, IRB 1959–44, p. 18.

§ 133. Schedule G; Transfers During Life; Transactions in Contemplation of Death; Preservation of Property.

Add note in fourth line of section on page 169:

. . . with life.[19a]

[19a] Brown v Comm, 19 TCM 1479, TC Memo 1960–265 (farm property in run-down condition, turned over to son to improve it by father, who although 73, was in good health). Acquiescence, 1959–1 CB 3.

p. 169; n. 2. Clark v U. S. (1962) 209 F Supp 895 (DC Colo).

§ 134. Schedule G; Transfers During Life; Transactions in Contemplation of Death; Amount of Transfer

p. 170, n. 19. Kniskern v United States (1964) 232 F Supp 7 (DC SD Fla) (transfer of 10% of estate not taxable).

§ 138. Schedule G; Transfers During Life; Transactions in Contemplation of Death; Evidence.

p. 174, n. 3. Where the decedent's doctor who treated decedent for cancer within three years of death was not called as a witness, the omission of such testimony, inter alia, constituted a failure to sustain the burden of proof. Hamar v Comm, 19 TCM 575, TC Memo 1960–107.

p. 175, n. 7. Where 18 months before her death in 1952 grantor-decedent amended an inter vivos trust to give widowed about-to-be-married daughter-in-law decedent's right to the income, to replace income from other trusts daughter-in-law would

lose by remarriage, and decedent simultaneously, to avoid having to pay income tax at a high rate on such income, relinquished powers over the trust, on which grandchildren-remaindermen paid gift taxes, there was no gift in contemplation of death. Studebaker v United States (1962) 211 F Supp 263 (DC ND Ind).

§ 139. Schedule G; Transfers During Life; Transfers with Retained Life Estate; The Problem.

p. 177, n. 18. A transfer for purposes of IRC Sec. 811(c) occurs when a distributee agreed with others in a family settlement that her share in parent's estate shall be placed in trust, income only to her life, and her estate cannot escape taxation on the value of trust (at least to the extent attributable to her share under the probated will) as a transfer direct from the parent, since she did not renounce her share, but agreed to a rearrangement of parent's estate. Vease v Comm (1963) 314 F2d 79 (CA 9).

§ 140. Schedule G; Transfers During Life; Transfers with Retained Life Estate; Evolution of Statute.

p. 178, n. 3. Under the Joint Resolution of March 3, 1931, referred to in the text, a reservation of a secondary life estate by grantor of insurance trust, created on June 4, 1932, rendered the transfer taxable, it being held irrelevant that the grantor in fact died before the intermediate life beneficiary. Comm v Arents (1962) 297 F2d 894 (CA 2), reviewing history of Resolution.

p. 179, n. 12. A "transfer" within the meaning of § 811(c)(1)(B) of the 1939 Code, excepting from taxability transfers with retained income and powers if made before March 4, 1931, was held not limited to irrevocable transfers; and in connection with a revocable trust created before March 4, 1931, commissioner's contention that the "transfer" took place, not on the date of creation of the trust, but after the critical date when the powers were relinquished and the trust became irrevocable, was overruled. Ridgeway v Comm (1960) 33 TC 1000, No. 111, affd 291 F2d 257 (CA 3); Cuddihy v Comm (1959) 32 TC 1171, No. 110.

Pre-1931 transfer referred to in § 2036 of the 1954 Code must be read to mean the transfer of legal title to a trust without regard to the reservation of certain powers over corpus, and to require that the transfer be complete and irrevocable as contended by the Commissioner would make nonsense of the Code, following Ridgway v Comm, supra. Comm v Canfield (1962) 306 F2d 1 (CA 2); Commissioner has noted nonacquiescence in the decision to the extent that it holds the transfer in trust occurred where trust was created rather than at the time the power of appointment was released (IRB 1964–1, p. 9).

Transfer of right to income of trust by mother to widowed daughter to replace income about to be forfeited by the latter upon her remarriage, and the necessary relinquishment of her power to revoke for income tax purposes, were held associated with life and not made in contemplation of death. Studebaker v United States (1962) 211 F Supp 263 (ND Ind).

Where inter vivos trust created in 1927 became irrevocable in 1943 upon grantor income beneficiary's relinquishment of broad powers to amend, revoke or terminate, there was no

"transfer" until 1943, and the corpus was taxable to grantor's estate on her death in 1952. Studebaker v United States (1962) 211 F Supp 263 (DC ND Ind), pointing out that it was the intent of congress, and the purport of the Supreme Court in the decisions interpreting the tax laws, that the exclusion from the incidence of the estate tax of transfers made before March 4, 1931 was limited to irrevocable transfers.

p. 179, n. 13. Property transferred in trust by decedent in 1929, with retained right to change beneficiary and trustees, otherwise than in his own favor, is taxable to his estate under IRC § 2038(a)(2). Although that section and § 2036 are not mutually exclusive, the exclusion from taxation, contained in § 2036, of transfers with retained right to designate beneficiaries when made before March 4, 1931 does not extend to transfers required to be taxed in donor's estate by § 2038. Florida Nat. Bank of Jacksonville (Ballard) v United States (1964) 336 F2d 598 (CA 3).

§ 141. Schedule G; Transfers During Life; Transfers with Retained Life Estate; Statutory Scheme.

p. 179, n. 14. The extension of duration of a trust, pursuant to a power of amendment by the affirmative vote of decedent and all of the other income beneficiaries, otherwise entitled to a distribution of corpus on the initial termination date, resulting in postponement of distribution of corpus until after the death of the decedent-income beneficiary, was held a relinquishment of a property right, tantamount to a transfer of decedent's property interest in the corpus with a retained life interest,

48

rendering decedent's share of trust corpus taxable in her estate under § 2036 of the 1954 Code. Sexton v United States (1962) 300 F2d 490 (CA 7).

Transfer of a vested remainder in widow's half of community property subject to certain powers of disposition during her life, made the value of her community as of the valuation date applicable to her estate, includible in her estate under § 2036. Vardell v Comm (1962) 307 F2d 688 (CA 5).

Where decedent by family property agreement settling will contest gave all her interest in an estate to her daughter, except the right to income for life, there was a taxable transfer with retained life estate under IRC § 2036. Union Commerce Bank (Baker) v Comm (1964) 339 F2d 162 (CA 6).

Disproportionate share of community property allocated to husband in connection with divorce is not "consideration" for the creation, as part of the settlement, of a trust for life of husband with remainder to children, so as to exclude trust from gross estate. Haskins v U. S. (1965) 240 F Supp 492 (DC ND Cal).

p. 180, n. 16. A transfer in trust made before March 4, 1931 is includible in the decedent's gross estate if such earlier trust was, in effect revoked and a distinct new trust created subsequent to that date, notwithstanding the fact that the trust corpus and one of the beneficiaries were the same. Maclean v United States, 275 F2d 936 (CA 9) (1960).

p. 180, n. 17. The words "or for any period not ascertainable without reference to his death," added June 7, 1932 to the provision on transfers with retained life estate, were held unnecessary to make taxable a transfer in trust created in February,

1932, whereunder settlor reserved to herself for life periodic payments of income, not less frequently than once each quarter, and directed that after death payments were to be made to named beneficiaries, but that no beneficiary should have any vested interest in income until paid over by trustee and then only if living on day of payment. Any income accrued in the trust since the last payment would vest in the next beneficiary only if he were alive on the date of the next periodic payment. Accordingly, the condition that terminated the decedent's actual or potential right to income was her death, and the phraseology of the statute as in effect between March 3, 1931 and June 7, 1932, included the transfer as one with income retained for a period "not ending before his death." Bayliss v United States (1963) 218 F Supp 97 (DC ED Va), aff'd 326 F2d 458.

p. 180, n. 18. Under the Joint Resolution of March 3, 1931, a reservation of a secondary life estate by grantor of insurance trust, created on June 4, 1932, rendered the transfer taxable, it being held irrelevant that the grantor in fact died before the intermediate life beneficiary. Comm v Arents (1962) 297 F2d 894 (CA 2).

p. 180, n. 19. Where decedent transferred assets to a trust, retaining the right to receive payment of $10,000 annually either by way of an annuity or by distribution from the trust; without the restrictions to pay such sums from income, it was held that since annual payments of $10,000 from principal for the number of years here involved would have exhausted the trust principal and since the trustees could have made the payments from principal or interest or both, then the trust balance remaining was not includible in the decedent's gross estate. Becklenberg v Comm, 273 F2d 297 (CA 7) (1959). Acquiescence, 1959–1 CB 3.

Where inter vivos trust provided for income payments of $100 per month each to grantor and his wife, and trust assets were inadequate, grantor was deemed to have a superior right to $100 per month, and the amount includable in grantor's estate was the amount necessary to yield $100 per month computed on an actuarial basis with a 3½ per cent return, plus a proportion of a discretionary illness payment fund. United States National Bank of Portland, Extr. v United States (1960) 188 F Supp 332 (DC Or).

Taxability of the corpus of an irrevocable inter vivos trust with a retained life estate may not be defeated by a sale of the life estate based upon the value of the expectancy, since Congress never intended to allow such an easy avoidance of the taxable incidence befalling reserved life estates, and the liability arises at the time of the inter vivos transfer. United States v Allen (1961) 293 F2d 916 (CA 10).

The fact alone that a transfer with a retained life estate into a trust is part of a property settlement agreement incident to a divorce is not sufficient to make the transfer of the decedent one for an adequate and full consideration; the value of what decedent received under the trust must be measured against the value of the property he transferred to the trust. United States v Past (1965) 347 F2d 7 (CA 9).

§ 142. Schedule G; Transfers During Life; Transfers with Retained Life Estate; Possession or Enjoyment.

p. 181, n. 20. Where deeds were delivered but not recorded, and

donor continued to receive income and to hold herself out as sole owner, transfer was held taxable. Bullock v Comm, 19 TCM 1080, TC Memo 1960–204.

p. 181, n. 2. National Bank of Commerce v Henslee, 179 F Supp 346 (MD Tenn) (1959) (trust for support of settlor's dependent daughter during minority).

Lee v Comm (1960) 33 TC 1064, No. 120.

Where Alabama law obligated husband to support his wife, the value of a husband's gift in trust, requiring trustee to pay all the income to wife for her "support and comfort" with right of invasion in case of insufficiency, was included in husband's estate under IRC § 2036(a), since grantor was merely transferring to the trustee his legal obligation of "support", even though wife was not required to account for her use of the income. First Nat. Bank of Montgomery v United States (1962) 211 F Supp 403 (DC MD Ala).

p. 181, n. 3. Uninterrupted receipt of income by grantor when coupled with a "prearrangement" to pay it, though there be no enforceable right, will satisfy the retention of enjoyment alternative in the statute; and where in connection with an irrevocable trust with a discretionary power in the trustee to pay income to the grantor, all income was in fact paid to her, and grantor had claimed a retained life interest when filing her gift tax return, the court found an informal prearrangement existed when the trust was created whereby the trustee agreed to pay her all of the income despite its discretionary power, thus rendering the trust taxable. The court pointed out "that every case of this sort must stand on its own facts and that the practice of assuming that a trustee, corporate or otherwise, is necessarily independent of the cestui whom he represents, need not be followed invariably but may be rebutted by the circumstances." Skinner v US (1963) 316 F2d 517 (CA 3); Uhl v Comm (1957 241 F2d 867 (CA 7).

Footnote cases distinguished on the basis that in those cases there existed no "prearrangement" for payment of income. McNichol v Comm (1959) 265 F2d 667 (CA 3), infra, note 7.

The value of a trust estate is not taxable in estate of settlor beneficiary of part of income, where trustees were given "absolute discretion" to use remaining income for her support, maintenance, comfort and enjoyment, since under Missouri law the decedent had no enforceable right to compel the trustees to exercise their discretion for her benefit. Lettice v United States, 237 F Supp 123 (DC SD Cal).

p. 182, n. 4. Nichols v Coolidge, cited in text, historically reviewed and deemed rejected by Joint Resolution of March 3, 1931. McNichol v Comm (1959) 265 F2d 667 (CA 3), infra, note 7.

p. 182, n. 6. Where decedent as settlor of trust provided for annual payments from income of $2,500 to each of four children, with appropriate gifts in remainder, retaining for herself life interest in balance of income, that part of trust corpus necessary to support such fixed payments is excluded from taxation in settlor's estate, being the amount of which $10,000 ($2,500 annual income for each of four children) is 3-1/2%, absent proof of other basis for valuation. Tomec v Comm (1963) 40 TC 134; the Commissioner has announced his acquiescence, IRB 1964-16 p. 7.

p. 182, n. 7. Where a joint interest in real property had been purchased by A and B, with each contributing

one-half the purchase price, and A and B executed joint and mutual wills under which the survivor of A and B was to receive a life estate in such real property, with a power of invasion, and C, the son of A and B, was to receive the remainder interest, it was held that, upon A's death, C acquired a remainder interest in fee which consisted of A's one-half interest in the real property and that B acquired a life estate. Upon B's death B's one-half interest was includible in B's gross estate as a transfer made originally upon A's death but over which B had subsequently retained right of possession and enjoyment. Olson v Reisimer, 271 F2d 623 (CA 7) (1959).

Where wife, holding policy on husband's life, before his death directed that proceeds be retained by company on his death, to pay interest and dividends to her for life with remainder to children, she then made a transfer with retained life estate, making the value of the proceeds held by insurer taxable to her estate under IRC § 2036; that the transfer by its terms was revocable until husband's death did not make the transfer taxable to his estate, instead of hers, or change the date of the transfer for purposes of determining the taxability of its value to her estate. Pyle (1962) 313 F2d 328 (CA 3).

Transfer of life insurance proceeds of policy taken out by wife on husband's life, takes effect on death of husband, so that where widow retains right to income for life, giving remainder to children, proceeds are subject to estate tax as part of her gross estate. Savage v United States (1964) 331 F2d 678 (CA 2) directions that proceeds be so disposed of, given under settlement option prior to March 4, 1931, were revocable up to date of husband's death occurring after the effective date of the Joint Resolution of March 3, 1931, amending IRC § 812(c).

Where donor caused U. S. Savings Bonds to be registered in names of great-grandchildren, but interest checks, endorsed to him, were deposited in savings accounts in names of donor "or" the minors, donor retaining both bonds and passbooks, the value of the bonds was taxable to donor's estate. Fitzsimmons v United States (1963) 222 F Supp 140 (DC ED Wash).

Where decedent purchased stock in the names of his wife and children, but arranged to receive directly all dividends declared during his lifetime, reimbursing his children for income taxes incurred by them through reporting the dividends on their tax returns, the value of the stock is taxable to his estate, since the right to the income of the shares was retained by donor until his death. Atkinson v United States (1964) 231 F Supp 933 (DC ED SC).

Where a decedent prior to his death transferred as a gift a residence to his wife, and after the transfer continued to reside there, such continued residence in and of itself was deemed insufficient as a matter of law to establish a transfer with a retention or reservation of the right to the possession or enjoyment thereof, and it was also deemed insufficient to imply an agreement to that effect. Stephenson v United States (1965) 238 F Supp 660 (DC WD Va), and Union Planters National Bank v United States (1964) 238 F Supp 883 (DC WD Tenn).

Where the decedent had conveyed income-producing realty to his children, orally reserving such income for life, such realty was includible in the decedent's gross estate although the oral reservation was unenforceable under the local Statute of Frauds. The test of includability, absent an enforceable right, is possession and enjoyment of the interest retained. McNichol v Comm (1959) 265 F2d 667 (CA 3). The court, however, had doubts whether the receipt of all income alone was sufficient, without an oral agreement, to satisfy the enjoyment clause, and though refusing to render an opinion thereon, indicated the need for some "prearrangement." See Skinner v United States (1961) 197 F Supp 726 (ED Pa) affd 316 F2d 517, supra, note 3.

p. 182, n. 10. But fact that wife paid premiums on her husband's life insurance policies held in an insurance trust created by her husband, of which she was a contingent life beneficiary, would not render the insurance proceeds taxable in her estate under § 2036(a)(1) of the 1954 Code, since the premium payments and the insurance proceeds were not one and the same, and there was "no retention by her of a life estate in the property she transferred." Goodnow v United States (1962) 302 F2d 516 (Ct Cls).

§ 143. Schedule G; Transfers During Life; Transfers with Retained Life Estate; Right to Designate Enjoyment.

p. 183, n. 12. Where a settlor created irrevocable inter vivos trusts in which he was designated a co-trustee with power to invest trust assets in securities other than legals, to allocate accretions to the trust property to principal or income as discretion should dictate, to select securities yielding high income or no income, and to be immune from liability except for wilful acts or defaults, it was held that the powers so reserved were so broad as to shift the economic benefits under the trusts between the life tenants and the remaindermen. In effect, the settlor thus "retained the right to designate the person who shall possess or enjoy the property or the income therefrom" and upon his death, the trust corpora were held includible in his gross estate. State Street Trust Co. v United States, 263 F2d 635 (CA 1) (1959).

Inter vivos trust property is not to be included in gross estate of settlor, though as sole trustee she had broad management powers, including sale and reinvestment, right to exercise conversion and voting rights, to determine what was principal or income, and the right to compromise tax claims. Peters v Comm (1964) 23 TCM 994, TC Memo 1964–167; refusing to follow State Street Trust Co. v United States, 263 F2d 635.

If the transfer was made before June 7, 1932, the right to designate must be retained by or reserved to the decedent alone to render the transfer taxable. Reg. § 20.2036–1 (a)(3)(ii), as amended Nov. 15, 1960, TD 6501.

Where life insurance proceeds were payable to a widow in a lump-sum, but she elected to leave the proceeds with the insurer, to draw interest thereon annually, to reserve a power to draw down the entire proceeds on any interest payment date and to designate her children as ultimate beneficiaries, the proceeds were held includible in the widow's gross estate as a transfer of property (to herself) with a retained life estate and further, a transfer subject to the widow's power to alter, amend or revoke. Rundle v Welch (1960) 184 F Supp 777 (DC Ohio).

p. 183, n. 16. A stock purchase agreement by family-owned corporation with price payable in specified number of installments or until death

of seller, is not a transfer with enjoyment of property retained as to those installments which were not paid after seller's death, where it was not shown that seller retained any control over stock, or over any part of the unpaid purchase price, or that the buyer was able to pay at any time the entire purchase price or that corporation had set aside the entire purchase price. Cain v Comm (1961) 37 TC 185, No. 24. Acquiescence, IRB 1962–41, p. 6.

p. 184, n. 3. Where decedent had transferred securities to a trust of which he was sole trustee, and retained the power to distribute trust property "should a special emergency arise," the power was held not limited by a definite external standard (despite a state court decision to the contrary which the federal court was not bound to follow) but was the equivalent of a power to invade or to terminate rendering trust corpus taxable under Sec. 811 (d)(2) of the 1939 Code; however, income accumulated on securities transferred to the trust was held not taxable, since adding undistributed income was a negation of power to invade. Michigan Trust Company v Kavanaugh (1960) 284 F2d 502 (CA 6).

p. 184, n. 4. Settlor's retention, as trustee, of the power to distribute or accumulate income is sufficient to cause inclusion in his estate of not only the value of the trust corpus but also the accumulated income, since he retained the power to designate who shall possess or enjoy the property or the income therefrom, and each accumulated income added to principal was subject to the same power, and therefore was a taxable transfer. United States v O'Malley (1966) — US —, 16 L ed 2d 145, 86 S Ct (rejecting the doctrine of Comm v McDermott (1955) 222 F2d 665 (CA 7)).

53

Where by inter vivos trust created in 1935 settlor retained the power to direc the accumulation of income, and to direct payments from income and principal to his children, the beneficiaries, the transfer is not complete, for purposes of making the value of the trust taxable to his estate, until the powers are finally relinquished at settlor's death, and there is no distinction in this respect between what is technically principal and securities purchased with retained and accumulated income, which are, until decedent's death, subject to those same powers of control that determine the taxability of the original principal. Round v Comm (1964) 332 F2d 590 (CA 1).

§ 146. Schedule G; Transfers During Life; Transfers Taking Effect at Death; Condition of Survivorship.

p. 187, n. 5. Employee's future services were held the consideration for which an agreement to pay his widow his annual basic salary after his death was made, and his entering into such agreement amounted in substance to a transfer to his wife, or whoever might be the ultimate beneficiary of the payment, rendering it includible in his estate under § 811 (c)(3) of the 1939 Code, though decedent was held to have no property right therein so as to render it taxable under § 811(a). The payment to the widow of a year-end bonus, which had been paid by company for the preceding ten years, and which was not included in the agreement because it was only an expectation was held not includible in decedent's estate, since decedent neither had a property right in it nor made any transfer of it. Worthen v United States (1961) 192 F Supp 727 (DC

54

Mass) (following Lehman v Comm discussed in § 151 of text).

Compensation for services rendered by decedent, in the form of bonuses awarded to decedent prior to, but payable after, death, and bonuses awarded after death, are income. But unpaid bonuses awarded to decedent before his death are property the value of which is includible in his gross estate subject to Federal estate tax. Revenue Ruling 65–217, IRB 1965–38, p. 5.

§ 147. Schedule G; Transfers During Life; Transfers Taking Effect at Death; Reversionary Interest.

Add note in ninth line on page 189:

. . . *express terms of the instrument.*[12a]

[12a] Richardson v United States (1961) 190 F Supp 369 (DC Wyo).

§ 149. Schedule G; Transfers During Life; Revocable Transfers.

p. 192, n. 17. Property transferred in trust by decedent in 1929, with retained right to change beneficiary and trustees, otherwise than in his own favor, is taxable to his estate under IRC § 2038(a)(2). Although that section and § 2036 are not mutually exclusive, the exclusion from taxation, contained in § 2036, of transfers with retained right to designate beneficiaries when made before March 4, 1931 does not extend to transfers required to be taxed in donor's estate by § 2038. Florida National Bank of Jacksonville (Ballard) v United States (1964) 336 F2d 598 (CA 3).

p. 193, n. 3. A new subsection (C) has been added to § 2038 of the

1954 Code, effective August 7, 1959, which excludes from the gross estate certain property held in trust where the decedent-grantor has reserved the right to change the trust beneficiaries but has otherwise divested himself of any interest in the property. If the decedent-grantor dying after August 16, 1954, was mentally incompetent for a period beginning at least 3 months prior to December 31, 1947 and continuing from that date to the date of death, and had not relinquished his power to change beneficiaries pursuant to the special relief granted under the 1939 Code § 811(d)(4), his estate is entitled to exclude the property from his gross estate.

Reg. 20.2038–1, amended May 28, 1962, Appendix B, this supplement.

p. 194, n. 12. National Bank of Commerce v Henslee, 179 F Supp 346 (MD Tenn) (1959).

Schuster v Comm (1962) 312 F2d 311 (power to revoke with written consent of beneficiary).

p. 194, n. 13. Settlor-beneficiary of a trust designated two persons in the trust instrument who could jointly terminate the trust at any time and pay the principal to the income beneficiary. Settlor-beneficiary also reserved a power, which she did not exercise during her lifetime, to substitute another person in place of either or both "co-terminators." Upon appeal from the District Court which had held that such trust was a revocable transfer includible in the settlor's gross estate, the Circuit Court considered but remanded for further proof the point whether the settlor, under local law (New York Real Property Law § 141) would have been barred from designating herself as a "terminator" of the trust in which event the taint of revocability would have been removed from the trust. Clark v United States,

267 F2d 501 (CA 1) (1959). Upon remand, it was held that the settlor would not be barred under New York Real Property Law § 141 from designating herself as a terminator of the trust. Clark v United States, 180 F Supp 696 (1960) (DC Maine).

p. 194, n. 17. Where the settlor reserved the right to appoint a successor if the named trustee should resign or cease to act, it was held that the trust was not thereby rendered a revocable transfer, since the right of appointment was restricted to acts not within the control of the settlor. Winchell v United States, 180 F Supp 710, (SD Cal) (1960), affd 289 F2d 212 (CA 9).

p. 195, n. 3. A reserved right to grant trustee "additional powers" was held not to render the trust taxable in the deceased settlor's estate under § 811(d)(2) of the 1939 Code, since any additional powers that might be granted, even if construed to be plenary, would be exercisable only by the trustee. Winchell v United States (1960) 180 F Supp 710 (SD Cal), affd 289 F2d 212 (CA 9).

p. 195, n. 6. Where the settlor reserved the right to grant "additional powers" to the trustees and upon a construction of the instrument it was determined that settlor intended to reserve administrative powers only and not the right to alter the beneficial enjoyment under the trust, it was held that trust property was not includible in the settlor's gross estate as a revocable transfer. Winchell v United States, 180 F Supp 710, (SD Cal) (1960), affd 289 F2d 212 (CA 9).

p. 195, n. 8. A power to invest as "may be deemed to be most advisable for the benefit of the estate, including the right to purchase life insurance, annuity contracts, and income bearing contracts", was held limited by a judicially established standard under the law of Kansas, and did not give the settlor, as co-trustee, a power to alter or amend so as to render the trust taxable in his estate under § 811(d) of the 1939 Code. United States v Powell (1962) 307 F2d 821 (CA 10).

p. 195, n. 14. Where settlor transferred property in trust with successive life estates to his wife and daughter, giving each a limited right of invasion and retaining the power to remove and appoint a successor and the power to control investment policy, these powers, together with the trustee's power to borrow money from itself, to charge expenses against principal and income, to allocate certain dividends to principal or income, and to do all acts that persons owning similar property would do did not constitute a power to designate or vary the enjoyment of the trust property or to alter, amend or revoke the trust, and the trust corpus was not includible in the decedent's gross estate. Wurts v Comm, 19 TCM 544, TC Memo 1960–102.

§ 150. Schedule G; Transfers During Life Revocable Transfers; Relinquishment of Power.

p. 196, n. 1. Where by inter vivos trust created in 1935 settlor retained the power to direct the accumulation of income, and to direct payments from income and principal to his children, the beneficiaries, the transfer is not complete, for purposes of making the value of the trust taxable to his estate, until the powers are finally relinquished at settlor's death, and there is no distinction in this respect between what is technically principal and securities purchased with retained and accumulated in-

come, which are, until decedent's death, subject to those same powers of control that determine the taxability of the original principal. Round v Comm (1964) 332 F2d 590 (CA 1).

p. 197, n. 6. Release of power to alter or amend a 1929 irrevocable trust was held not made in contemplation of death where grantor's predominant motive in originally creating the trust was to provide his wife with an independent income, and the release, executed upon advice of counsel in order to avoid estate tax due to a change in the regulations, was but a step in the integrated transaction. Wardwell v Comm, 20 SCM 1530, TC Memo 1961–295.

§ 151. Schedule G; Transfers During Life; Reciprocal Trusts.

p. 198, n. 10. See § 106, this supplement where principle of Lehman v Comm, discussed in text, was applied to case involving payment of salary to widow of an employee pursuant to an agreement between employee and company.

p. 198, n. 12. Reciprocity was established by the fact that each trust was executed within two days of each other, each in consideration of the other, and both prepared by the same attorney, although the executor sought to establish different motives for each trust. Carter v Comm. 31 TC 1148, No. 117.

§ 152. Schedule G; Transfers During Life; Annuity Combined with Life Insurance.

p. 199, n. 19. Rev Rul 54–552 cited in the note to the text was modified by Rev Rul 65–69, IRB 1965–11, p. 21, to conform with the

56

decision in Fidelity-Philadelphia Trust Co. (Haines) v Smith (1958) 356 US 274, 2 L ed 2d 765, 78 S Ct 730, which case decided that where decedent was divested of all interest in a single premium life insurance policy, bought in connection with an annuity, the policy proceeds were not includible in his estate, since the annuity payments were not conditioned on the continued existence of the contract of life insurance. In an accompanying ruling (Rev Rul 65–57, IRB 1965–11, p. 7) the CIR stated that the insurance policy in such single premium cases involved no risk to insurer, and was not to be treated as "insurance" under various IRC provisions (e. g. § 302(g) of Rev Act of 1926; § 101(a) of 1954 Code).

p. 199, n. 2. The proceeds of an annuity contract, payable to a named beneficiary on the death of the annuitant before the annuity matured, which consisted of annual premiums contributed in part by the annuitant's employer voluntarily but not as part of a remuneration agreement, were taxable to the extent of the annuitant's paid-in premiums attributable to the total benefits received. Provident Trust Co. v United States, 170 F Supp 74, (ED Pa) (1959). The government has acquiesced in this decision, and will not appeal.

§ 153. Schedule G; Transfers During Life; Overlapping Taxability of Reserved Powers.

p. 200, n. 4. Where in accordance with property settlement on judicial separation decedent gave up her share of the community and received certain property plus a million dollars which she then placed in trust,

she to have income for life and the remainder to go to others, the value of the trust was taxable to her estate as a transfer with retained economic benefit, despite contention that under Louisiana law she had under the circumstances "obtained" rather than "retained" the life interest. First National Bank of Shreveport (Fain) v United States (1965) 342 F2d 415 (CA 5).

§ 155. Schedule G; Transfers During Life; Insufficient Consideration.

p. 201, n. 14. Where widow had elected under husband's will, to allow her half of the community property to pass on her death under his will, accepting a life estate defeasible on remarriage in his half of the community, the value of her community as of the valuation date applicable to her estate was included in her estate under § 2036, and a credit allowed under § 2043(a) for the value of the life estate she received as of the date she elected, or the sums actually received before remarriage, whichever is less. Vardell v Comm (1962) 307 F2d 688 (CA 5).

p. 201, n. 17. Where the decedent created an inter vivos trust for the support of his daughter during her minority and such trust was includable in his gross estate as a transfer with a retained life estate, it was held that the death of the decedent prior to his daughter's attaining majority did not exempt from the gross estate the value of the daughter's right of support under the trust from the date of decedent's death to the date of her majority. The value of the daughter's interest could not be excluded from the gross estate on the theory that such interest was given to the daughter in consideration of the decedent's obligation for future support until she reached majority. National Bank of Commerce v Henslee, 179 F Supp 346, (MD Tenn) (1959).

§ 157. Schedule G; Transfers During Life; Valuation.

p. 203, n. 5. Where decedent as settlor of trust provided for annual payments from income of $2,500 to each of four children, with appropriate gifts in remainder, retaining for herself life interest in balance of income, that part of trust corpus necessary to support such fixed payments is excluded from taxation in settlor's estate, being the amount of which $10,000 ($2,500 annual income for each of four children) is 3-1/2%, absent proof of other basis for valuation. Tomec v Comm (1963) 40 TC 134; the Commissioner has announced his acquiescence, IRB 1964–16 p. 7.

p. 203, n. 8. Where a gift by husband to wife by trust to be distributed at end of ten years was, when made, subject to revocation by donor under Louisiana Code provisions as to corpus but not as to increases or income, the valuation of the items given, for purposes of determining the amount to be included in donor's estate by reason of IRC Sec. 811(d) is measured by value of gift at time when the trust instrument was executed. Whited v United States (1963) 219 F Supp 947 (DC WD La).

Where by inter vivos trust created in 1935 settlor retained the power to direct the accumulation of income, and to direct payments from income and principal to his children, the beneficiaries, the transfer is not complete, for purposes of making the value of the trust taxable to his estate, until the powers are finally relinquished at settlor's death, and

58

there is no distinction in this respect between what is technically principal and securities purchased with retained and accumulated income, which are, until decedent's death, subject to those same powers of control that determine the taxability of the original principal. Round v Comm (1964) 332 F2d 590 (CA 1).

Settlor's retention, as trustee, of the power to distribute or accumulate income is sufficient to cause inclusion in his estate of not only the value of the trust corpus but also the accumulated income, since he retained the power to designate who shall possess or enjoy the property or the income therefrom, and each accumulated income added to principal was subject to the same power, and therefore was a taxable transfer. United States v O'Malley (1966) — US —, 16 L ed 2d 145, 86 S Ct (rejecting the doctrine of Comm v McDermott (1955) 222 F2d 665 (CA 7)).

Add text at end of section:

Where an interest in insurance on the life of another is transferred with a right to receive income on the proceeds retained, the face value of the proceeds held by insurer are taxable to transferor's estate (at least where all premiums were paid by him), and this is so although the transfer is made by directions to insurer given before the death of insured.[11a] Where a decedent, as donor by inter vivos trust instrument, retained the right to change the beneficial interests in the principal of the trust, so that the transfer was subject to estate tax in donor's estate, the actuarial value of the gift to a beneficiary of the right to receive the income of the fund, which donor could not reduce, was excluded from the amount subject to tax.[11b]

11a Savage v United States (1964) 331 F2d 678 (CA 2); proceeds of insurance taken out in 1928 by wife on life of husband with retained right to change beneficiaries, or the settlement option, was irrevocably transferred on husband's death in April 1931, when settlement option became effective giving widow right to income for life and remainder to children, and taxability to widow's estate is determined by code as effective after March 3, 1931.

11b Walter v United States (1965) 341 F2d 182 (CA 6).

§ 158. Schedule G; Transfers During Life; Meaning of Adequate Consideration.

p. 205, n. 2. Where business as well as marital rights were settled by a property settlement agreement which was incorporated into a divorce decree, a transfer of property, though with a retained life interest, was held supported by adequate consideration, rendering the transfer nontaxable. McCoy v Comm (1961) 20 TCM 224, TC Memo 1961-40.

§ 159. Schedule G; Transfers During Life; Preparation of Schedule.

FORM NO. 20

Schedule G of Form 706, as revised January 1966 contains an additional item:

5. If a Federal gift tax return(s) was ever filed, state the year(s) covered and the Internal Revenue district in which filed.

§ 161. Schedule H; Powers of Appointment; Statutory Provisions Generally.

p. 209, n. 14. See § 168, this supplement.

§ 162. Schedule H; Powers of Appointment; Evolution of the Statute.

p. 209, n. 17. Helvering v Grinnell, cited in text, was held no longer decisive under § 2041(a)(1)(B) of the 1954 Code. Gartland v Comm (1961) 293 F2d 575 (CA 7).

p. 210, n. 1. See § 168 as to date

of "creation" in connection with releases of powers of appointment.

§ 164. Schedule H; Powers of Appointment; Definition.

p. 211, n. 7. Where under civil law in effect in state of decedent's domicile powers of appointment are not recognized, exclusion from decedent's taxable estate of a transfer with retained life estate, made by decedent as part of property settlement under separation agreement, on theory that remainders had been created by completed exercise of a power, and the life estate received, rather than retained, under the agreement in exchange for transfer of rights in the community, was denied. First National Bank of Shreveport (Fain) v United States (1963) 224 F Supp 747 (DC WD La), aff'd (1965) 342 F2d 415 (CA 5).

Add new note at end of first sentence, 5th paragraph of text page 211:
. . . "of his estate."[8a]

[8a] Power to appoint corpus of trust to life tenant's estate but not to herself, was a general power, making the value of the property subject thereto includible in her gross estate, the use of the word "or" in Code § 2041(b)(1) being disjunctive. Edelman (1962) 38 TC 972.

Maryland National Bank (Wilson) v United States, 236 F Supp 532 (DC Md); (power not exercisable in favor of donee's creditors, her estate, or its creditors, under state law).

Where the sole corporate trustee of a testamentary trust was given broad discretion to invade principal for health, comfort and welfare of the widow and other members of testator's family, widow's rights to compel trustees to exercise discretion in her favor were subject to trustee's legal duty to protect the rights of other beneficiaries, and could not be construed to any extent whatever as a general power to appoint under IRC § 2041(b)(1). Security-Peoples Trust Co. v United States (1965) 238 F Supp 40 (DC WD Pa).

Add new note in eighth line from bottom on page 211:
. . . of appointment.[9a]

[9a] Whether widow had an unlimited power to consume is a matter of state law, to be determined by decisions of its courts of last resort and not necessarily by local tax and probate decrees; and where widow was given full power to dispose of principal during her life "in such manner as she may see fit", with a gift over, it was held that under Kentucky law she had the unlimited power to appoint herself as unqualified owner during her life, rendering the property undisposed of on the date of her death taxable in her estate, though she had no testamentary control thereof. Snyder v United States (1962) 203 F Supp 195 (WD Ky).

Where widow, as income beneficiary of testamentary trust, is given power to request trustee at any time to sell certain stock and pay proceeds to her, she is a donee of a general power of appointment for purposes of IRC § 2041, and the value of the stock subject to the power is taxable to her estate, though the power is never exercised. Ewing v Rountree (1964) 228 F Supp 137 (DC MD Tenn) aff'd 346 F2d 471. Under state law remaindermen could not have restrained widow from requesting a sale even though she did not require the proceeds for her reasonable support and maintenance, the power under Tennessee law not being limited by an ascertainable standard of such support.

Testamentary power to invade trust principal whenever "necessary or advisable in order to provide" for "needs," "proper expenses" or "benefit" of life tenant is to be construed as a general power of appointment, requiring corpus to be taxed to life tenant's estate on her death in 1956; the requirement of Pennsylvania law that such power must be exercised in good faith does not provide an ascertainable standard under IRC § 2041(b)(1)(A), and the will was found not to restrict the life beneficiary's consumption of principal exclusively to support and maintenance. Strite v McGinnes (1964)

330 F2d 234 (CA 3) aff'g 215 F Supp 513 (DC ED Pa).

§ 165. Schedule H; Powers of Appointment; Exceptions to Definition.

p. 215, n. 1. Stafford v United States (1964) 236 F Supp 132 (DC ED Wis) (gift of life estate "with full power of sale and making other disposition", together with right to use principal for "care, comfort or enjoyment", was taxable to life tenant's estate, as property subject to a general power not limited by an ascertainable standard).

p. 215, n. 2. Where a widow was given a life estate with power to consume, invade or appropriate the estate property for her benefit, but only if necessary to maintain for her the standard of health, support and/or maintenance to which she was accustomed, and she was given the concurrent power to convey such property during her lifetime, it was held that the twofold power to consume and convey was not limited by an ascertainable standard and was taxable as a general power of appointment. Phinney v Kay, 275 F2d 776 (CA 5) (1960).

Where the decedent had been given a power to invade trust principal "as he may from time to time request, he to be the sole judge of his needs," the power given was limited by an ascertainable standard consisting of decedent's needs and was not includible in decedent's gross estate. Pittsfield National Bank v United States, 181 F Supp 851 (D Mass) (1960).

p. 216, n. 4. Where a widow is given income for life under a trust with a power to invade corpus when necessary for her maintenance, support and comfort, the power of invasion is thereby limited by a fixed

standard capable of measurement and such power is not free of the trust and does not qualify for the marital deduction. Noble v Comm. 31 TC 888 (1959).

§ 166. Schedule H; Powers of Appointment; Created Prior to October 21, 1942.

p. 217, n. 11. Where decedent, having a general power of appointment under a 1929 trust providing for payment of "so much of income to decedent as the trustee in his discretion shall deem advisable", requested, in 1931, payment of the entire income to himself for life, and in 1945 executed a release of the general power of appointment, it was held that the 1931 request constituted an exercise of the power and that when decedent released the power in 1945, after taking the life income, he thereby caused the remainder to become vested at that time, and resulted in the exercise of a power of appointment of the type described in § 2041(a)(1)(B) of the 1954 Code, rendering the trust taxable in his estate although no property actually passed by the exercise. Gartland v Comm (1961) 293 F2d 575 (CA 7).

§ 167. Schedule H; Powers of Appointment; Created Subsequent to October 21, 1942.

Add new note in third line of section, p. 217: . . . at the time of his death.[15a]

[15a] Where decedent dies before probate of a will whereby she receives a life estate subject to . general power, the value of the property subject to the power is not taxable to her estate, since the power is a personal privilege, not an interest in property, and she did not have or possess it at time of death. Town-

send v United States (1964) 232 F
Supp 219 (DC ED Tex).

p. 218, n. 17. The rule of IRC §
2041(a)(3) making appointive property taxable in the estate of the
donee, under certain conditions,
where a successive power is created,
does not apply where the second
donee is a person in being at date of
original donor's death, so that vesting is not postponed beyond limitations ascertainable with reference to
such date. Ball (1964) 43 Misc 2d
1032, 252 NYS2d 894, the court re-
ferring to text for discussion of the
taxability of property subject to suc-
cessively created powers, affd — AD
2d —, 259 NYS2d 1005.

§ 168. Schedule H; Powers of Appointment; Date of Creation of Power.

*Substitute for first sentence of
second paragraph on page
219:*

Regulation § 20.2041–1(e) has
been amended to provide that
a power of appointment created
by an inter vivos instrument is
considered as created on the
date the instrument takes effect.
Such a power is *not* considered
as created at some future date
merely because it is not exercisable on the date the instrument takes effect, or because it
is *revocable,* or because the identity of its holders is not ascertainable until after the date the
instrument takes effect.[1a]

The amendment was issued as
a result of the court's disagree-
ment with former Regulation

62

§ 20.2041–1(e). The effective
date of the inter vivos instrument (trust or insurance settlement agreement) had been determined by the courts to be
the date of "creation" under
IRC § 2041(a)(1), dealing with
releases of powers of appointment before or after the critical
date, and whether the power
was revocable or not was held
to have nothing to do with its
date of creation for purposes
of this section of the Code. The
commissioner had contended
that the later date of death of
the appointee of the power governed. Accordingly, where the
inter vivos instruments involved
were executed prior to October
21, 1942, though revocable, subsequent releases of the powers
were held to render the trust or
insurance proceeds nontaxable.[1b]

[1a] Regulation § 20.2041–1(e), as
amended Dec. 11, 1961 by TD 6582.
See App B, this supplement.

[1b] Turner v United States, 178 F
Supp 239, affd 287 F2d 821 (CA 8)
(1961); United States v Hubner
(1960) 285 F2d 27 (CA 9); Hyman
Extr. v United States (1960) 187 F
Supp 661 (SD NY); Rosenthal v
Comm (1960) 34 TC 144. Commissioner has acquiesced in this decision. 1963–1 CB 4.

Prior to issuing the amended regulation the Commissioner had announced that he would follow the
Turner decision (supra), and revoked
Rev Rul 278, 1953–2 CB 267, cited
in text. Rev Rul 63–74, 1963–1 CB
176.

[Harris Tax Supp]

§ 170. Schedule H; Powers of Appointment; Failure to Exercise; Lapse.

p. 221, n. 9. Turner v United States, 178 F Supp 239 (WD Mo) (1959), affd 287 F2d 821 (CA 8).

§ 172. Schedule H; Powers of Appointment; Disclaimer or Renunciation.

p. 223, n. 16. The provisions of IRC § 2041(a)(2), rendering property which is the subject to a general power of appointment created after October 21, 1942 taxable in the estate of a donee of power who dies, after statute became effective, in 1951, are not unconstitutional as taking property without due process of law, though the value of such property was not previously subject to tax in such estate, since the provisions for disclaimer or renunciation of the power by the donee afford such donee an opportunity to avoid the imposition of taxes in donee's estate, and the statute is thus not arbitrary, or unconstitutionally retroactive. Ewing v Rountree (1964) 228 F Supp 137 (DC MD Tenn), affd 346 F2d 471.

§ 173. Schedule H; Powers of Appointment; Exercise or Release Taxable Under Other Sections.

p. 224, n. 20. Where decedent, having a general power of appointment under a 1929 trust providing for payment of "so much of income to decedent as the trustee in his discretion shall deem advisable", requested, in 1931, payment of the entire income to himself for life, and in 1945 executed a release of the general power of appointment, it was held that the 1931 request constituted an exercise

of the power and that when decedent released the power in 1945, after taking the life income, he thereby caused the remainder to become vested at that time, and resulted in the exercise of a power of appointment of the type described in § 2041(a) (1)(B) of the 1954 Code, rendering the trust taxable in his estate although no property actually passed by the exercise. Gartland v Comm (1961) 293 F2d 575 (CA 7).

§ 174. Schedule H; Powers of Appointment; Legal Disability.

p. 225, n. 11. Though settlor, establishing inter vivos trust in 1935, made provision for relinquishment, on his death, resignation, or incapacity, of retained powers that rendered the trust taxable to his estate, the subsequent appointment of a conservator of his property, upon his own petition does not operate as a relinquishment of the powers, since it does not permanently remove him from his trusteeship without possibility of resumption of duties as co-trustee when the incapacity comes to an end. Round v Comm (1964) 332 F2d 590 (CA 1).

§ 177. Schedule H; Powers of Appointment; Return.

p. 227, n. 7. A residual death benefit or lump sum payable, upon the death of a railroad employee, to a person designated by him, as allowed by the Railroad Retirement Act of 1937, § 5 (f) (2), is includible in the gross estate of the deceased railroad employee. Rev Rul 60–70 IRB 1960–6, p. 21.

§ 178. Schedule I; Annuities; Generally.

p. 230, n. 12. An annuity or other lump-sum payment payable by virtue of § 5 of the Railroad Retirement Act of 1937 to any person under subsections (a), (b), (c), (d) or (f) (1) is not includible in the gross estate of the deceased railroad employee because the statutory beneficiaries thereof do not derive such benefits from a contract or agreement. Rev Rul 60–70, IRB 1960–6, p. 21.

§ 179. Schedule I; Annuities; Definition of Terms.

Add note in 7th line on page 231:

. . . employment[18a]

[18a] Payments to widow under railroad's unqualified deferred compensation and death benefit plans held taxable under IRC § 2039. Bahen v United States (1962) 305 F2d 827 (Ct Cls).

Where decedent on his retirement became entitled to retirement allowances during his life under employer's Annuity Plan, and on his death widow received twelve monthly payments measured by decedent's allowances, under a Death Benefit Plan, the payments receivable by her are taxable to decedent's estate; the Death Benefit and Annuity Plans are, under Reg. § 20.2039–1, to be considered as integrated into a single plan. All v McCobb (1963) 321 F2d 633 (CA 2). The unfunded Death Benefit Plan to which no periodic contributions were made involved no insurance element, or shifting of risk, and was not treated as "insurance".

Retirement contract with decedent's company calling for annual payments over 15 years, unless after retirement he should engage in competing business, gave decedent an enforceable right so long as he refrained from competition, binding on the company, and the commuted

64

value was includible in his estate. Wadewitz (1964) 339 F2d 980 (CA 7).

Where widow's death benefits were declared by decedent's employer's board of directors, after his death, out of year's profits, and his salary continued, pursuant to consistent long standing policy not based on contract or agreement, decedent had a hope but no right to expect payments to be made to his widow, and had himself no property right requiring sums paid widow to be included in his estate as annuities, or otherwise. Barr (1963) 40 TC 227. The Commissioner has announced acquiescence, IRB 1964–16 p. 6.

p. 231, n. 19. Where employee had a right under a retirement pension contract to receive future payments, to continue as long as he did not engage in competitive activities, the value of the annuity is taxable to his estate, though he dies before retirement, the company's obligation being fixed and nonforfeitable and subject to defeat by acts within employee's control only. Wadewitz (1964) 339 F2d 980 (CA 7).

p. 231, n. 20. Wadewitz (1964) 339 F2d 980 (CA 7) where the court pointed out that interpretation developed under IRC § 2036 are relevant to a determination of whether a decedent's right to receive payments is for a period determined with reference to the date of his death.

§ 180. Schedule I; Annuities; Amount Includible.

Add note in sixth line of section on page 232:

. . . by the decedent.[2a]

[2a] The entire value of an annuity payable under the Uniformed Services Contingency Option Act of

1953 is includible in the gross estate of the deceased retired member of the uniformed service. Rev Rul 59–254, IRB 1959–32, p. 8.

Lump-sum payments under a qualified retirement annuity contract which represent simply a refund of decedent's contributions toward the cost of the contract are includable in gross estate in their entirety. Comm v Albright (1966) 356 F2d 319 (CA 2).

p. 233, n. 5. Where contributing employer was beneficiary and owner of pension fund annuity policies which provided death benefits for employee-decedent's widow, if surviving, the value of employer's con tingent rights is not taxable to employee's estate, but is deductible from the estate-tax return value of the annuities, since employer did not take from decedent, but reserved its right when it bought the annuities. Allen (1963) 39 TC 817. Commissioner acquiesced, IRB 1964–17 p. 5.

p. 234, n. 9. For calendar years beginning after December 31, 1962, contributions or payments made on behalf of the decedent while self-employed (See 401(c)(1)) are considered to have been made by decedent under § 2039(c).

§ 181. Schedule I; Annuities; Exemptions Under Qualified Plans.

p. 235. n. 15. Reg. 20.2039–2, amended Jan 18, 1961 to include annuity contracts.

Internal Revenue Service procedures for issuing determination letters relating to the initial qualification of pension, annuity, profit sharing and bond purchase plans which include self-employed individuals have been set forth in Rev Proc 63–23, IRB 1963–41 p. 84, 26 CFR 601.201.

For calendar years beginning after December 31, 1962 the requirement of § 403(a), not of the paragraphs of § 401(a), are to be met. See IRC § 2039(c).

§ 184. Nonresidents Not Citizens; Gross Estate; Generally.

p. 238, n. 4. Effective October 23, 1963 Reg §§ 20.2031–1, 20.2103–1, and 20.2105–1 are amended to reflect the elimination of the exclusion from the gross estate of real and tangible property situated outside the United States.

p. 238, n. 5. But see §§ 185, 186, this supplement for amendment to IRC affecting estates of decedents dying after September 14, 1960.

§ 185. Nonresidents Not Citizens; Property Within the United States.

p. 239, n. 8. Where decedent, a nonresident widow, had been given under German law the equivalent of a life estate with power of invasion followed by a remainder to her son, and had purchased out of corpus American securities held in custodian accounts in the country, the American securities were treated as funds of the decedent's husband's estate and were not includible in decedent's gross estate. Zietz v Comm (1960) 34 TC 351, No. 35. Acquiescence, 1960–2 CB 7.

p. 240, n. 4. Amounts owing by brokerage firm in New York to nonresident alien not engaged in business in the U. S. constitute property situated in the U. S.; although broker maintained balances in banks the estate did not succeed in showing that the deposits were made by broker as decedent's agent. Ogarrio,

40 TC 242 (1963); affd 337 F2d 108 (CA Dist Col).

p. 240, n. 7. A new United States-Canadian Estate Tax Convention was signed Feb. 17, 1961, to become effective when ratified by both countries, and will apply to estates of decedents dying on or after January 1, 1959.

Add new text at end of section, page 241:

With respect to estates of decedents dying after September 14, 1960, a resident of a United States possession shall for estate tax purposes be considered a nonresident not a citizen of the United States if he acquired his United States citizenship solely by reason of his being a citizen of such possession or his birth or residence within such possession (added to IRC § 2209 by PL 86–779). The estate of a decedent dying after September 14, 1960, who is thus considered a nonresident not a citizen of the United States, shall be entitled to an estate tax exemption which shall be the greater of (a) $2,000, or (b) that proportion of $60,000, which the value of that part of his gross estate situated at his death in the United States bears to the value of his entire gross estate wherever situated (added PL 86–779).[8a]

[8a] Regs. 20.0–1, 20.2011–1, 20.2014–1, 20.2053–9, 20.2106–1, 20.2208–1, 20.2209–1, as amended, Jan 18, 1961.

Effective October 23, 1963 Reg §§ 20.2031–1, 20.2103–1, and 20–2105–1

are amended to reflect the elimination of the exclusion from the gross estate of real and tangible property situated outside the United States.

The additional instructions, revised Form 706, see § 26, this supplement, reflect the changes made by the above statute.

§ 186. Nonresidents Not Citizens; Property without the United States.

p. 241, n. 9. See IRC § 2209, Regs. 20.0–1, 20.2011–1, 20.2014–1, 20.2053–9, 20.2106–1, 20.2208–1, 20.2209–1, as amended, Jan 18, 1961.

p. 242, n. 10. Where trust income payable to a nonresident French beneficiary was withheld after June 17, 1940 by the trustee, a New York trust company, pursuant to an executive order and was deposited by it in its banking department in its own name for the income account of said beneficiary, such accumulated income was held a bank deposit not situated within the United States and not includible in the deceased beneficiary's gross estate. City Bank Farmers Trust Co. v United States, 174 F Supp 583 (SD NY) (1959).

§ 187. Nonresidents Not Citizens; Return.

Add new text at end of section on page 245:

The Non-resident Alien Estate Tax Return Form 706NA, Schedule B, and paragraph 3 of the instructions accompanying the return were amended to reflect the removal by the Revenue Act of 1962 of the exclusion from the gross estate of real and tangible personal property situated outside the United States. The value of such property, in the case of decedents dying on or after July 1, 1964, and, in the case of decedents dying between October 17, 1962 and June 30, 1964 the value of such property acquired by decedent (or by his donor, if acquired by gift) after January 31, 1962, is to be included in the value of the gross estate, as reported in Schedule B. The proportion of expenses that may be deducted, and the amount of the "prorated exemption", will be correspondingly reduced.

The changes made by the revision of April, 1962 reflect the Canadian Estate Tax Convention of that year (Schedule B of return, paragraphs 10 and 11 of the instructions, § 312 this supplement), and the requirement where decedent made transfers of $1000 or more within three years of death Form 706 must be used (instructions, paragraph 2, § 26 this supplement).

In January 1965 form 706NA was revised by requiring information as to whether decedent at date of death personally or by agent had access to a safe deposit box in the United States.

CHAPTER 3

TAXABLE ESTATE

New sections added:
§ 197.1. Income Tax and Estate Tax Deductions; Administration Expenses.
§ 211.1. Schedule K; Claims against Estate; Medical Expenses; as Income or Estate Tax Deductions.
§ 232A. Schedule M; Marital Deduction; Illustrative Clauses of Conditioning Interest of Spouse on Survival for Limited Period.
§ 251.1. Schedule N; Transfers for Public, Charitable or Religious Uses; Illustrative Clauses.

§ 190. Taxable Estate; Definition.

Add note at end of first paragraph:

. . . two terms.[1a]

[1a] The definition of "net estate" in subchapter A applies in determining the additional tax under subchapter B. Reg. 80, Art. 1. Hurwitz v United States, 208 F Supp 594 (DC SD Tex), affd 320 F2d 911 (CA 5).

§ 191. General Considerations.

p. 250, n. 16. Trustee's final distribution fee, attorneys fees, and cost of documentary stamps on transfer of trust, the value of assets of which were included in decedent's estate for estate tax purposes as a transfer with retained life estate, were expenses "occasioned by decedent's death", although not actually incurred until later death of decedent's brother, co-beneficiary, since decedent's death was a condition precedent to the expense. The Union Commerce Bank v Comm (1963) 39 TC 973; affd oth gr 339 F2d 163 (CA 6), where the court also held that interest for periods after decedent's death on overdue gift taxes was deductible as a proper administration expense, absent bad faith or willful tax evasion.

Where the value of the assets of an inter vivos trust were included in decedent's gross estate due to death within three years of transfer, but were not part of the Kansas probate estate, the fees of the trustees for various sevices were treated as follows by the Tax Court:

1) preparation of estate tax returns being an executorial function, trustee's fees for these sevices were deductions for estate tax purposes, as made to probate estate and could not be taken against trust income on trust's fiduciary returns;

2) to the extent performed after decedent's death, fees for other administration services, essentially the distribution of the assets due to termination at death, related to property not subject to claims, and could be taken against gross estate as deductions, or against trust income; and

3) such deductions could be taken in part against fiduciary income, and in part against the gross estate, since the prohibition in IRC § 642(g) against using the same deduction for income and estate tax purposes ap-

68

plies to estate income but not to trust income. Burrow v Comm (1963) 39 TC 1080; the deduction of trustees' fees, allowed as estate tax deduction, from the income tax returns of the trust, was upheld on appeal. Comm v Burrow (1964) 333 F2d 66 (CA 10).

§ 193. Effect of Court Decree.

p. 252, n. 8. Declaratory judgment of state court, based on documentary evidence, oral testimony, briefs and an analysis of West Virginia law, was held not "collusive" and "non-adversely", though not opposed by residuary legatees, otherwise entitled to remainder, who were made parties and fully advised of issues. The state court proceeding, begun after bequest was questioned by IRS, in conference, involved substantial property interests with rival claimants, was based on reason and authority (as reviewed by the federal court in the tax refund action) and would in any event have been necessary for instruction and protection of trustees. Parkersburg Nat. Bank (Gordon) v United States (1964) 228 F Supp 375 (DC ND W Va); the federal court followed the state court in holding charitable gift a valid trust.

State court decree in action instituted by trustees was deemed conclusive as to property rights of parties though trustors did not resist the action, where the federal tax authorities had notice of the state court action, the District Director of Internal Revenue having been originally made a party to the action, and the result was correct under state law (California). Flitcroft v Commissioner of Internal Revenue (1964) 328 F2d 449 (CA 9) (ten-year trust agreement reformed to express irrevocability found to have been intended, resulting in tax-

[Harris Tax Supp]

ation of income to trust, rather than settlor).

p. 252, n. 9. As between a state court decree allowing a claim against an estate after an adversary hearing on the merits and a subsequent ex parte order adjusting the same debt, the final court decree takes precedence and is controlling in determining the deductible indebtedness. Cole v Granquist, 179 F Supp 440 (DC Or).

Where state trial court decree entered in an adverse proceeding between remainderman and widower that widower, who had been given a life estate with power to use the corpus as necessary for his comfort, maintenance, and well being, had a general power of appointment even in the absence of language in the will expressly conferring such power, such life estate was not a terminable interest, and therefore qualified for marital deduction. Willcox v United States (1965) 244 F Supp 500 (DC ED Va).

p. 252, n. 11. Ohio Probate Court order allowing executrix, as an administration expense, reasonable attorneys' fees for "extraordinary" services for successfully defending the will although executrix in her capacity as the sole residuary legatee would receive the benefit of the deduction, was held valid under Ohio law, and therefore controlling for estate tax purposes. Cadden v Welch (1962) 298 F2d 343 (CA 6).

Decree directing payment, out of the estate, of contestant's counsel fees in effecting settlement of will contest was held controlling, there not being sufficient clarity in New York law to make it possible to state that the Surrogate was without power to so charge the estate. Sussman v United States (1962) 236 F Supp 507 (ED NY).

p. 252, n. 13. Also see § 242 as to effect of state court decree upon marital deduction.

§ 194. Exemption.

p. 253, n. 5. Rev Rul 62–83, IRB 1962–23, p. 10 (Osage Indians).

Inherited allotted lands and trust fund cash, held by the United States in trust for a non-competent Indian, is exempt from federal estate taxes where no patent in fee simple was ever issued to the deceased Indian prior to his death or to his restricted non-competent Indian heir. Nash v Wiseman (1963) 227 F Supp 552 (DC WD Okla).

§ 196. Schedule J; Funeral Expenses.

Add note in 8th line, page 255:
". . . local law."[17a]

[17a] Funeral annd last illness expenses of Pennsylvania married woman predeceasing husband, paid pursuant to her will and allowed by the local probate court as a charge against gross estate, are deductible estate tax deductions. A wife may by will thus relieve her husband from the common law obligation for such expenses, provided he does not elect against the will. If the wife does not make such provision, such expenses are not deductible, unless the husband is insolvent, in which event they are deductible. Rev Rul 65–300, IRB 1965–50, p 30.

§ 197.1. Income Tax and Estate Tax Deductions; Administration Expenses (New).

The executor or administrator may elect to deduct administration expenses, or a portion

thereof, though payable out of principal, on the estate fiduciary income tax returns, rather than on the estate tax return.[1] Where the applicable estate tax rate is relatively low in comparison with the income tax rate, considerable tax savings may be possible, in which case a failure to take the deduction for income tax purposes may subject the executor or administrator to criticism.

Since estate fiduciary income tax returns are prepared on a cash basis, administration expenses are deductible thereon only if, and in the year, paid. They may not be estimated, as when taken on the estate tax return. With proper tax planning from the inception of the estate, actual payments of administration expenses may be scheduled and measured to offset income received in a particular year. Delaying the consideration of these tax aspects until the approach of the due date for filing the estate tax return may result in a loss of possible tax savings. However, preliminary computations may also indicate that it is more advantageous to take the deductions on the estate tax return.

The Code sets forth certain waiver requirements which are discussed further in Section 223 of the main text.

[1] IRC §§ 642(g), 2053. See § 238 (effect of election on marital deduc-

70

tion); and § 255 (effect of election on charitable deduction).

The double deduction of fees allowed to trustees of a trust whose assets are included for tax purposes in settlor's gross estate on her death in 1956, once in decedent's estate tax return and again in the trust's income tax return, is not prohibited by IRC §§ 642(g) and 2053, since the trust was an independent taxable entity at settlor's death, and the deductions are therefore claimed by two separate and independent taxable entities. Comm v Burrow (1964) 333 F2d 66 (CA 10).

Estate which deducted attorney's fees in its Federal estate tax return may, even though the statute of limitations on assessment of estate taxes has expired, elect to deduct such fees in its Federal income tax return, where such fees are subject to disallowance as estate tax deductions in connection with disposition of a validly filed claim for refund of Federal estate taxes. Rev. Rul. 63–240, IRB 1963–46, p. 16.

§ 198. Schedule J; Administration Expenses; Trustees' Commissions; Other Administration Expenses.

p. 259, n. 5. Attorney's fees incurred in Tax Court in connection with contesting inclusion in gross estate of certain property not subject to claims, and if paid within 60 days after the decision of the Tax Court becomes final (IRC § 6503 (a)(1)), even though more than three years after filing the return constitute an allowable deduction under IRC § 2053(b). Rev Rul 61–59, IRB 1961–14, p. 12.

p. 260, n. 13. Attorney's fees and expenses incurred and paid in connection with the successful defense of litigation attacking validity of

inter vivos trusts, which were expenses incurred in administration of property not subject to claims but included in decedent's gross estate, were held deductible under IRC § 2053; in addition, expenses incurred in determining the estate tax liability were held deductible. Central Trust Company of Cincinnati, Ohio v Welch (1961) 193 F Supp 336 (SD Ohio), affd 304 F2d 923 (CA 6).

§ 199. Schedule J; Administration Expenses; Attorneys' Fees.

p. 261, n. 17. Failure to claim deduction for attorney's fees at inception of proceeding contesting payment of an estate tax deficiency did not bar the executors from later claiming such deduction after judgment against them was reversed and a remand was ordered for further proceedings. Silverman v McGinnes, 170 F Supp 813, (ED Pa) (1959).

p. 261, n. 18. Ohio Probate Court order allowing executrix, as an administration expense, reasonable attorneys' fees for "extraordinary" services for successfully defending the will although executrix in her capacity as the sole residuary legatee would receive the benefit of the deduction, was held valid under Ohio law, and therefore controlling for estate tax purposes. Cadden v Welch (1962) 298 F2d 343 (CA 6); Swayne v Comm (1964) 43 TC 190, No. 18 (counsel fees paid for attempt to probate a will are a deductible expense though chargeable by statute pro rata against the shares of the beneficiaries).

Where decree directed that contestant's counsel fees in effecting compromise of will contest be paid out of the estate, the fees were held deductible from the gross estate, the said payment not being clearly contrary to New York law, and the court noting that wills which are so drafted or drafted in such circumstances that they are set aside without trial to the extent of half their dispositive effect must provoke special classes of administration expense of which the legal cost of the contest to arrive at the right rule of distribution is one. Sussman v United States (1962) 236 F Supp 507 (ED NY).

Where executor after denial of refund claim distributed and closed the estate, and the heirs recovered the overpayment of federal estate taxes in a class action brought by themselves in the District Court, the attorney's fees and cost of litigation incurred therein are deductible administration expenses. Altendorf v United States (1964) 228 F Supp 969 (DC ND). Reg § 20.2053–3(c)(3) does not apply since heirs should not be penalized for executor's failure to bring court action in his official capacity, expenses of which action would be clearly deductible.

p. 261, n. 20. Attorney's fee deduction held limited to amount fixed by state court. Bullock v Comm, 19 TCM 1080, TC Memo 1960–204.

Attorneys' fees and expenses allowed by probate court to executor named in will that was denied probate for lack of testamentary capacity were deductible as expenses of administration, since the named executor had a duty to present the will. Peck (1963) 40 TC 238. The Commissioner has announced acquiescence, IRB 1964–16 p. 7.

Where under Connecticut statutes an executor named in a will must present it for probate, and his counsel fees in a contest, whether or not the will is admitted, are chargeable pro rata against the beneficiaries and distributees of the estate, such fees, as allowed by the probate court,

and state tax commission, are deductions for federal estate tax purposes, though propounding executor who retained the counsel was to receive greater benefits under the will denied probate than under the one admitted by compromise agreement. Swayne v Comm (1964) 43 TC 190, No. 18.

p. 262, n. 7. Testator may not cause administration expenses and estate attorney fees, to extent required by Texas law to be allocated to widow's share of community, to become deductions from his estate under IRC 1939 § 812(b) for purposes of computing Federal estate tax, by testamentary provision that such charges be paid entirely from his share of community. To permit the allowance of such deductions would be contrary to statutory purpose to tax transmission of wealth at death, and to equalize tax treatment of marital property in common law and community property states. United States v Stapf (1963) 375 US 118, 11 L ed 2d 195, 84 S Ct 248.

Although under the facts of a specific case the outcome of estate tax litigation, involving the size of the marital deduction and the apportionment of estate taxes, inured primarily to the benefit of the widow's share, the entire attorneys' fee was nevertheless allowed as an estate tax deduction where the estate had been in administration for over 7 years and had also involved protracted state court litigation. First National Bank of Topeka (Graham) v United States (1964) 233 F Supp 19 (DC Kan).

p. 262, n. 11. First National Bank of Topeka (Graham) v United States (1964) 233 F Supp 19 (DC Kan); where attorneys' fee in $1,200,000 estate, supported by proper affidavits and by record in estate litigation, was allowed, overruling commission-

72

er's determination that $32,500 provided by county minimum fee schedule should be the measure of the deduction.

§ 200. Schedule J; Administration Expenses; Miscellaneous.

p. 264, n. 14. Reg § 20.2053–3(d) was am (see Appendix B) to provide that expenses for selling property of the estate are deductible of the sale is necessary in order to pay the decedent's debts, expenses and administration, or taxes, to preserve the estate, or to effect distribution. The phrase "expenses for selling property" includes brokerage fees and other expenses attending the sale, such as the fees of an auctioneer if it is reasonably necessary to employ one. Where an item included in the gross estate is disposed of in a bona fide sale (including a redemption) to a dealer in such items at a price below its fair market value, for purposes of this paragraph there shall be treated as an expense for selling the item whichever of the following amounts is the lesser: (i) the amount by which the fair market value of the property on the applicable valuation date exceeds the proceeds of the sale, or (ii) the amount by which the fair market value of the property on the date of the sale exceeds the proceeds of the sale. The principles used in determining the value at which an item of property is included in the gross estate shall be followed in arriving at the fair market value of the property for purposes of this paragraph. See §§ 20.2031–1 through 20.2031–9. [p. 2651]

p. 264, n. 4. Swayne v Comm (1964) 43 TC 190, No. 18, fees of guardian ad litem in will contest settled by compromise agreement.

§ 201. Schedule J; Administration Expenses; Taxes.

P. 265, n. 14. California real property taxes which become a lien on the first Monday in March preceding the fiscal year for which the taxes are levied, become enforceable obligations on that day, and therefore accrue at that time for purposes of Federal estate tax. If decedent dies after that day, whether before or after fiscal year commences, such taxes are deductible. Rev Rul 65–274, IRB 1965–47, p. 49.

p. 265, n. 17. As to amendments to IRC, § 2053 (d) (1954 Code) see § 214, this Supplement.

§ 202. Schedule J; Return.

FORM NO. 25

Schedule J on Form 706, as revised January 1966 provides:

A. Funeral expenses:

B. Administration expenses:

1. Executors' commissions—amount estimated/agreed upon/paid. (Strike out words not applicable) ....

2. Attorneys' fees—amount estimated/agreed upon/paid. (Strike out words not applicable) ....

3. Miscellaneous expenses: ....

§ 203. Schedule K; Claims against Estate; Generally.

p. 267, n. 5.

Testator may not by directing payment of "all" of community debts, including the half thereof for which under Texas law the widow is primarily liable, make such debts as were chargeable to the widow "claims" against the estate, deductible from testator's gross estate for purposes of determining the amount of the Federal estate tax (IRC 1939 § 812(b)), since they were not contracted for an adequate and full consideration in money; fact that testator may have been secondarily liable as surety did not constitute widow's share of the community debts "personal obligations" of testator under the Regulations (Treas. 105 § 81.36); such an interpretation would afford unwarranted tax advantages to couples holding community property. United States v Stapf (1963) 375 US 118, 11 L ed 2d 195, 84 S Ct 248.

§ 204. Schedule K; Claims against Estate; Interest.

p. 268, n. 17. Estate is not entitled to an expense of administration deduction for the interest on delayed payments of the federal estate tax. Ballance v United States (1965) 347 F2d 419 (CA 7).

Where state probate court allowed post-death interest on claims against estate, incurred by postponing payment of claims to avoid sale of assets at a sacrifice, such interest is an allowable deduction for purpose of arriving at net value of estate for federal estate tax purposes. Ballance v United States (1965) 347 F2d 419 (CA 7).

§ 205. Schedule K; Claims Against Estate; Contracts; Generally.

p. 268, n. 19. Payments alleged to have been made to decedent from principal of trust may not be deducted as claims against the estate, where it is not shown that trustee requested refund from decedent, or that she was aware that trustees had exceeded their discretion. Caplan v Comm (1964) 42 TC 446.

p. 268, n. 4. Wolf v Comm. 264 F 2d 82, (CA 3) (1959).

Balance due on a running account payable at the convenience of the deceased was held not barred by the Statute of Limitations, and therefore deductible as a claim against decedent's estate. Kerr v Comm. (1961) 199 F Supp 447 (ED Va).

§ 208. Schedule K; Claims against Estate; Contracts; Matrimonial Obligations.

p. 271, n. 9. Rev Rul 60–160, IRB 1960–17, p. 12, reaffirms the rule that an indebtedness founded upon a property settlement incorporated into a divorce decree is deductible from the decedent's gross estate. This ruling adds that if a court does not have the power to disregard the provisions of a pre-existing property settlement agreement, a deduction is allowable only to the extent that the transfer does not exceed the reasonable value of the support rights of the wife. In other words, the value of the consideration given by the wife in exchange for the property settlement agreement measures the maximum indebtedness deductible from the decedent's estate.

Where a separation agreement incorporated into a divorce decree required the husband to leave by will one-third of his net estate to his ex-wife, such amount was a deductible claim against his estate. Florida National Bank & Tr. Co. v United States (1960) 182 F Supp 76 (SD Fla).

Where executors' computation of the amount of the deduction available to the estate by reason of alimony payments payable until death or remarriage was supported by accepted actuarial tables as being the fair discounted value of the obligation as of decedent's death, but did not make any allowance for the effect on such value of their contesting the estate's liability for such obligation, deduction for only such alimony payments as were actually paid to date of remarriage was allowed. Gowetz v Comm (1963) 320 F2d 874 (CA 1).

§ 211. Schedule K; Claims Against Estate; Miscellaneous Claims.

p. 273, n. 8. Rosenman v United States, cited in text, revd oth gds, 323 US 658, 65 S Ct 536, 89 L ed 535.

§ 211.1. Schedule K; Claims against Estate; Medical Expenses; as Income or Estate Tax Deductions (New).

Medical expenses incurred by the decedent may be taken as a deduction in Schedule K, provided they are allowable as a claim against the estate by the laws of the jurisdiction under which the estate is being administered.[1] Where under local law a surviving husband is liable for medical expenses incurred for his wife's last ill-

[Harris Tax Supp]

ness,[2] the expense will generally be disallowed as a deduction in the wife's estate. If, due to financial or other circumstances, such liability had been assumed by the wife during her lifetime, her medical expense has been held to be a valid claim against her estate.[3]

The executor or administrator may elect to deduct medical expenses incurred by the decedent, which are paid out of the estate within one year after death, on either the estate tax return, or on decedent's final prior-to-death income tax return, whichever proves most beneficial.[4] The Code sets forth certain waiver requirements to be complied with in making the election.[5]

[1] IRC § 2053; Reg. § 20.2053–1.
[2] Rusuli (1959) 22 Misc 2d 590, 194 NYS2d 1009.
[3] Totten, 137 AD 273, 121 NYS 942; Tate v O'Malley, 52 F Supp 834 (DC WD Pa).
[4] IRC § 213.
[5] IRC §§ 213, 643g, 2053; and see § 223, main text.

§ 212. Schedule K; Claims against Estate; Taxes; Generally.

p. 273, n. 20. Where joint income tax return was filed prior to death of decedent, deduction of any part of the joint federal income tax payment from decedent's gross estate was disallowed where executor failed to establish a basis for determining decedent's portion of the tax. Pridmore v Comm (1961) 20 TCM 47, TC Memo 1961–12.

§ 214. Schedule K; Claims against Estate; Death Taxes.

Insert in text at end of second line of section on page 275:
. . . and foreign[12a]

[12a] See note 19, infra.

p. 275, n. 16. Provident Trust Co. of Philadelphia v United States, 268 F2d 779 (CA 3) (1959).

Add new note in third from last line on page 275:
. . . transferee,[18a]

[18a] Whether the deduction inures solely to the benefit of the charitable legatee is determined by state law, and in order that state court decree be binding it is not necessary that it be the result of a contest, provided there is no collusive arrangement. Darlington v Comm (1962) 302 F2d 673 (CA 3). Also see § 234 as to effect of state court decree.

p. 276, n. 19. The 1954 Code § 2053 (d) was amended in 1959, effective as to estates of decedents dying after July 1, 1955 to provide that an executor may elect to take a deduction for an estate, succession, legacy, or inheritance tax imposed by, and actually paid to, any foreign country with respect to property situated within that foreign country if the property is included in the gross estate of a citizen or resident of the United States and is property which would otherwise be transferred for public, charitable, or religious uses. The same treatment is accorded to foreign death taxes as is now provided by present law for state death taxes.

Code § 2014(f) was enacted at the same time to provide in effect that where a deduction is taken for foreign death taxes under § 2053(d), as amended, no foreign tax credit is allowable under § 2014 for the foreign taxes so deducted. Reg. 20.2011–2, 20.2014–1, 20.2014–2, 20.2014–3, as amended, and Reg. 20.2014–7, 20-.2053–10, as adopted, May 28, 1962, Appendix B, this supplement. Also see §§ 283, 309 and 310, this supplement.

p. 276, n. 20. Instructions to Schedule K, revised Form 706, see § 26, this supplement, provide that if difficulty is experienced in computing the deduction for death taxes a request for computation may be submitted to the Commissioner.

§ 215. Schedule K; Claims Against Estate; Gift Taxes.

p. 277, n. 5. Interest accruing after death in unpaid gift taxes may be proper deductions as administration expenses where allowed by state law, and where delay is not due to bad faith. Union Commerce Bank (Baker) v Comm (1964) 339 F2d 163 (CA 6).

§ 216. Schedule K; Claims against Estate; Income Taxes.

p. 278, n. 15. Reg. § 20.2053–6(f) governing apportionment and deduction of joint income tax liability has been held valid. McClure v United States (1961) 288 F2d 190 (Ct Cls).

§ 219. Community Property; Funeral and Administration Expenses; Claims Against Estate; Mortgages and Liens.

p. 280, n. 15. Testator may not cause administration expenses and estate attorney fees, to extent required by Texas law to be allocated to widow's share of community, to become deductions from his estate under IRC 1939 § 812(b) for purposes of computing Federal estate tax, by testamentary provision that such charges be paid entirely from his share of community. To permit the allowance of such deductions would be contrary to statutory purpose to tax transmission of wealth at death, and to equalize tax treatment of marital property in common law and community property states. United States v Stapf (1963) 375 US 118, 11 L ed 2d 195, 84 S Ct 248.

p. 280, n. 16. Testator may not by directing payment of "all" of community debts, including the half thereof for which under Texas law the widow is primarily liable, make such debts as were chargeable to the widow "claims" against the estate, deductible from testator's gross estate for purposes of determining the amount of the Federal estate tax (IRC 1939 § 812(b)), since they were not contracted for an adequate and full consideration in money; fact that testator may have been secondarily liable as surety did not constitute widow's share of the community debts "personal obligations" of testator under the Regulations (Treas. 105 § 81.36); such an interpretation would afford unwarranted tax advantages to couples holding community property. United States v Stapf (1963) 375 US 118, 11 L ed 2d 195, 84 S Ct 248.

§ 200. Schedule K; Claims Against Estate; Mortgages and Liens; Return.

FORM NO. 26

The legend appearing before the items on Schedule K of Form 706, as revised January 1966 reads:

Debts of Decedent—Creditor and nature of claim, and allowable death taxes.

§ 221. Schedule L; Net Losses and Support of Dependents.

Add note at end of first sentence of fourth paragraph of section:

. . . September 23, 1950.[14a]

[14a] A family allowance is deductible from the gross estate, but the amount of the deduction is subject to review to accord with the actual needs of the dependents. Vogel v Comm (1960) 278 F2d 548 (CA 9).

§ 222. Schedule L; Expenses Incurred in Administering Property Not Subject to Claims.

p. 284, n. 17. The double deduction of fees allowed to trustees of a trust whose assets are included for tax purposes in settlor's gross estate on her death in 1956, once in decedent's estate tax return and again in the trust's income tax return, is not prohibited by IRC §§ 642(g) and 2053, since the trust was an independent taxable entity at settlor's death, and the deductions are therefore claimed by two separate and independent taxable entities. Comm v Burrow (1964) 333 F2d 66 (CA 10).

§ 223. Income Tax and Estate Tax Deductions.

p. 285, n. 4. Duly filed election to take administration expenses as income tax deductions under 1939 and 1954 Codes were binding and could not be revoked so as to permit a part thereof to be taken as estate tax deductions during the course of examination of fiduciary income and estate tax returns. Darby v Wiseman (1963) 323 F2d 792 (CA 10).

p. 285, n. 5. In applying and clarifying the rule as discussed in the text, the Treasury Department has ruled that the portion of any administration expenses attributable to the earning of tax-exempt income is allowable as a deduction for Federal estate tax purposes provided that the deduction has not also been taken by an estate for Federal income tax purposes. The representative may thus be allowed to apportion the total cost of producing tax-exempt income between the estate tax return and the income tax return, but he cannot use the same

deduction twice. Rev Rul 59-32, IRB 1959-4, p. 17; Rev Rul 63-27, IRB 63-10, p. 7.

Statement that administration expenses had not been claimed on the estate tax return, or allowed as estate tax deductions, and waiver of right to so claim them need not be filed with the income tax return but may be filed at any time prior to the expiration of the statutory limitation applicable to the taxable year for which deduction is sought. Darby v Wiseman (1963) 323 F2d 792 (CA 10).

Administration expenses are payable from corpus in the absence of testamentary direction, but where life tenant was to receive income "immediately following" death, they are to be deducted in determining value of charitable bequests of remainder, though executor elected to claim them as income tax deductions and claimed to have paid them out of income. Republic National Bank of Dallas (George) v Comm (1962) 39 TC 85, affd (1964) 334 F2d 348 (CA 5).

§ 224. Schedule L; Net Losses and Expenses Incurred in Administering Property Not Subject to Claims; Return.

FORM NO. 27

The legend appearing before the items on the expense portion of Schedule L of Form 706, as revised January 1966 reads:

Expenses incurred in administering property not subject to claims (indicate whether estimated, agreed upon, or paid)

§ 225. Schedule M; Marital Deduction; Generally.

Add text at end of first paragraph of section:

The marital deduction is mandatory and cannot be waived by the representative of the deceased spouse.[12a]

[Harris Tax Supp]

12a Where a husband and wife die within a short time of each other, a situation may arise whereby the estate representatives may seek to utilize the marital deduction and other estate tax benefits in order to increase the net estate, after taxes, passing to the ultimate beneficiaries of the deceased spouse dying last. However, the Treasury Department has ruled that the estate tax marital deduction is mandatory and cannot be waived by the estate of a spouse first to die in order to reduce the estate taxes on the property passing from the surviving spouse's estate, nor can the marital deduction be waived for any other purpose. Thus, the estate of the spouse first to die is not allowed to waive the marital deduction in order to reduce the size of the estate passing to the surviving spouse and in order to give the estate of the surviving spouse a credit for tax on prior transfers. Rev Rul 59–123, IRB 1959–15, p. 18.

p. 288, n. 14a. Boyd v Gray, 175 F Supp 57 (D Ky) (1959).

§ 228. Schedule M; Marital Deduction; Interest in Property Passing.

p. 290, n. 1. United States v Stapf (1963) 375 US 118, 11 L ed 2d 195, 84 S Ct 248.

Where husband and wife were killed in an accident, and there was no evidence as to who died first, and husband had furnished entire consideration for property held by the entirety, if Uniform Simultaneous Death Act applies, a presumption of survivorship in the wife is created with respect to half of the property, which half passes to and is includible in her estate, and the husband's estate is entitled to a marital deduction to the extent of the one-half interest

passing to the wife. Rev Rul 66–60, IRB 1966–11, p. 14.

p. 291, n. 7. See § 239, p. 310, n. 4, this supplement.

But a statutory right under Ohio law of a surviving spouse to purchase certain specified property from the estate of the deceased spouse was held not to be an interest in property passing from the decedent to his surviving spouse, and that such estate assets purchased pursuant to such a right do not qualify for the marital deduction. Crichfield v Comm, 32 TC 844, No. 72 (1959).

Where estate personalty had been exhausted to pay decedent's debts and the decedent's widow had thereafter advanced her own funds to the estate in order to receive from the estate her widow's allowance and support as provided under Ohio law, it was held that such funds so set apart as a widow's allowance did not pass from the decedent to his surviving spouse and thus did not qualify for the marital deduction. Denman v Comm, 33 TC 277, No. 44 (1959), affd 287 F2d 725 (CA 6).

§ 229. Schedule M; Marital Deduction; Nondeductible Interests.

Add note in twenty-fifth line on page 292:

. . . adequate and full consideration.[11a]

11a Where contributing employer was beneficiary and owner of pension fund annuities with death benefits for employee-decedent's widow should she survive him, the full value of the annuity, less the value of that part attributable to decedent's contribution, was allowable as part of the marital deduction; the employer's execution and assumption of obligations of the pension agreement constituted full and adequate consideration, so that disallowance under IRC Sec. 2056(b)(1) was not required. Allen (1963) 39 TC 817. Commissioner acquiesced, IRB 1964–17 p. 5.

p. 293, n. 15. Where retired Federal employee elects to receive a reduced civil service retirement annuity so that his widow will receive a survivor's annuity payable until death or remarriage, the value of the annuity does not qualify for a marital deduction in his estate, unless decedent designated the widow or her estate as the beneficiary of unrecovered contributions, or unless all decedent's contributions, plus interest, have been recovered by the date of his death. Rev Rul 64–310, IRB 1964–48, p 15.

p. 293, n. 16. Where, under mutual wills, each spouse irrevocably leaves his entire property to the other absolutely with an alternative gift over to their children in case one spouse has predeceased the other, it has been held that, where under state law upon the death of the first spouse the interest passing to the surviving spouse is absolute, and not terminable, it thus qualifies for the marital deduction. The fact that the surviving spouse is under a contractual obligation not to revoke his will which disposes of all his property to his children does not reduce the property received from the first spouse to a terminable interest since his right to alienate such property during his lifetime is unrelated to the obligation not to revoke his will. Newman v United States, 176 F Supp 364 (SD Ill) (1959); McLean v United States (1963) 224 F Supp 726 (DC ED Mich) (joint and mutual will devising property held by the entirety).

Provision in joint will giving property to surviving spouse, and any-

thing left upon death of survivor to children, lacked any indicia of intent to effect contractual disposition of property or to limit survivor to life interest, and therefore survivor's interest was absolute and qualified for marital deduction. Dekker v United States (1965) 245 F Supp 255 (DC SD Ill).

§ 230. Schedule M; Marital Deduction; Exceptions to Terminable Interest Rule.

p. 294, n. 19. Where trustees are given uncontrolled discretion to use income of trust for widow for benefit of sons, widow's interest is not such an unconditional right for life to all the income as to qualify for the marital deduction. This result is not affected by trustee's failure to make any such use, or by widow's right to use residential property, where she directed a sale of the residence and the proceeds were added to the trust. Thomas v United States (1962) 207 F Supp 609 (DC ND Oh), affd (1963) 317 F2d 519 (CA 6).

§ 232. Schedule M; Marital Deduction; Interest of Spouse Conditional on Survival for Limited Period.

p. 297, n. 11. Smith v U. S. noted in the text has been acquiesced in by the government.

§ 232A. (New) Schedule M; Marital Deduction; Illustrative Clauses of Conditioning Interest of Spouse on Survival for Limited Period.

Cases where conditional limitations, construed under state

law, have been considered in determining whether a gift to a surviving spouse is terminable, and so not available in computing the marital deduction, are compared in the following chart.

CASE	PROVISION IN WILL	STATE LAW	HOLDING
Lamar v Bookwalter (1963) 323 F2d 644 (CA 8).	Gift to wife "absolutely", but gifts over should she "not survive the administration of my estate", and in two other events.	Under Missouri law clear and conclusive language, as here, is sufficient to cut down a fee; administration is mandatory, and ends on a day certain, though not knowable at decedent's death.	*for government.* "Administration of my estate" has a clear meaning, and widow's interest would terminate on failure to survive it.
US v Mappes (1963) 318 F2d 508 (CA 10).	Absolute gift, but if wife dies "before my estate is administrated", to his sons.	Oklahoma law requires "clear and distinct" words to cut down absolute gift.	*for government.* Wife's interest was subject to defeasance by occurrence of an uncertain event; her survival beyond the conclusion by judicial decree of the process of administration, and so was terminable under 1954 Code.
Martinson v Wright (1959) 181 F Supp 534 (D Idaho).	Gift over if wife dies in common disaster or "prior to the distribution of my estate".	State probate court held that property had vested absolutely and indefeasibly.	*for taxpayer.* State court judgment determining persons entitled to succeed to estate, and their respective interests was controlling (1939 Code).
Roberts v US (1960) 182 F Supp 957 (D Cal).	Absolute gift of half of estate to wife, if cohabiting with testator at his death; pecuniary legacy to step-son if wife die prior to "distribution of my estate".	California law required expressed interest of testator, not speculation regarding possible unexpressed wishes, to be considered.	*for taxpayer.* Wife's half interest not affected by condition attached to the pecuniary legacy. (1939 Code).

82

§ 233. Schedule M; Marital Deduction; Valuation of Interest Passing to Surviving Spouse.

p. 298, n. 14. Where bequest to surviving spouse is conditioned on relinquishment of her community property interest, so that it would pass to a trust for children, the testamentary interest passing to surviving spouse upon such relinquishment will qualify for the marital deduction only to the extent that such bequest exceeds in value the relinquished share of the community. United States v Stapf (1963) 375 US 118, 11 L ed 2d 195, 84 S Ct 248 (the court indicated that the applicable Regulation 105, § 81.47c (b)(3)(1949), now § 20.2056(b)-4(b) Example (3)(1958), set forth in App B p 994 of text, is directly based on expressions of Congressional intent, and was not inconsistent with the Code provisions).

Where in settlement of extended litigation involving the validity of intestate's second marriage, the widow agrees to make a substantial payment, individually, to her stepchildren, the value of her intestate share is not reduced by the amount of such payment, as an encumbrance, under IRC § 2056(b)(4), since the payment was not imposed by decedent, but was agreed to by surviving spouse in consideration of the avoidance of further litigation after her rights had become vested on decedent's death. First National Bank of Topeka (Graham) v United States (1964) 233 F Supp 19 (DC Kan).

p. 299, n. 3. Absent statutory provision or conclusive judicial precedent directing the apportionment of federal estate taxes, the intestate share of a surviving spouse, qualifying in its entirety for the marital deduction, will be treated as ex-

cluded from the gross taxable estate and so will not be required to share the burden of the estate taxes. First National Bank of Topeka (Graham) v United States (1964) 233 F Supp 19 (DC Kan). (The court reasoned that the Kansas legislature might hav omitted to pass an apportionment statute so as not to defeat the purpose of Congress in providing a marital deduction to equalize tax treatment of marital gifts in common law and community property states.)

§ 234. Schedule M; Marital Deduction; Life Estate with Power of Appointment in Surviving Spouse.

p. 300, n. 5.
Annotation: Construction of § 2056(b)(5) of the 1954 Internal Revenue Code providing for marital deduction if surviving spouse has life estate with power to appoint. 90 ALR2d 414.

p. 300, n. 9. Property passing to widow by joint, mutual and contractual will, with gift over to children on death of survivor, was held to qualify for the marital deduction, and not to be treated as a life estate, where testators' intent was clear that survivor should have full control and power o disposition over the moderate sized estate; the property had been accumulated during fifty years of marriage and of joint operation of a construction business, and will provided that should wife survive, son would take equipment of business, but surviving husband would take such equipment. United States v Spicer (1964) 332 F2d 750 (CA 10) (The court observed that husband would not be able to operate the business without control of the property, and since daughters were grown and married, there was no basis for finding that widow's control was intended to be limited).

Where administrative power granted to trustees to retain cash without investment is subject to the right of the spouse under State law to require that trustees either make the property productive or convert it within a reasonable time, and power to allocate receipts and disbursements between principal and income is subject to reasonable limitations under applicable State law, the granting of such powers does not evidence an intention to deprive the surviving spouse of the beneficial enjoyment required by the statute, and a marital deduction may be allowed for the value of the bequest notwithstanding these powers. Rev Rul 66–39, IRB 1966–8, p. 48.

p. 302, n. 3. Bourke v Comm, 19 TCM 496, TC Memo 1960–94.

p. 302, n. 4. Where under joint wills each spouse agreed not to make any testamentary disposition other than therein provided, but each had the unrestricted right to dispose during lifetime of any property received under the will, the property passing under the will qualified for the marital deduction, even though there had been no power to devise. Nettz v Phillips (1962) 202 F Supp 270 (SD Iowa).

p. 304, n. 14. Right of wife, as holder of life estate in family residence with absolute power, to sell and convey without accounting for the proceeds, was held, under Missouri law, to vest wife with an absolute right to dispose of the property during her lifetime by gift, as well as by sale, thus qualifying the bequest for the marital deduction under § 812(e)(1)(F) of the 1939 Code. Geyer v Bookwalter (1961) 193 F Supp 57 (WD Mo).

Where surviving widow is given life estate in decedent's residence with power to sell for purposes of buying a more suitable home in fee simple, the power is not exercisable in all events, and the gift does not qualify for the marital deduction. United States v First Nat. Trust & Sav. Bank of San Diego (Vajen) (1964) 335 F2d 107 (CA 9).

p. 304, n. 16. Gelb v Comm (1962) 298 F2d 544 (CA 2).

Where surviving spouse as life tenant and trustee was required to provide for maintenance and support of son from income and principal, her power of invasion was limited and the gift did not qualify for the marital deduction. Flesher v United States (1965) 238 F Supp 119 (DC ND W Va).

Where surviving spouse as life tenant of trust to pay her income for life had the right to withdraw up to $5,000 each year, it was held that she had the power to appoint and receive income from a specific portion of corpus, and therefore such sum qualified for the marital deduction. Allen v United States (1965) 250 F Supp 155 (DC ED Mo).

p. 304, n. 17. Boyd v Gray (1958) 175 F Supp 57 (DC WD Ky).

Bequest of entire estate to wife on condition she execute an agreement approved by Surrogate to leave unused portions of his estate equally to his children, otherwise all but a specified portion of the estate was bequeathed to one child, was a bequest of a terminable interest, since viewed as of the moment of death—which is the determining factor—bequest was subject to contingencies, upon failure of which the estate was to pass to one other than spouse for less than an adequate consideration, who would enjoy the property upon the termination of the spouse's interest. Allen v United States (1966) — F2d — (CA 2), affg 242 F Supp 687.

84

Add text at end of section:

The determination of whether a power to invade or consume with a gift over qualifies for the martial deduction has been held to be dependent upon two factors: (1) The surviving spouse must be given the unrestricted right to appoint the principal of the estate to himself or herself as unqualified owner *or* to appoint it to his or her estate, and (2) whether the particular power given to the surviving spouse meets the foregoing requirement is to be determined by state law.[19a]

An examination of the cases which seem to present conflicting conclusions reveals that there is no conflict as to principle, but rather a difference in the scope and extent of the power to consume in light of the applicable state law. The powers in some instances are limited to maintenance and comfort, and others are more extensive. The decisions may be reconciled to some extent by applying the foregoing principles.[19b]

[19a] Where testator on his death in 1953 gave widow a life estate with power to expend for her benefit, but no power to give it away or dispose of it by will, the interest was terminable, not qualifying for the marital deduction. Piatt v Gray (1963) 321 F2d 79 (CA 6).

Where state trial court decree entered in an adverse proceeding between remainderman and widower that widower, who had been given a

life estate with power to use the corpus as necessary for his comfort, maintenance, and well being, had a general power of appointment even in the absence of language in the will expressly conferring such power, such life estate was not a terminable interest, and therefore qualified for marital deduction. Willcox v United States (1965) 244 F Supp 500 (Dc ED Va).

[19b] In New York the right to invade or consume, in absence of provision to the contrary, is limited by a standard of good faith, and since it would not be exercisable in all events it would not qualify for the marital deduction. Lincoln Rochester Trust Company v United States (1962) 297 F2d 891 (CA 2); May v Comm (1959) 32 TC 386, No. 38, aff'd 283 F2d 853 (CA 2).

Widow's power to expend principal of life estate "whenever in her opinion it shall be necessary for her maintenance, comfort or well being", found under Kentucky law not to give her power to waste the property nor to give it away nor dispose of it by will, is thus not to be exercisable in all events, and does not qualify for the marital deduction. Piatt v Gray (1963) 321 F2d 79 (CA 6).

Provision in will for gift over of property undisposed of by widow at time of her death limited widow's power to alienate the property by gift or by will under Kentucky law, and defeated the marital deduction. Collings v United States (1961) 201 F Supp 266 (WD Ky).

Where testator's widow is given property in trust for life, she to have the income and "such portions of the principal as in her judgment may be necessary for her comfortable support and maintenance, she to be the sole judge as to what may be necessary", the right to principal is contingent under Massachusetts law on a good faith determination, and is thus not for purposes of IRC § 2056 to be deemed a power to appoint to herself exercisable in all events, so that the property may qualify for the marital deduction. Stedman v United States, 233 F Supp 569 (DC Mass).

Under Ohio law a power of invasion allowing the widow to withdraw any amounts she might deem advisable for her maintenance, comfort and general welfare is deemed a limited power which, when coupled to a life interest in trust disqualifies such interest from the marital deduction. Comer v Comm, 31 TC 1193, No. 123 (1959).

Where the widow was life income beneficiary of a trust with a power to encroach upon principal for her own benefit without being required to account to the remaindermen, the widow's interest did not qualify for the marital deduction since, under local law, the power to encroach upon principal did not enlarge the widow's interest into a fee. Semmes v Comm, 32 TC 1218, No. 119 (1959), affd 288 F2d 664 (CA 6).

Under Alabama law, where widow was given a life estate with a complete power to sell and dispose of or convert estate to her own use with a gift over, the power was held unrestricted and included power to make inter vivos gifts, thus qualifying bequests for marital deduction. Carlson v Patterson (1961) 190 F Supp 452 (ND Ala).

Bequest to widow of interest in estate with absolute power to convey such interest during her lifetime and gift over if she should die before settlement of estate, qualified as a deductible nonterminable interest even though will probated in 1952 further provided that until settlement of estate executor should have full and complete charge and management of the estate.

Robertson v U. S. (1962) 310 F2d 199 (CA 5).

An unrestricted power of invasion with a gift over to remaindermen of unconsumed principal qualifies for the marital deduction where the widow was clearly granted a right to consume any amount of principal and thereby to cut off remainder interests. Hoffman v McGinnes (1960) 277 F2d 598 (CA 3); Bone v United States (1965) 238 F Supp 97 (DC WD Ark) (widow given property for life with right to "use the same as she deems best and proper without limitation", together with appropriate power to sell and convert, despite gift over on widow's death).

Holder of a legal life estate under German will having unfettered power to invade principal was taxable under the 1939 Code as an individual, not as a fiduciary. Hirschmann v United States (1962) 309 F2d 104 (CA 2).

A bequest of residuary estate to wife "to do as she pleases without bond for life and after her death the balance to be divided" in a specified manner, does not qualify for marital deduction, since under Kentucky case law she could not wilfully waste or give corpus away so as to extinguish the remainder interests, and therefore she was not given an unrestricted power of appointment over the corpus. Duvall v United States (1965) 246 F Supp 378 (DC ED Ky).

§ 235. Schedule M; Marital Deduction; Life Insurance or Annuity Payments with Power of Appointment in Surviving Spouse.

p. 305, n. 4. Limitations not disqualifying for marital deduction on widow's power to appoint insurance proceeds were: that she shall have

[Harris Tax Supp]

given at least 90 days' notice of intent to withdraw principal, which was payable only on interest dates, and that if she dies within one year, principal not withdrawn would pass to decedent's estate. Since an application for withdrawal submitted to the insurance company would give widow an unqualified right to proceeds, she had a power exercisable in all events. Jennings (1962) 39 TC 417; the commissioner has acquiesced in this decision.

Where the widow was given power, under an insurance settlement provision paying her interest on the proceeds of insurance for life, to withdraw the insurance proceeds, in whole or in part only on monthly interest payment dates, it was held that such power of appointment, first available one month after decedent's death, was not exercisable in all events and thus disqualified for the marital deduction. T. C. Werbe v United States, 273 F2d 201 (CA 7) (1959); the Tax Court has held that provisions giving widow power to withdraw entire insurance proceeds on any interest date, 30 days after receipt by insurer of proof of death, with power retained by insurer to defer payment for not more than six months, were made for administrative convenience of insurer, and did not prevent the withdrawal rights from coming into existence on decedent's death, or the qualification of the proceeds for the marital deduction. Cornwell v Comm (1962) 37 TC 688; the commissioner has acquiesced, IRB 1964–17, p. 5.

§ 237. Schedule M; Marital Deduction; Entire Interest or Specific Portion.

p. 307, n. 1. Meyer v United States (1959) 275 F2d 83 (CA 2), affd 364

US 410, 5 L ed 161, 81 S Ct 210 (policy not qualified for marital deduction under 1939 Code).

p. 308, n. 5. "The liberalization in the provision as to trusts, made in the 1954 Code and applied to earlier years by the Technical Amendments Act, was evidently designed to permit certain normal testamentary dispositions without the total forfeiture of the deduction that the 1939 Code had occasioned in some instances. That Congress gave a fractional interest as an example of a 'specific portion' does not warrant a construction that Congress did not mean to include other instances fairly within the language and the underlying policy. We disapprove Regulations 105, § 81.47a(c)(3) [1954 Code —Regs. § 20.2056(b)–5(c)] insofar as it would limit a 'specific portion' to 'a fractional or percentile share.' " Gelb v Comm (1962) 298 F2d 544 (CA 2), holding that widow's power to appoint the entire corpus, less a sum determinable by actuarial calculations (or less a given dollar amount) was exercisable over a "specific portion" of residuary trust, qualifying said portion for the marital deduction. Citizens Nat. Bank of Evansville v United States (1966) — F2d — (CA 7).

Where widow was not given entire income of marital trust, but was to receive $300 per month for life, payable from income and corpus, the amount of corpus which would yield an income of $300 per month for widow's life, actuarially computed, qualified for the marital deduction. Northeastern Pennsylvania National Bank & Trust Co. (Young) v United States (1964) 235 F Supp 941 (DC MD Pa).

Where surviving spouse as life tenant and trustee was required to provide for maintenance and support of son, the spouse's share of income was indefinite, not determinable, and the gift did not qualify for the marital deduction. Flesher v United States (1965) 238 F Supp 119 (DC ND W Va).

Where surviving spouse as life tenant of trust to pay her income for life had the right to withdraw up to $5,000 each year, it was held that she had the power to appoint and receive income from a specific portion of corpus, and therefore such sum qualified for the marital deduction. Allen v United States (1965) 250 F Supp 155 (DC ED Mo).

p. 308, n. 6. Where contributing employer was beneficiary and owner of pension fund annuities with death benefits for employee-decedent's widow should she survive him, the full value of the annuity, less the value of that part attributable to decedent's contribution, was allowable as part of the marital deduction; the employer's execution and assumption of obligations of the pension agreement constituted full and adequate consideration, so that disallowance under IRC Sec. 2056(b)(1) was not required. Allen (1963) 39 TC 817. Commissioner acquiesced, IRB 1964-17 p. 5.

§ 238. Schedule M; Marital Deduction; Limitation on Aggregate of Deductions.

p. 309, n. 8. Marital deduction will be reduced to reflect abatement of widow's legacy for payment of debts and expenses in accordance with rule generally followed in Minnesota, and Commissioner would not be bound by a more favorable probate court decree rendered in a non-adversary proceeding. Stevens v Comm (1960) 36 TC 184. See § 242.

p. 309, n. 11. *Contra:* Where administration expenses incurred by the fiduciary of an estate had been

claimed on the estate fiduciary income tax return, the same administration expenses were held deductible in computing the adjusted gross estate for purposes of the estate marital deduction, where under state law they were chargeable to the legacy. Roney v Comm, 33 TC 801, No. 89, aff'd — F2d — (CA 5).

p. 309, n. 14. Where widow was bequeathed a share of the residuary estate, the marital deduction must be reduced by the administration expense chargeable to her share of the residue under state law, even though the executors chose to pay the expense out of income. Ballantine v Tomlinson (1961) 293 F2d 311 (CA 5).

Where will provides for an outright gift to surviving spouse in an amount equal to half of value of "adjusted gross taxable estate" as determined for federal estate tax purposes, after deduction of "all debts and . . . administration expenses," the widow being also the beneficiary of a residuary trust, the election, by executors, to take such administration expenses as income tax deductions does not permit an increase of the outright gift as provided in the will, and thus does not affect the amount of the marital deduction. Empire Trust Co. (Mixsell) v United States (1963) 226 F Supp 623 (DC SD NY).

§ 239. Schedule M; Marital Deduction; Other Interests Which Qualify for the Marital Deduction.

p. 310, n. 15. See § 286, this supp.

p. 310, n. 20. A widow's right of dower under Alabama law which at husband's death is a chose in action, and does not become a property interest until either lands are admeasured, giving her a life estate, or the award of an outright cash payment by equity decree which is vested absolutely, is not terminable, and qualifies for the marital deduction. United States v Hiles, 318 F2d 56 (1963); Wachovia Bank & Trust Co. (Kiser) v United States (1964) 234 F Supp 897 (DC MD NC) (applying North Carolina law).

The existence of a statutory right, and not the invocation of a statutory remedy, is the condition that permits a non-terminable dower right to qualify for the marital deduction under IRC § 2056. Therefore, under Kentucky law which gives widow a right to bring a court action to fix the cash value of her interest, and direct the sale of indivisible real property, amounts received by her from the heirs in exchange for relinquishment of her rights, determined by statutory formula, may be taken as marital deductions, although statutory court action was not commenced. Moore v United States (1963) 214 F Supp 603 (DC WD Ky).

Where Virginia law is found to be that dower until assigned is no more than a right to sue for and compel the setting aside of an interest in property, and where it cannot be so set aside to take annual payments, or a commuted value in cash, the payment to widow who elects against the will, and takes the commuted value, qualifies for the marital deduction. The decisive factor is what the spouse actually receives from decedent; here it was held to be a right to have the dower interest commuted or alternatively to take annual payments terminating at death plus a lien on the land. The interest she opted was not terminable. First Nat. Exchange Bank of Roanoke (Pell) v United States (1963) 217 F Supp 604 (DC WD Va), affd (1964) 335 F2d 91 (CA 4).

National Bank of Orange (Sims) v United States (1963) 218 F Supp 907 (DC ED Va).

p. 310, n. 2. Distribution to widow in accordance with a settlement agreement with executor recognizing her bona fide right of election, and having court approval, qualified for the marital deduction. Indiana National Bank v United States (1961) 191 F Supp 73 (SD Ind). See § 242.

Reg 20.2056(e)–2(d) does not apply in the case of payments made in settlement of litigation involving rights of distributees of intestate estates. First National Bank of Topeka (Graham) v United States (1964) 233 F Supp 19 (DC Kan).

p. 310, n. 4. *Widow's allowance: Vested and qualified for marital deduction:*

Georgia. First National Bank & Trust Co. of Augusta v United States (1960) 191 F Supp 446 (SD Ga), affd 297 F2d 312 (CA 5); overruled U. S. v Edmondson (1964) 331 F2d 676 (CA 5) (on authority of Jackson v U. S. (1964) 376 US 503, 11 L ed 2d 871, 84 S Ct 869 infra, this note, this supp).

Illinois. Molner v United States (1959) 175 F Supp 27 (ND Ill).

Iowa. United States v Shafer (1961) 293 F2d 629 (CA 8).

Maine. Gale v Comm (1960) 35 TC 215, No. 27, wherein husband's allowance was held qualified. Acquiescence, IRB 1962–37, p. 6; withdrawn and non-acquiescence substituted, IRB 1964–32, p. 7.

Massachusetts. Rudnick v Comm (1961) 36 TC 1021. Acquiescence, IRB 1962–26, p. 7; withdrawn and non-acquiescence substituted, IRB 1964–32, p. 7.

Michigan. Reynolds v United States (1960) 189 F Supp 548 (DC ED Mich); Rensenhouse v Comm (1959) 31 TC 818, No. 81. Acquiescence, 1959–1 CB 5; withdrawn and non-acquiescence substituted, IRB 1964–32, p. 7.

Missouri. Bookwalter v Phelps (1963) 325 F2d 186 (CA 8), holding that under Sec. 138A, 1955 Mo. Probate Code a lump sum payment is a non-terminable interest, and qualifies for the marital deduction; Gardner v United States (1963) 220 F Supp 196 (DC ED Mo) Sec 474.260 Missouri RS 1959 makes no substantial change and spouse's allowance thereunder qualifies for marital deduction.

Avery v Comm (1963) 40 TC 392.

New York. The allowance for support of a surviving spouse given by Surr Ct A § 200, qualifies for the marital deduction under state law. Forness (1957) 4 AD2d 168, 164 NYS 2d 258.

Not vested and not qualified for marital deduction:

California. Cunha v Comm (1960) 279 F2d 292 (CA 9).

Where under state law widow's right to an allowance is not vested at date of death (in 1951) of spouse, is lost on death or remarriage before securing an order of allowance, and abates on remarriage subsequent to such order, the interest is terminable. Jackson v United States (1964) 376 US 503, 11 L ed 2d 871, 84 S Ct 869 (terminability must be determined as of date of death and not as of date of decree).

Connecticut. Second Nat'l. Bank of New Haven (Brewster) v United States (1963) 222 F Supp 446 (DC Conn) (Conn 1958 Gen Stat § 45–250). [Executor's appeal from failure to include widow's allowance as part of marital deduction was abandoned, and case was reversed on oth gds 351 F2d 489 (CA 2).]

Nebraska. United States v Quivey (1961) 292 F2d 252 (CA 3).

North Carolina. Wachovia Bank & Trust Co. (Kiser) v United States (1964) 234 F Supp 897 (DC MD NC).

Oklahoma. Darby v Wiseman (1963) 323 F2d 792 (CA 10).

Oregon. United States National Bank of Portland, Extr. v United States (1960) 188 F Supp 332 (DC Or).

Tenessee. Hamilton Nat. Bank of Knoxville v United States, 353 F2d 930 (CA 6).

Wisconsin. Wiener v United States (1964) 235 F Supp 919 (DC ED Wis), holding that under 1960 Wisconsin law widow is entitled to an allowance only if as found by county judge she has a need for it, and that such need would terminate with her death or remarriage.

p. 310, n. 5. A tenancy by the entirety is not made a terminable interest by the fact that the surviving spouse under the terms of a joint will is required to convey one-half of the vested interest to another. Schildmeier v United States, 171 F Supp 328, (SD Ind) (1959).

p. 311, n. 13. Where a widow's homestead right is a life interest vesting at husband's death, a cash payment therefor is made for a terminable interest, and its amount is not to be included in determining the marital deduction. United States v Hiles, 318 F2d 56 (1963).

p. 311, n. 14. A "family" allowance for widow and minor children under Georgia law will not qualify for the marital deduction. Hailey v Comm (1961) 36 TC 120.

§ 241. Schedule M; Marital Deduction; Election by Surviving Spouse.

p. 313, n. 6. Marital deduction allowed where husband after electing his intestate share, gave such share to the son's children, the purpose to reduce taxes, and consistency of such disposition with decedent's apparent wishes, were immaterial. Harter, 39 TC 511, No. 50 (1962). Commissioner acquiesced, IRB 1963–34, 6.

p. 313, n. 8. United States v Hiles, 318 F2d 56 (1963).

First National Exchange Bank of Roanoke (Pell) v United States (1964) 335 F2d 91 (CA 4).

Dougherty v United States (1961) 292 F2d 331 (CA 6).

§ 242. Schedule M; Marital Deduction; Will Contests.

p. 313, n. 9. The controversy referred to in Reg. 20.2056(e)–2(d) means any controversy, with relation to the decedent's disposition of his entire estate, settled by the widow's giving up some part of the estate subject to the United States estate tax which, but for the controversy, she would have been entitled to retain; and widow's surrender of power to appoint under American will in settlement of contest of separate foreign will resulted in loss of the marital deduction. United States Trust Co. of New York (Davenport) v Comm (1963) 321 F2d 908 (CA 2).

Widow's intestate share qualifies in its entirety for the marital deduction, though in settlement of extended litigation involving the validity of intestate's second marriage, she agreed to make a substantial payment to her step-children, individually. Although the payment was in fact made directly from the estate, and deducted from her share, it nevertheless "passed" to her within the meaning of IRC § 2056, and the requirement of Reg. 20.5056(e)–2(d) of a judicial determination on the merits of widow's enforceable rights in an adversary proceeding applies only by its terms to will contests. First National Bank of Topeka (Gra-

ham) v United States (1964) 233 F Supp 19 (DC Kan).

p. 314, n. 13. Northwest Security National Bank of Sioux Falls v Welsh (1962) 203 F Supp 263 (DC SD).

Property received by widow in settlement of her claim to estate qualified for marital deduction where (a) the controversy was genuine; (b) she received substantially her statutory interest on a renunciation; and (c) the settlement was approved by Orphan's court order obtained in good faith, without purpose to affect tax liabilities, even though such court had no jurisdiction to decide questions affecting title to realty. Duca v United States (1964) 236 F Supp 747 (DC Md).

p. 314, n. 14. Faulkerson v United States (1961) 193 F Supp 410 (ND Ind), aff'd 301 F2d 231 (CA 7).

Add new text at end of section on page 314:

However, uncertainty exists as to the precise definition of the word "collusion".[14a] In some circuits, the word is treated as synonomous with "nonadversary".[14b] In others, the collusive nature is determined on a case-by-case basis after a consideration of all the factors involved.[14c] Where the decree was clearly contrary to state law and had been entered ex parte, on consent, it was found to be collusive.[14d] In another case, it was held that the government failed to sustain its burden of proving the state court decree was obtained by collusion, though rendered in a nonadversary proceeding.[14e]

14a Northwest Security National Bank of Sioux Falls v Welsh (1962) 203 F Supp 263 (DC SD).

As to "collusive" and "non-adversary" decrees, see also §§ 6, 193, this supp.

14b Stallworth v Comm (1958) 260 F2d 760 (CA 5); Sweet v Comm (1956) 234 F2d 401 (CA 10); Newman v Comm (1955) 222 F2d 131 (CA 9).

14c Faulkerson v United States (1961) 193 F Supp 410 (ND Ind) aff'd 301 F2d 231; Gallagher v Smith (1955) 223 F2d 218 (CA 3).

Where nisi prius state court adopted testator's widow's interpretation of her power of appointment over trust corpus without any independent research, in a proceeding where other necessary parties, all duly cited, offer no opposition, though some might have adverse interests, and the only effect of the state court decree was found to be the qualification of the testamentary trust for the marital deduction, the tax court disregarded the state court decision in holding that the trust corpus did not qualify for the deduction. Pierpont v Comm (1964) 336 F2d 277 (CA 4) (the federal court found that under Maryland law the widow's power was not general and exercisable in all events, contrary to widow's contention.)

Evidence of collusion found wanting in a proceeding for construction of an inter vivos trust, where after the state district court had orally announced that it would decide one point in such a way as to make surviving spouse's interest non-terminable, thus qualifying for the marital deduction, the parties sought to negotiate a settlement, and thereafter the state court, after considering briefs by the parties, gave surviving spouse a fee in one-half instead of one-third of the trust fund, thus increasing the estate's marital

deduction, and decreasing the share of the daughters. Coleman v United States (1963) 221 F Supp 39 (DC D Kan).

Probate court proceeding is collusive, and properly disregarded by tax court, where estate counsel, after obtaining CIR ruling that testamentary gift of life estate to widow, with power of invasion for "comfortable maintenance," was terminable (and so not qualifying for marital deduction), conferred with probate judge as to interpretation of will, and thereafter filed petition for interpretation, without notice to CIR, acting on behalf of widow, though childrens' interests were adverse; and where at the hearing opposing side of issues was not completely argued, but federal tax saving that would result from holding that widow actually was given a fee was emphasized in counsel's memorandum. The Minnesota probate court decree to effect that widow received fee simple absolute was not supported by state statute or case law. Peyton v Comm (1963) 323 F2d 438 (CA 8).

14d Faulkerson v United States (1961) 193 F Supp 410 (ND Ind) aff'd 301 F2d 231.

14e Northwest Security National Bank of Sioux Falls v Welsh (1962) 203 F Supp 263 (DC SD).

Where state probate court construed a marital gift of 40% of testator's "estate" to include not only a percentage of the probate estate (totalling $294,222) but also of the corpus of an inter vivos trust ($341,176), though aware that the resulting increase in the marital gift (from $173,770 to $254,160) would almost eliminate the residuary of the probate estate, the state court decree was effective in the tax litigation to determine the value of property available for the marital deduction.

The property rights determined were the same as those involved in the tax case, and the state court proceeding was not collusive as a matter of law, although the petition for the construction of the will was consented to by the residuary legatees, including brothers and minor nieces and nephews; all parties were represented by the same counsel, and there was no appeal. The IRC imposes no criteria for the determination of taxability of such testamentary interests other than the determination, under state law, of the persons entitled, and the state court decree is controlling, absent evidence of collusion, rather than more suspicion. Old Kent Bank & Trust Co. (Campbell) v United States (1964) 232 F Supp 970 (DC WD Mich).

§ 244. Schedule M; Marital Deduction; Return.

p. 317, n. 10. The revised instructions to Schedule M, Form 706, see § 26, this supplement, indicate that a separate pamphlet of supplemental instructions for Schedule M is again obtainable from the District Director.

§ 245. Schedule N; Transfers for Public, Charitable, and Religious Uses; Statutory Provisions.

Add note in seventh line of text:
. . . or transfers[15b]

[15b] Escheat to the state under intestacy laws is not a transfer made by decedent. Senft v United States (1963) 319 F2d 642 (CA 3).

§ 246. Schedule N; Transfers for Public, Charitable, and Religious Uses; Uses Qualifying.

p. 323, n. 9. Operation of dining room, and conduct of social activities, were held minor in nature and merely incidental to predominant activities of Providence Art Club, and would not disqualify club as charitable organization. Industrial National Bank of Providence v United States (1960) 187 F Supp 810 (DC RI).

p. 324, n. 18. Contributions to college for constructing housing for a fraternity held deductible. Rev Rul 60–367, IRB 1960–49, p. 11.

p. 325, n. 9. Bequest to a medical society was denied exemption from estate tax where many of its activities were primarily of benefit to its members only, it was active politically to the extent of endorsing candidates for election, it sought to influence legislation not necessarily affecting the profession, and while it maintained a grievance committee, such committee was without legal powers or authority. Hammerstein v Kelley (1964) 255 F Supp 60 (DC ED Mo), affd 349 F2d 928.

p. 325, n. 14. Where the Carmelite Order was vested with the personal property rights of member nuns after each had taken solemn vows of poverty, but prior to the date that her daughter had taken solemn vows the testatrix had executed a will bequeathing property to her daughter who was then a Carmelite nun, it was held that the execution date of the will determined whether the testamentary gift was individual or charitable and in the absence of the daughter's having taken solemn vows at that time no charitable deduction was allowable. Callaghan v Comm, 33 TC 870, No. 99 (1960).

No charitable deduction was allowed under 1947 will for a bequest to a son designated by name, followed by "S. J.", who did not until 1952, three years before testator's death, take final vows requiring him to renounce to the Society all property rights devolving to him, since testator did not intend to bequeath property directly to the order, and thus to treat this son differently from his other children. Barry v Comm (1962) 311 F2d 681.

Cox v Comm, 19 TCM 1470, TC Memo 1960–260, aff'd 297 F2d 36 (CA 10) (legatee a member of Society of Jesus); Lamson v United States (1964) 338 F2d 376 (Ct Cls) (legatee member of Capuchin Order).

p. 325, n. 15. It has been held that gifts to three bar associations, incorporated in the State of New York, qualified for the charitable deduction where activities such as the regulation of the unauthorized practice of law, disciplining of the legal profession, improving court procedure and endorsement of judicial candidates and influencing legislation were carried on primarily to promote a public or educational purpose and not for self interest or gain. Dulles v Johnson (1959) 155 F Supp 275, (SD NY), mod 273 F2d 362 (CA 2).

Rhode Island Hospital Trust Co. v United States, cited in note to text, is reported in 159 F Supp 204 (DC RI).

Under Rev Rul 59–152, IRB 1959–18, p. 9, a bequest to a state bar association which exercises governmental functions and is exempt from Federal income tax as an instrumentality of the state is a charitable bequest which may be deducted.

p. 325, n. 16. A transfer to the League of Women Voters does not qualify for the charitable deduction, since its main purpose is to influence legislation. League of Women Voters

of the U. S. v United States, 180 F Supp 379, (Ct Cl).

p. 326, n. 19. Gifts to the Secretary of Commerce are exempt from Federal estate and gift taxes, and gifts heretofore made to the US Merchant Marine Academy have been transferred to him. Pub L 88–611.

§ 247. Schedule N; Transfers for Public, Charitable, and Religious Uses; When Not Deductible; Validity of Gift.

p. 326, n. 2. Charitable deduction is to be computed on the basis of the amount actually received by the charitable legatee, and moneys paid in settlement of will contest, will decrease the deduction, even though payment was made to contestant with independent funds of charitable legatee which were later reimbursed by gifts. Wilcox, Extr. v United States (1960) 185 F Supp 385 (NC Ohio).

Declaratory judgment of state court, based on documentary evidence, oral testimony, briefs and an analysis of West Virginia law, was held not "collusive" and "nonadversary," though not opposed by residuary legatees, otherwise entitled to remainder, who were made parties and fully advised of issues. The state court proceeding, begun after bequest was questioned by IRS, in conference, involved substantial property interests with rival claimants, was based on reason and authority (as reviewed by the federal court in the tax refund action) and would in any event have been necessary for instruction and protection of trustees. Parkersburg Nat. Bank (Gordon) v United States (1964) 228 F Supp 375 (DC ND W Va).

p. 327, n. 8. To qualify for a charitable deduction, the amount to be used for charitable purposes (the amount of deduction) must be established to be accurately calculable. Hammerstein v Kelley (1965) 349 F2d 928 (CA 8).

Only charitable bequests capable of being stated in terms of money are deductible; conditional bequests are not. Hammerstein v Kelley (1965) 349 F2d 928 (CA 8).

§ 250. Schedule N; Transfers for Public, Charitable, and Religious Uses; Conditional Gifts.

p. 329, n. 14. Where the charity is provided with a vested remainder gift consisting of a stated percentage of the value of its real property payable if the charity can raise a matching fund of a certain percentage which, when combined, is to be used for construction purposes, and under local law, a gift without a gift over or a provision that it shall be void if the condition is not fulfilled is deemed absolute, it was held that the vested remainder qualified for the charitable deduction, since the only uncertainty was the date of payment. Polster v Comm, 274 F2d 358, (CA 4) (1960).

p. 330, n. 3. Rev Rule 60–162 IRB 1960, p. 17 clarifies whether a charitable deduction is allowable in the case of a charitable remainder in a wasting asset, namely, the surface and subsurface rights in land where no provision has been made for a reserve for depletion of subsurface deposits. In such a case there is a pro tanto diversion of corpus each year to the income beneficiary comparable to an invasion of corpus. Ascertainment of the value of such a remainder interest may be shown by determining the quantity of subsurface resources and the maximum feasible rate at which the subsurface

resources could be withdrawn during the period of the income beneficiary's interest in order to arrive at the resources remaining at the inception of the charitable remainder.

p. 330, n. 4. Charitable bequest of half of residue, conditioned on approval of decedent's sister, who otherwise would benefit from entire residue, will not be allowed as a deduction, since the likelihood, as of date of death, that such wholly discretionary consent will be exercised is in law a mere speculation. Rev Proc 64–129, IRB 1964–17, p. 15.

p. 330, n. 5. A trust remainder payable to a charity but subject to consumption at a stated annual rate in favor of the life beneficiary was held not a qualified charitable deduction. Moffett v Comm. 269 F2d 738 (CA 4) (1959).

p. 330, n. 8. The probability of issue in a childless woman over 54 years of age is so remote as to be negligible; thus a charitable deduction will be allowed for a remainder to charity contingent upon the failure of such issue. Rev Rul 59–143, IRB 1959–17, p. 13.

Where life beneficiary of trust at decedent's death was 54 years old, a childless eccentric bachelor, not known to have had association with women since a brief marriage 31 years before, living alone in a trailer in squalor, in poor health, a heavy smoker, with poor dietary habits, jury verdict that the possibility of his . aving issue was so remote as to be negligible would not be overruled. Hamilton National Bank of Chattanooga (Long) v United States, 236 F Supp 1005 (DC ED Tenn).

p. 330, n. 9. Probability of issue in a married childless woman 47 years of age was not so remote as to be negligible, and charitable deduction was disallowed. Bankers Trust

Co. (Newman) v United States (1960) 190 F Supp 671 (DC SD NY), affd 299 F2d 938 (CA 2).

p. 330, n. 11. Where the estate involved in a tax proceeding consisted of a vested remainder in the corpus of a trust created by decedent's mother, which provided for the erection of certain memorials at costs not to exceed specified amounts, the problem of whether or not the trust qualified as a charitable deduction because of uncertainty was held irrelevant since decedent did not create the trust. The only problem is the determination of the value of decedent's remainder interest at time of mother's death in this particular trust, which is arrived at by considering the uncertainties and probabilities involved. Utley v United States (1961) 290 F2d 188 (CA 9).

Bach v McGinnes (1963) 218 F Supp 914 (DC ED Pa) (60% actuarial possibility that a named legatee would survive to defeat charitable gift not so negligible as to justify charitable deduction), affd on this ground (1964) 333 F2d 979 (CA 1).

Although bequest to charity of excess of purchase price of annuity over sum of annuity payments to annuitants transfers a legal interest with an ascertainable actuarial value, the gift is not so effective as to qualify for estate tax deduction where there is a greater than 20% chance that annuitants will live long enough to preclude any refund. Choffin v United States (1963) 222 F Supp 34 (DC SD Fla).

§ 251. Schedule N; Transfers for Public, Charitable, or Religious Uses; Subject to Diversion.

p. 331, n. 12. Where trust instrument provides that capital gains (as from a regulated investment company) be treated as income distributable to the life beneficiary, the value of the charitable remainder is uncertain, and the charitable deduction will not be allowed. Rev Rul 60-385, IRB 1960-52, p. 15.

p. 331, n. 16. The unlikelihood that the corpus ever will be invaded is of no consequence. Marine Trust Co. of Western N. Y. v United States (1965) 247 F Supp 278 (DC WD NY).

p. 331, n. 6. Direction to trustee not only to pay the income and so much of the corpus as may be necessary to maintain the life income beneficiary in the living standard she enjoyed at decedent's death, but also to invade corpus for funds needed by reason of her sickness, accident, misfortune or "any other circumstances", defeated a remainder interest to charity, since there was an unlimited power of invasion, not limited to some objective standard, thereby precluding a present valuation of the remainder. Marine Trust Co. of Western N. Y. v United States (1965) 247 F Supp 278 (DC WD NY).

p. 331, n. 7. See § 251.1 for illustrative clauses.

Any ascertainable standard having been stated by authorization to invade to enable widow-life beneficiary to maintain accustomed living standard and to be provided with proper medical care was negated by further authorization to "give sympathetic consideration to any request" made by her, and deduction was denied. Union Trust Co. v Tomlinson (1966) 355 F2d 40 (CA 5).

p. 331, n. 8. Power to invade for widow's maintenance, welfare, comfort or happiness, when coupled with a direction for restraint, was held limited by a fixed standard and did not give the settlor power to alter or amend the trust under § 811(d)

(2) of the 1939 Code. United States v Powell (1962) 307 F2d 821 (CA 10).

p. 332, n. 16. Mercantile-Safe Deposit & Trust Co. v United States (1959) 141 F Supp 546 (D Md).

§ 251.1. Schedule N; Transfers for Public, Charitable or Religious Uses; Subject to Diversion; Illustrative Clauses.[1]

[1] The chart of cases, concluding with Commerce Trust Co. v United States (167 F Supp 643) and their analysis, was appended by District Judge Charles F. Paul to his enlightening opinion in Kline v United States, 202 F Supp 849, aff'd 313 F2d 633 (CA 4).

CASE	STANDARD FOR INVASION, CRUCIAL LANGUAGE	LIFE BFCY	HOLDING & COMMENT
In re Bartlett's Estate, 153 F Supp 674 (ED Pa 1957);	"best interests" during "illness or emergency of any kind."	servant, 71 limited means, limited demands	*for government.* "Best interests" is as subjective and incapable of ascertainment as "happiness" and "pleasure" (see Supreme Court decisions).
Commerce Trust Company v United States, 167 F Supp 643 (WD Mo 1958).	"illness, injury, or any circumstances of emergency affecting her welfare or health".	daughter, 65 and healthy, with income in excess of needs	*for government.* Missouri courts interpret "welfare" broadly; standard not referable to "accustomed mode"; invasion conceivable.
Lincoln Rochester Trust Co. v C. I. R. 181 F2d 424 (2nd Cir, 1950);	"necessary for her proper care, support, and maintenance".	nurse, 72, small means	*for taxpayer.* Standard set up is referable to her accustomed mode, Clark, J.
Blodget v Delaney, 201 F2d 589 (1st Cir, 1953).	"for her comfort and welfare".	sister, 84 blind	*for taxpayer.* Relying on Massachusetts law, Ithaca Trust held controlling.
Lincoln Rochester Trust Co. v McGowan, 217 F 2d 287 (2nd Cir, 1954).	"unusual demands, emergencies" . . . "from sickness, accident or failure of investments".	widow	*for taxpayer.* Medina, J., considers issue of post-death evidence; decides trustee's discretion adequately bound. Swan dissents.
Third National Bank and Trust Co. of Springfield v United States, 228 F2d 772 (1st Cir, 1956);	if trustee in "its opinion shall deem wise".	mother, 69, frugal	*for government.* "Deem wise" furnishes no standard.
Seubert v Shaughnessy, 233 F2d 134 (2nd Cir, 1956);	"for any purpose which may add to her comfort or convenience" Beneficiary filed an affidavit to effect that she had no intention of invading.	sister, 73, maiden, frugal, of own means	*for government.* Clark, J. looks at nothing beyond the will; "add" the crucial word.
DeCastro's Estate v C. I. R. 155 F2d 254 (2nd Cir, 1946) cert denied	if income not enough, "due to illness, accident or other unforeseen emergency"; no one to call in question propriety of	widow, 75, frugal	*for government.* Case governed by Supreme Court's decision in Merchants Bank,

98

Citation	Language	Beneficiary	Result
329 US 727, 67 S Ct 82, 91 L ed 630.	wife's invasion.		
Newton Trust Co. v C. I. R. 160 F2d 175 (1st Cir, 1947);	"use and benefit".	widow	*for government.* "Use and benefit" furnishes no ascertainable standard; Massachusetts cases don't confine standard. Excellent analysis and review.
National Bank of Commerce of San Antonio v Scofield, 169 F2d 145 (5th Cir, 1948) cert denied 335 US 907, 69 S Ct 410, 93 L ed 441;	"maintain her in our home or a location of her choosing, provide with necessities and comforts in life to which she is accustomed"; trustee to provide "liberally".	widow, 82	*for government.* Amount of corpus that will remain a matter of conjecture, not accurately calculable; strong dissent.
Berry v Kuhl, 174 F2d 565 (7th Cir 1949);	"accident, illness, or other cause". . . "treatment, support, maintenance".	widow, then daughter, of means, frugal	*for taxpayer.* Uncertainty of "other causes" cured by later words referable to accustomed standard of living. Minton, J.
Hartford - Connecticut Trust Co. v Eaton, 36 F2d 710 (2nd Cir, 1929);	for what trustee deems "necessary or advisable for her comfortable maintenance and support."	widow	*for taxpayer.* Under Connecticut law, words tantamount to "station in life", hence Ithaca Trust controls.
Gammons v Hassett, 121 F2d 229 (1st Cir, 1941) cert denied 314 US 673, 62 S Ct 136, 86 L ed 539;	"so much as my wife may need or desire"	widow, 93, of own means	*for government.* "Extremely remote" possibility of invasion, but "desire" imports subjectivity.
C. I. R. v Bank of America, 133 F2d 753 (9th Cir, 1943);	$250 a month from trust property and if required "by reason of accident, illness, or other unusual circumstances, more. Beneficiary uppermost in mind.	sister, 79, $25,000 net worth	*for taxpayer.* Majority says "look at actualities." Dissent.
C. I. R. v Wells Fargo Bank & Union Trust Co., 145 F2d 130 (9th Cir, 1944);	"sickness, accident, want or other emergency";	niece, 54, $54,000 net worth	*for taxpayer.* Follows Bank of America, above, says then-recent Merchants Bank distinguishable.

CASE	STANDARD FOR INVASION, CRUCIAL LANGUAGE	LIFE BFCY	HOLDING & COMMENT
Wells Fargo Bank & Union Trust Co. v C. I. R. 145 F2d 132 (9th Cir, 1944);	"in event of sickness, accident, want, or other emergency"	widow, 60, thrifty, healthy, own means	*for taxpayer.* Tax Court reversed because it considered post-death events (invasion).
Ithaca Trust Co. v United States, 279 US 151, 49 S Ct 291, 73 L ed 647 (1929);	any sum "necessary to suitably maintain her in as much comfort as she now enjoys".	widow	*for taxpayer.* "Standard was fixed in fact and capable of being stated in definite terms of money," and trust income sufficient.
Merchants National Bank of Boston v C. I. R. 320 US 256, 64 S Ct 108, 88 L ed 35 (1943);	"comfort, support, maintenance, and/or happiness"; liberal discretion granted to provide for wife, whose interest is to come first.	widow, 67, of means	*for government.* No fixed standard because of "happiness" language and liberal instruction to trustee.
Henslee v Union Planters National Bank & Trust Co. 335 US 595, 69 S Ct 290, 93 L ed 259 (1949).	$750 a month from trust income, to be used as beneficiary "sees fit"; invasion of corpus for her "pleasure, comfort, and welfare". First object of trustees to provide for beneficiary as "she may desire".	mother, 85, of frugal habits, and means	*for government.* Remote possibility of wasting corpus, but still possibility.
Helvering v Union Trust Co. 125 F2d 401 (1942), cert denied 316 US 696, 62 S Ct 1292, 86 L ed 1766;	"additional sums for the proper care and comfort of the husband, should illness, accident or misfortune so require."	widower, 76	*for government.* However, another ground controls the decision.
C. I. R. v Robertson's Estate, 141 F2d 855 (1944);	"if in the judgment of the said trustee, the best interests of my sister should so require."	sister, 76, wife of clergyman and of means	*for taxpayer.* Looks to actualities, holds no possibility of charity not getting all. Validity of case somewhat questionable because rule of Dobson v C. I. R. 320 US 489, 64 S Ct 239, 88 L ed 248; 321 US 231, 64 S Ct 495, 88 L ed 691, overruled by statute,

Case	Language	Beneficiary	Holding
Bowers v South Carolina National Bank of Greenville, 4 Cir, 228 F2d 4 (1955);	to pay, if trust income be insufficient, monthly sums to sisters and for their medical expenses and for upkeep of house.	2 sisters, 1 cousin, elderly	*for taxpayer.* Actualities, including post-death evidence (a probate order), looked to.
Mercantile-Safe Deposit, etc. v United States, 141 F Supp 546 (DC Md 1956).	for "comfortable support" and "in event of accident, illness, misfortune, or other emergency." Beneficiary of primary concern, but trustee bound to consider her entire resources before invading.	elderly sister, of own means	*for taxpayer.* Ithaca Trust controls, *for taxpayer.* Relies heavily on CCA 4 decisions, looks to actualities and decides no invasion likely.
United States v Powell (1962) 307 F2d 821 (CA 10).	"to use some portion of principal for maintenance, welfare, comfort or happiness" and "provided that the trustee shall deem that the purpose for which the payments are to be made, justifies the reduction in the principal of the trust properties."	widow	*for taxpayer.* Settlor intended restraint be used in invading principal. Happiness equated with basic maintenance.
Kline v United States (1962) 202 F Supp 849 (ND W Va).	to provide maintenance and support "to the same generous extent that I, if living, could do" and "to invade the corpus of the trust as circumstances may require"	son, age 74, independent income	*for government.* Trustees to apply subjective test of desire and not objective test of need.
State Street Bank & Trust Co. v United States (1963) 313 F2d 29 (CA 1)	"in their uncontrolled discretion may deem necessary or advisable for her comfortable support and maintenance and for any other reasonable requirement"	widow, age 59, large estate of her own	*for government.* "Comfortable support and maintenance" would provide continuance of present standards; the added words authorized a higher, and immeasurable standard, and the risk of uncertainty should be testator's not government's.
Vaccaro v United States (1963) 224 F Supp 307 (DC D Mass)	"in their uncontrolled discretion, such amounts . . . as in the judgment of the Trustees will adequately provide for her support, maintenance and comfort, including luxuries, or will be for her best interest to receive"	widow	*for government.* Provision, "or will be for her best interest to receive", renders value of remainder unascertainable.

CASE	STANDARD FOR INVASION, CRUCIAL LANGUAGE	LIFE BFCY	HOLDING & COMMENT
Harris v Comm (1964) 23 TCM 635, TC Memo 1964-109;	trustees to use any portion of corpus necessary for support, comfort, and "happiness"	brother, 89 extremely frugal	*for government.* Word "happiness" introduced a subjective standard, incapable of being confined within ascertainable limits.
Wood v Comm (1963) 39 TC 919	To provide for "support, maintenance welfare and comfort" as trustees in absolute discretion should deem "necessary or advisable."	brother-in-law 69 with living expenses of $4000, income $5000 before trust's $10000.	*for taxpayer.* The possibility of invasion was so remote as to be negligible; in the context "comfort and welfare" rounded out the standard of living concept.
James v Comm (1963) 40 TC 494	"Emergency clause" to provide for "comfortable maintenance and support educational requirements, illness, operations, or for any reason whatsoever."	income to relatives remainder to charity	*for government.* General heading "Emergency clause" did not restrict broad powers; words "or for any reason whatsoever" were not limited by ejusdem generis; and fiduciary duty did not supply requisite restriction.
Zentmayer v Comm (1964) 336 F2d 488 (CA 3)	"support, maintenance, welfare and comfort" "and for any other purpose which my trustees shall deem expedient, necessary or desirable"	sister, 80, frugal with ample funds	*for government;* no ascertainable standard.
Union Trust Co. v Tomlinson (1966) 355 F2d 40 (CA 5).	To enable beneficiary to maintain standard of living and have proper medical care, "and to give sympathetic consideration to any request" made by her.	widow, 81	*for government;* no ascertainable standard.

[Harris Tax Supp]

§ 252. Schedule N; Transfers for Public, Charitable, and Religious Uses; Disclaimer.

p. 333, n. 1. However, death was not equivalent to a disclaimer under former § 812(d) of the 1939 Code. City National Bank & Trust Co. of Columbus v United States (1962) 203 F Supp 398 (SD Ohio) affd 312 F2d 118 (CA 6).

§ 253. Schedule N; Transfers for Public, Charitable, or Religious Uses; Payments in Compromise.

p. 334, n. 8. Although the amount of the charitable deduction available to an estate should be reduced to the extent of the value of the corpus received by intestate heirs as a result of a compromise of a will contest, such reduction should not include that part of the compromise payment attributable to the estate's net income up to the time of settlement, which is not part of the estate for tax purposes. The part so attributable is arrived at by applying that percentage to the total value of the compromise payment which the net income of the estate bears to the total corpus and income available for payment of the compromise, after deducting debts, then-existing administration and funeral expenses. Oldham v Campbell (1963) 217 F Supp 819 (DC ND Tex) (compromise arrived at two years from death after sale of mineral leases had resulted in substantial bonus income, and the final size of the bonuses was determinative of the amount finally offered in compromise).

§ 255. Schedule N; Transfers for Public, Charitable, or Religious Uses; Death Taxes Payable Out of Bequests.

Add new note in fourth from last line of section on page 335:
. . . administration expenses,[7a]

[7a] Administration expenses are to be deducted from the gross estate before determining the present value of the residuary estate passing to charity, even though the executor had elected to deduct administration expenses, presumably payable out of corpus, on the fiduciary income tax return rather than on the estate tax return, the court having applied the rule that the charitable deduction is limited to the amount actually available for charitable uses. Luehrmann v Comm (1960) 287 F2d 10 (CA 8).

Administration expenses are payable from corpus in the absence of testamentary direction, but where life tenant was to receive income "immediately following" death, they are to be deducted in determining value of charitable bequests of remainder, though executor elected to claim them as income tax deductions and claimed to have paid them out of income. Republic National Bank of Dallas (George) v Comm (1962) 39 TC 85, affd (1964) 334 F2d 348 (CA 5).

§ 257. Schedule N; Transfers for Public, Charitable, or Religious Uses; Return.

FORM NO. 30

Form 706, as revised January 1966, provides space in Schedule N for information about payment of Federal estate and other death taxes from charitable bequests:

If the transfer was made by will—

(a) Has any action been instituted to have interpreted or to contest the will or any provision thereof affecting the charitable deductions claimed in this schedule? Yes.... No....

(b) According to the information and belief of the person or persons filing the return, is any such action designed or contemplated? Yes.... No....

At the bottom of Schedule N on the January 1966 revised form 706 appear these new items:

TOTAL ....

Less: (a) Federal estate tax payable out of above-listed property
interests ....

(b) Other death taxes payable out of above-listed property
interests ....

Total of items (a) and (b) ....

§ 258. Nonresidents Not Citizens.

p. 341, n. 8. Reg. 20.2106–1, amended Jan 18, 1961.

CHAPTER 4

COMPUTATION OF TAX

§ 260. Valuation; Alternate; Generally.

p. 346, n. 2. Shares of stock are to be valued as of the date of the order of the local probate court directing their distribution, rather than as of the date of their physical delivery. Hertsche v United States (1965) 244 F Supp 347 (DC D Or).

p. 346, n. 4. The general instructions to revised Form 706, see § 26, this supplement, specify that the election of alternate valuation is not valid unless made on the return within the time prescribed by law and regulations. Prior to the issuance of the revised return it was ruled that whether an election to use the alternate method of valuation has been made is to be determined from all the facts disclosed in the estate tax return, and failure to designate an election in the box on the estate tax return would not preclude an election where the executor otherwise reported alternate valuations in the appropriate schedules and computed the tax by the alternate valuation method. Rev Rul 61–128, IRB 1961–28, p. 7. However, it would seem more prudent practice to fill in the box (Item 21, general information) as required by the instructions to the revised return.

§ 262. Valuation; Alternate; Operation as to Real Estate, Stocks and Bonds.

Add note in third paragraph, fifth line:

. . . disposition as a result.[16a]

[16a] Securities devolving upon a surviving joint tenant are not "disposed" of by a transfer to a revocable trust under which the joint tenant-settlor has retained an absolute power of disposition. Rev Rul 59–213, IRB 1959–24, p. 16.

p. 350, n. 18. Where the estate of the decedent received additional stock as a result of a stock dividend before the alternate valuation period expired, such additional stock must be included in the gross estate; Schlosser v Comm (1959) 32 TC 262, No. 25, aff'd 277 F2d 268. See also Rev Rul 58–576, IRB 1958–47, p. 8, which prescribes the treatment of stock rights, stock dividends, insurance proceeds, and interest bearing obligations received or disposed of within the year following decedent's death.

Add new text at end of section:

In the determination of the value of a decedent's gross estate, dividends declared before death, on stock includible in the gross estate, payable to stockholders of record after the decedent's death, must be considered in making an adjustment in the ex-dividend quotation of the stock at the date of the decedent's death. But such dividends are not included in the gross estate under the alternate method of valuing the gross estate either as a separate asset or as an adjustment of the ex-dividend quoted value of the stock as of one year or as of some intermediate date. Under the alternate valuation method, stock includible in the gross estate and selling ex-dividend is to be valued at its ex-dividend quoted selling price as of one year after the date of the decedent's death or at any intermediate valuation date, increased by the amount of dividends declared on the stock during the alternate valuation period payable to stockholders of record subsequent to the date which is one year after the date of the decedent's death or such intermediate date. No part of the value so determined is to be deemed excluded property in determining the value of the gross estate.[18a]

[18a] Rev Rul 60–124, IRB 1960–14, p. 12.

§ 263. Valuation; Alternate; Operation as to Assets Affected by Mere Lapse of Time.

p. 351, n. 19. For the purpose of alternate valuation of right to receive share of future partnership earnings, compromise agreement entered into between remaining partners and beneficiaries, and circumstances surrounding it, should be taken into consideration in fixing its value. The compromise was not a factor affecting value by mere lapse of time. Hull v Comm (1962) 38 TC 512; for app on oth issue see Hull v Comm, 325 F2d 367 (CA 3) § 131 this supp.

p. 353, n. 4. Where decedent held

106

insurance policies on the life of another person, who died within one year of holder's death, the resulting increase in value of the policies is not excluded from the value of decedent's gross estate as determined at the alternate valuation date, as attributable to "mere lapse of time", and the value of the entire proceeds is includible. Rev Rul 63–52 IRB 1963–13 p. 14.

§ 276. Deduction for Property Previously Taxed; Statutory Provisions.

p. 360, n. 2. In computing the deduction for property previously taxed available to the estate of one dying in 1952, administration expenses and estate taxes incurred by the prior 1947 estate must be prorated between property taxable to the 1947 estate and property deductible in that estate as previously taxed; the 1952 estate may not obtain in effect a second deduction for part of the property deducted in the 1947 by charging all expenses of the 1947 to property there deductible (but taxable in the 1952 estate) thus increasing the amount of the net fund or estate reported in the 1952 estate as property taxed in the prior estate. Benjamin (1963) 312 F2d 428.

§ 278. Deduction for Property Previously Taxed; Limitations.

p. 364, n. 16. Provident Trust Co. of Philadelphia v United States, 268 F2d 779 (CA 3) (1959).

§ 279. Deduction for Property Previously Taxed; Operation.

Add new note in twelfth line on page 367:

. . . computation made.[20a]

20a The deduction otherwise allowable under the 1939 Code for property previously taxed should not be proportionately reduced by that portion of the marital deduction, comprised of insurance and jointly owned property passing to the widow, not allocable to or payable out of property previously taxed. Roth v Welch (1960) 183 F Supp 559 (SD Ohio), affd 290 F2d 919 (CA 6).

§ 283. Death Taxes Payable Out of Transfers for Public, Charitable, or Religious Uses.

p. 373, n. 14. Foreign death taxes upon transfers for public, charitable, or religious uses may now be taken as a deduction, rather than a credit, and the limitations discussed in the text as applicable to State death taxes are also applicable to foreign death taxes. 1954 Code §§ 2053(d), 2014(f), as amended in 1959; Reg. 20.2011–2, 20.2014–1, 20.2014–3, as amended, and Reg. 20.2014–7, 20.2053–10, as adopted May 28, 1962, Appendix B. See also § 214, this supplement.

§ 286. Marital Deduction; Valuation.

p. 376, n. 6. The Internal Revenue Service will disallow the marital deduction where the gift to the surviving spouse may be satisfied by distribution of securities at estate tax valuations, unless by local law by terms of the governing instrument, or by agreement of interested parties the distribution must be made in such a way that accretions or depreciation in value of all available securities are fairly represented in the distribution to the surviving spouse. Rev Proc 64–19, IRB 1964–15, p. 30.

p. 377, n. 8. Where bequest to surviving spouse is conditioned on relinquishment of her community property interest, so that it would pass to a trust for children, the testamentary interest passing to surviving spouse upon such relinquishment will qualify for the marital deduction only to the extent that such bequest exceeds in value the relinquished share of the community. United States v Stapf (1963) 375 US 118, 11 L ed 2d 195, 84 S Ct 248.

Add text at end of section:

The Internal Revenue Service has issued a Revenue Procedure[8a] stating that in the case of an instrument executed on and after October 1, 1964 which provides a pecuniary bequest or transfer in trust to be satisfied in kind, with assets selected at the discretion of the fiduciary, and valued as finally determined for federal estate tax purposes, the full amount of the marital deduction will be allowed if it is clear under state law[8b] or under the express or implied terms of the instrument (a) that the fiduciary, in order to implement the bequest or transfer, must distribute assets, including cash, having an aggregate fair market value at the date or dates of distribution amounting to no less than the amount of the pecuniary bequest or transfer as finally determined for federal estate tax purposes; or (b) that the fiduciary must distribute assets, including cash, fairly representa-

107

tive of appreciation or depreciation in the value of all property available for distribution in satisfaction of the pecuniary bequest or transfer.

Examples are given of cases where the "problem" does *not* arise (Sec. 4.01):

"(1) In a bequest or transfer in trust of a fractional share of the estate, under which each beneficiary shares proportionately in the appreciation or depreciation in the value of assets to the date, or dates, of distribution.

(2) In a bequest or transfer in trust of specific assets.

(3) In a pecuniary bequest or transfer in trust, whether in a stated amount or an amount computed by the use of a formula, if:

(a) The fiduciary must satisfy the pecuniary bequest or transfer in trust solely in cash, or

(b) The fiduciary has no discretion in the selection of the assets to be distributed in kind, or

(c) Assets selected by the fiduciary to be distributed in kind in satisfaction of the bequest or transfer in trust are required to be valued at their respective values on the date, or dates, of their distribution."

In the case of instruments executed before October 1, 1964 the marital deduction will be allowed, even if the foregoing conditions are not satisfied, if both

the fiduciary and the surviving spouse execute and forward to the Internal Revenue Service agreements that the assets of the estate available for distribution will be so distributed between the marital gift and the balance of the estate available for distribution in satisfaction of the marital gift that the marital gift is fairly representative of the net appreciation or depreciation of the assets available on the date or dates of distribution. The execution of such an agreement will not constitute a gift by the surviving spouse to other beneficiaries, but failure to abide by the agreement will be treated as a gift. It should be observed that the Release carefully avoids the flat assertion that pecuniary bequests or transfers will be totally disallowed if the new requirements are not met. It does say that if they are not met, the marital gift will be considered unascertainable as of the date of death (sec. 2.03).

In effect, the purport of this Release is that the surviving spouse must receive at the date of distribution property having a value at least as great as the value of the marital gift as determined for estate tax purposes, unless the spouse shares with other beneficiaries the risks of appreciation or depreciation in the estate assets available for satisfaction of the marital gift. If she shares these risks, the fact that the property actually passing to her upon distribution may have an aggregate value which is less than the value of the marital gift for estate tax purposes is not objectionable, for this is due to economic conditions beyond human control. It does not depend on the fiduciary's discretion in selecting assets to satisfy the gift. If the executor has the power to satisfy the marital gift by distribution of property in kind, he may not fund the marital deduction legacy with assets that have decreased in value at the time of distribution so that the estate would be entitled to the full marital deduction although the spouse received less.

The Treasury Department has also explained the rules for determining the basis of assets distributed in kind by an executor where a beneficiary, including a trust, is required to treat as gross income a portion of the fair market value of assets distributed.[8c]

8a Technical Information Release 553, Rev Proc 64–19 (IRB 1964–15, April 13, 1964).

8b Executor as beneficiary of marital legacy measured by one half of "adjusted gross estate" must exercise authority to distribute appreciated securities at date of death values fairly and equitably, so that trust for son shares proportionately in appreciation and depreciation of security values with marital gift. Bush (1956) 2 AD2d 526, 156 NYS2d 897, affd other gr (1957) 3 NY2d 908, 167 NYS2d 927. (The court noted that the pur-

ported authority to use discretion in making distribution, given by the will, conflicted with Dec Est L § 125.)

Where will authorizes executors to satisfy bequests in kind, valuing securities for that purpose at federal estate tax values, and the surviving spouse, beneficiary of a maximum marital deduction trust is also an executor, the testatrix is deemed clearly to have intended that the aggregate gains in security values should be distributed proportionately to values at date of distribution to the maximum marital deduction trust and to the residuary trust for a son. Inman (1959) 22 Misc 2d 573, 196 NYS2d 369.

Where executors are authorized to satisfy a marital bequest in cash, or in kind, or partly in kind, property to be valued at date of distribution or at federal estate tax values whichever shall be the lower, the legacy when satisfied in cash must include a proportionate share of the appreciation realized on sales made by executors during the period of administration. McDonnell (1965) 45 Misc 2d 57, 256 NYS2d 149. On a motion for an order amplifying its ruling, the court held that in order to arrive at an equitable apportionment, there being no discernible fraction, the widow's right to share in the gains, was that portion of net appreciation (after taxes and administration expenses) that the amount of the marital deduction trust bore to the total value of all trusts after exclusion of appreciations during the period of administration. McDonnell (1965) 45 Misc 2d 1062, 258 NYS2d 591.

Callahan v Peltier (1936) 121 Conn 106, 183 A 400 (legacies expressed in dollars "or the equivalent thereof", ordered satisfied in kind equal to cash value at date of distribution).

Where distribution of stock in a family corporation is made to one legatee, another legatee, entitled to a larger and controlling number of shares, should also receive her share in kind, not in cash, since all beneficiaries in a particular class are entitled to equal treatment. Comiskey (1960) 24 Ill App 2d 199, 164 NE2d 535.

Where in an estate consisting of stock in a rapidly growing company, a pecuniary obligation of decedent is assumed by a legatee who otherwise is to share equally in the residue, the number of shares in the growth stock to be deducted from such legatee's share (and added to the share of the other residuary legatee) to compensate for shares originally sold by the estate to pay off the debt, is determined by actual date of transfer in distribution, not by date of decree directing distribution, or by the number of shares previously sold, or the equivalent of such number after 3 for 1 split. Barrett v Macdonald (1963) 264 Minn 560, 121 NW2d 165.

Simpson (1954) 32 NJ Super 85, 107 A2d 827 (where executors were authorized to pay pecuniary legacy in kind "in securities I may be possessed of at the time of my decease", distribution was to be made at current market values when distribution made).

In New York, by statute (Pers Prop L § 17-f, add L 1965, ch 693, eff July 2, 1965) it is provided that where a will or trust agreement authorizes the estate fiduciary to satisfy a pecuniary gift wholly or partly in kind, and no valuation date is prescribed, unless the instrument expressly provides otherwise, the assets selected for that purpose shall be valued at their respective values on the date of distribution. If, however, the will or trust agreement prescribes a valuation date other than the date of distribution, unless the

instrument expressly provides otherwise, the assts selected for that purpose together with any cash distributed, shall have an aggregate value on the date or dates of distribution amounting to no less than, and to the extent practicable to no more than, the amount of such gift as stated in or determined by the formula stated, in the instrument.

8c Where assets are distributed in kind and the beneficiary is required to include in gross income a portion of the fair market value of the assets so distributed, a pro rata portion of each item is considered as having been included in income, and is added to (or, in the case of loss deducted from) the income tax basis of the property. Rev Rul 64–314, IRB 1964–50, p. 6 (giving example of method of computation).

§ 287. Marital Deduction; Effect of Death Taxes.

p. 377, n. 9. Where under state court decisions a surviving spouse's share in the residuary is not to bear any part of the federal estate tax, to the extent that such share qualifies for the marital deduction, and there is no mandate by will as to payment of such taxes, the estate is entitled to a marital deduction undiminished by federal taxes. Dodd v United States (1963) 223 F Supp 785 (DC D NJ), aff'd 345 F2d 715.

In determining the effect of death taxes on the amount of a marital deduction the situation at date of decedent's death must be considered, and the value of an inter vivos trust, included in decedent's gross estate, must be reduced, as qualifying for the marital deduction, by the amount of estate taxes to which it is subject, though decedent's trustees were given discretion, in fact later exercised, to pay such taxes from the corpus of a non-qualifying trust. Boston Safe Deposit & Trust Co. (Rice) v Comm (1965) 345 F2d 625, (CA 1).

§ 288. Marital Deduction and Death Taxes; Interrelation; Generally.

p. 378, n. 13. Where under state court decisions a surviving spouse's share in the residuary is not to bear any part of the federal estate tax, to the extent that such share qualifies for the marital deduction, and there is no mandate by will as to payment of such taxes, the estate is entitled to a marital deduction undiminished by federal taxes. Reg § 20.2056(b)–4(c)(4) (App B of text, p 994) is not to be interpreted to require the marital deduction to be reduced by a share of the federal estate tax where this is contrary to local law. Dodd v United States (1963) 223 F Supp 785 (DC D NJ), affd 345 F2d 715.

Add new note in sixth from last line on page 378:

. . . such share[14a]

[14a] Where will gave one-half of residue outright to wife (rather than a separate bequest of equivalent of maximum marital deduction), and one-half of residue in trust, and provided that estate taxes be paid out of residue, estate taxes were held payable out of residuary estate as a whole, this being clearly the intent of the testator, one-half thereof out of widow's half, reducing her marital deduction accordingly, despite state law placing entire tax burden on trust share. Weiss v Comm, 19 TCM 1223, TC Memo 1960–219.

Where provision in will explicitly provided against proration of death taxes, federal estate tax was pay-

able before residuary estate was determined, widow's trust of one-third of residuary was subject to payment of one-third of federal estate tax, and amount of her marital deduction was to be reduced by tax. Second Nat. Bank of New Haven v United States (1965) 351 F2d 489 (CA 2).

Add note in first line on page 379:

. . . Marital Deduction.[14b]

[14b] The revised instructions to Schedule M, Form 706, see § 26, this supplement note that a separate pamphlet of supplemental instructions for Schedule M is again obtainable from the District Director.

§ 296. Specific Exemption.

p. 394, n. 15. Reg. 20.2106–1, amended Jan 18, 1961.

§ 302. Schedule R; Credit for Tax on Prior Transfers; Comparison to Deduction for Property Previously Taxed.

Add new note at end of section on page 405:

. . . means simple.[1a]

[1a] Credit for tax on prior transfers would not be governed by events existing as of date of second decedent's death, and where a deficiency in estate of husband who died first, was paid by wife's estate and credit claimed, and subsequently, due to a change in the law, a refund was received by the wife's estate, the credit for tax on prior transfers and the claim for the deficiency shown in her return were disallowed. Shedd v Comm (1963) 320 F2d 638 (CA 9).

§ 303. Schedule R; Credit for Tax on Prior Transfers; General Rule.

p. 406, n. 2. Where transferor-husband left no taxable estate, and so paid no estate tax, transferee-decedent's estate gets no credit for tax on prior transfers, although the property taxed to her estate had in fact been taxed to husband's transferor's estate within four years of decedent's death in 1955. Since there is no taxable estate, there is no credit under IRC § 2013. Although husband would have had a taxable estate but for the marital deduction, and though original transferor's property is taxed twice in ten years, the statutory language controls. United States v Denison (1963) 318 F2d 819 (CA 5).

§ 304. Schedule R; Credit for Tax on Prior Transfers; "Property" and "Transfer" Defined.

p. 407, n. 9. Where settlement plan under decedent's annuity contract, which provided for retention of the proceeds by insurer and payment of income to decedent's surviving spouse for life, gave such spouse during the first contractual year, the unlimited right to withdraw all or any part of the amount retained by the insurer, such spouse had a general power of appointment for purposes of the credit for tax on prior transfers. Regardless of date of spouse's death (decedent-transferee) the value of the entire amount retained by the insurer represents a transfer of a beneficial interest in the property passing to her from the transferor. Rev Rul 66–39, IRB 1966–8, p. 48.

112

§ 305. Schedule R; Credit for Tax on Prior Transfers; Valuation of Property Transferred.

p. 409, n. 12. The estate of a decedent who had been a life income beneficiary under a testamentary trust is entitled to a credit for all or any part of the Federal estate tax paid with respect to the transfer of such property by the prior estate, although the value of such life estate is not included in the gross estate of the decedent. Rev Rul 59–9 IRB 1959–2 p. 13.

§ 306. Schedule R; Credit for Tax on Prior Transfers; Limitation on Credit.

p. 410, n. 19. For illustrations of the methods of computing the credit for tax on prior transfers under the 1954 Code, see Rev Rul 59–73, IRB 1959–10, p. 33.

p. 411, n. 4. Where the amount of the marital deduction or charitable deduction depends on the amount of the Federal estate tax due, the method for computing the credit for tax on prior transfers is governed by Rev Rul 61–208, IRB 1961–48, p. 13 which provides: "The marital deduction and charitable deduction to be used in computing the tax described in subparagraph (A) of section 2013(c)(1) are the same as the respective amounts actually allowed as marital and charitable deductions in the final determination of the decedent's taxable estate. They (subject to the 50-percent limitation as to the amount of the marital deduction) are also the actual amounts which pass, after taxes, to the surviving spouse and to charity.

The amount of the charitable deduction which is referred to as "otherwise allowable" in subparagraph

(B) of section 2013(c)(1) is the amount actually allowed as a charitable deduction in the final determination of the taxable estate, which, in turn, is the amount actually passing to charity, after payment of all death taxes chargeable to the charitable interest."

The substance of this ruling is reflected in the new instructions to part II of Schedule R in the latest edition of the estate tax return, Form 706, revised July, 1961, and applies to returns filed after Nov. 27, 1961.

p. 411, n. 6. Rev Rul 60–161, IRB 1960–17, p. 10, clarifies § 20.2013–3(b) by holding that no proportionate adjustment to deductions otherwise allowable, except that provided for in cases involving a charitable deduction, is to be made in computing the tax on the reduced gross estate of the transferee. Also, in computing the estate tax on the reduced gross estate, the maximum deduction applicable is 50% of the reduced adjusted gross estate.

§ 309. Schedule S; Credit for Foreign Death Taxes; In General.

p. 419, n. 16. Reg. 20.2014–1(a) amended Jan. 18, 1961.

Foreign death taxes upon transfers for public, charitable, or religious uses may now be taken as a deduction, rather than a credit; and an election to take one rules out the other. The election must be filed within the period of limitation for assessment. 1954 Code §§ 2053(d), 2104 (f), as amended in 1959; Reg. 20.2011–2, 20.2014–1, 20.2014–2, 20-.2014–3, as amended, and Reg. 20-.2014–7, 20.2053–10, as adopted, May 28, 1962, Appendix B, this supplement. See also §§ 214 and 310, this supplement.

§ 310. Schedule S; Credit for Foreign Death Duties; Limitations on Credit.

p. 421, n. 5. The limitations imposed by IRC § 2014 (b) (1954 Code) are extended and apply to the deduction now allowed under IRC § 2053 (d) as amended in 1959 and effective as to estates of decedents dying on or after July 1, 1955; Reg. 20.2014–1, 20.2014–2, 20.2014–3 as amended, and Reg. 20.2014–7, as adopted (with a further example) May 28, 1962, Appendix B, this supplement. Also see §§ 214 and 309, this supplement.

§ 311. Schedule S; Credit for Foreign Death Taxes; Where Death Duty Convention.

p. 427, n. 13. General instructions to Form 706, revised July, 1961, lists countries with which there are estate tax conventions. See §§ 185 and 312.

§ 312. Schedule S; Credit for Foreign Death Taxes; Where Death Duty Convention; Tax by Foreign Country and Political Subdivision.

p. 430, n. 19. A new Canadian Estate Tax Convention came into force on April 9, 1962, retroactive to Jan. 1, 1959. Where Canada imposes tax solely by reason of the property being situated therein, Canada shall, if the decedent was a citizen of or domiciled in the United States, (a) for the purpose of computing the tax apply a rate not to exceed 15% in respect of the property situated in Canada, and (b) exempt from tax property situated in Canada where the aggregate value thereof does not exceed $15,000.00, but if the aggregate value exceeds $15,000.00 the amount of the tax shall not be greater than the amount by which the aggregate value exceeds $15,000.00. Rules are provided for determination of situs of property, and it is provided that stocks and bonds shall be deemed to be situated at the place where the company is incorporated.

Due to its retroactive nature, refund claims may be filed, based upon foreign estate tax credit, for taxes paid to Canada in estates of decedents dying after Jan. 1, 1959. Refund claims are to be made within the time provided in the Code, or within six years of date of death, whichever is later.

§ 314. Schedule S; Credit for Foreign Death Taxes; Proof of Credit.

p. 433, n. 6. Form 706 CE revised July, 1961, to delete Canada pending ratification of death tax convention. (But on April 9, 1962, a new Canadian Death Tax Convention came into force retroactive to Jan. 1, 1959, see § 312, this supplement).

§ 318. Credit for State Death Taxes; Generally.

Add new text at end of section:

In the event that two states claiming jurisdiction on the basis of domicile impose a state death tax on intangible property, a credit will be allowed for the amount paid to each state, up to the maximum total credit permitted by § 2011 of the 1954 Code.[8a]

[8a] Rev Rul 60-88, IRB 1960-10, p. 20.

§ 319. Computation of the Tax; Credit for State Death Taxes; Period of Limitations on Credit.

Add new note at end of paragraph (3) on page 444:

. . . is later.[8b]

[8b] Reg. 20.2011-1, amended Jan 18, 1961.

p. 445, n. 11a. If the time for payment of the tax has not expired on February 26, 1964, the two-year period provided for by IRC § 6163 (b) of 1954 Code, and IRC § 925 of 1939 Code may be extended to three years (as am Rev Act 1964 § 243).

§ 322. Deduction for State Death Taxes.

p. 449, n. 18. Reg. 20.2053-9 amended Jan. 18, 1961.

§ 323. Credit for Gift Taxes; In General.

p. 451, n. 20. No gift tax credit accrues unless a gift tax was actually due and payable. Chapman v Comm. (1959) 32 TC 599, No. 53.

§ 326. Credit for Death Taxes on Remainders.

p. 456, n. 12. Reg. 20.6163-1, amended Jan. 18, 1961.

p. 456, n. 12a. If the time for payment of the tax has not expired on February 26, 1964, the two-year period provided for by IRC § 6163 (b) of 1954 Code, and IRC § 925 of 1939 Code may be extended to three years (as am Rev Act 1964 § 243).

p. 456, n. 14. Reg. 20.2015-1, amended Jan. 18, 1961.

CHAPTER 5

PRACTICE AND PAYMENT

§ 330. Declaration of Fiduciary and Attorney.

p. 462, n. 4. Reg. 20.6061–1 and 20.6065–1, adopted May 28, 1962, in Appendix B, this supplement, as to signature and verification of returns.

p. 462, n. 4a. Form 706, revised Sept 1963, see § 26, this supplement, indicates that the verification may now be made by a firm, as well as by an individual.

§ 332. Authorization of Attorney.

p. 464, n. 6. Practice by former government employees before the Internal Revenue Service is subject to restrictions as to matters in which they had participated or which had been under their official responsibility. 31 CFR Part 10 § 10.32; IRB 1964–19, p. 23.

An enrolled attorney or agent may not assist or accept assistance from or share fees with anyone who participated personally and substantially in a matter as a government employee, nor assist, accept assistance from, or share fees with a government employee appearing personally before the Service, within one year after such employment is terminated, and in a matter which was under his official responsibility within a year prior to such termination. 31 CFR Part 10 § 10.34; IRB 1964–19, p. 23.

Admission requirements for representation in matters before the Revenue Service have been abolished for licensed attorneys and certified public accountants. Under Public Law 89–332, a lawyer in good standing in his home state is automatically admitted by simply filing a written declaration with the Revenue Service that he is currently qualified to practice law in his state and is authorized to represent the client involved.

p. 464, n. 7. The Internal Revenue Service provides forms for general (FORM 2848) and limited (FORM 2848–A) powers of attorney, use of which is not mandatory.

The requirements with respect to powers of attorney are set forth in detail in Rules on Administrative Procedure §§ 601.502–507, as am Mar. 13, 1964 (29 FR 3398). These rules have been relaxed in certain particulars, so that 1) a power of attorney is not required of an attorney or agent at a conference also attended by the taxpayer; 2) a power of attorney is not required of an attorney of record for the estate in the probate court, who prepared the return, and who is enrolled to practice before the IRS, even though the estate representative does not attend the conference; 3) a power granted by a corporation need not be attested, or be under seal, unless required by local law; 4) a power may be acknowledged by an attorney or agent enrolled to practice when granted to him; and 5) copies reproduced by photographic process need not be certified as true copies.

The Rules provide generally that only one power, naming all delegated attorneys or agents, shall be in effect in an office of the Service in any one matter, and additional copies are not required to be filed with regional offices unless requested. The power may designate the address to which copies of correspondence are to be sent. New powers of attorney supersede older ones, but a new limited power does not revoke an earlier general power except as to matters referred to in the limited powers.

Authority may be delegated to sign closing agreements and protests.

FORM NO. 52

General Power of Attorney

[Adopted March 1964. *Substitute for form in text*]

Form 2848
(Mar. 1964)

U. S. Treasury Department—Internal Revenue Service

GENERAL POWER OF ATTORNEY

(IMPORTANT—Please read instructions on reverse before completing this form)

Name and address of principal(s) ....
....

hereby appoint(s) (Name and address of appointee(s)) ....
....

as attorney(s)-in-fact to represent the principal(s) before any office of the Internal Revenue Service with respect to (specify Internal Revenue tax matter(s) and year(s) or period(s),

Said attorney(s)-in-fact shall, subject to revocation, have full power to perform any and all acts that the principal(s) can perform, including the power to receive (but not to endorse and collect) checks in payment of any refund of Internal Revenue taxes, penalties, or interest; to delegate authority or to substitute another attorney or agent; to execute waivers of restrictions on assessment or collection of deficiencies in tax; to execute consents extending the statutory period for assessment or collection of taxes; to execute a closing agreement (under section 7121 of the Internal Revenue Code) in respect of a tax liability or a specific matter; and to execute a protest to a determination of taxes by a district director.

Copies of correspondence addressed to the taxpayer in proceedings involving the above matter(s) should be sent to:

Any prior powers of attorney filed with this office by the principal(s) relating to the matter(s) and the year(s) or period(s) specified above are hereby revoked.

Signature if Principal is Individual or Husband and Wife
Signature of Principal   Date

. . . .

Signature of Principal   Date

. . . .

CORPORATE SEAL
(If applicable)

Signature if Principal is Partnership, Estate, Corporation, Etc.

Under penalties of perjury, I declare that I have the authority to execute this power of attorney on behalf of the principal.

Signature for Principal   Title   Date

. . . .

Signature for Principal   Title   Date

. . . .

Notarization   or   Witnessing

. . . .

The above-named person(s) signing as or for the principal(s) appeared this day before me and acknowledge this power of attorney as his/her/their voluntary act and deed.

NOTARIAL SEAL
(If required)

Signature of Notary

. . . .

Date

. . . .

This power of attorney was signed by or for the principal(s) by a person or persons known to, and in the presence of, the two disinterested witnesses whose signatures appear below:

Signature of Witness   Date

. . . .

Signature of Witness   Date

. . . .

Certification by Enrolled Attorney or Agent in Lieu of Witnessing or Notarization

I certify that I am in good standing and enrolled to practice before the Internal Revenue Service (the following is applicable only if the principal is other than an individual or husband and wife) and that to the best of my knowledge and belief, the person(s) signing above has/have the authority to execute this power of attorney on behalf of the principal.

Signature of Attorney-In-Fact

....

Enrollment Card Number

....

Expiration Date on Card

....

If a Limited Power of Attorney is Desired, Use Form 2848-A

INSTRUCTIONS

GENERAL

No formal rules govern the preparation of a power of attorney other than that the instrument should clearly express the scope of the authority granted the attorney or agent, the tax matters and taxable years or periods to which it relates, and that it should follow the instructions set forth in Subpart E, Conference and Practice Requirements of the Statement of Procedural Rules (Part 601, Title 26 of the Code of Federal Regulations). This form is made available simply as a convenience. Its use, therefore, is not mandatory.

This form may be used with respect to any matters affecting any tax imposed by the Internal Revenue Code, except alcohol or tobacco taxes. If alcohol or tobacco taxes are involved, Form 1534 should be used.

If a prior power of attorney was filed, this form may be used to constitute a new authorization of all attorneys or agents to represent the principal with respect to specified matters and years or periods before the office of the Internal Revenue Service where this power is filed. This will serve to automatically revoke all prior powers of attorney with respect to the same matters and years or periods filed in that office of the Internal Revenue Service.

A true copy of the power of attorney must be filed with each office of the Service in which the attorney or agent is to represent the principal, together with one additional copy for each taxable year or period in excess of one. However, when a copy of the power is filed with the office of a district director who has the matter under consideration, it shall not be necessary to file another copy of the power with the office of a regional commissioner or regional counsel who subsequently has the matter under consideration, unless an additional copy is specifically requested. Copies reproduced by photographic processes need not be certified as true and correct. Copies reproduced by other methods must be certified either by the attorney or agent (if enrolled), or by a notary public who shall state that he has personally compared the copy with the original and found it to be a true and correct copy.

SPECIFIC INSTRUCTIONS

Name and address of principal(s).—If a joint return is involved, enter the name and address (if different) of both husband and wife.

Example: "John J. Smith, 831 First Ave., Atlanta, Georgia; and Mary M. Smith, 1200 Pine St., Miami, Florida."

If a corporation, partnership, or association is the principal, enter the name and business address.

Example: "The A B C Corporation, (address"; "A–B Partnership, (address)"; etc.

If an estate or trust is the principal, enter the name, title, and address of the executor, administrator, trustee, etc., and the name of the principal.

Example: "Joseph Jones, (address), Executor of the Estate of Ruth Green."

Specify Internal Revenue tax matter(s) and year(s) or period(s).—The year(s) or period(s) to which the power relates must be clearly identified. Any number of specified years or periods and types of taxes may be listed in the same power, but a mere reference to "all years", "all periods", or "all taxes" will not be acceptable. If the matter relates to estate tax, enter the date of decedent's death instead of the year(s) or period(s).

Authority delegated.—If this form is used, none of the delegations of authority printed on the face of the form may be deleted. If a limited delegation of authority is desired, Form 2848–A may be used.

Signature of principal(s).—If a joint return is involved, both husband and wife must sign unless one spouse duly authorizes the other in writing to sign for both. In such a case, the authorization should accompany the power.

If the principal is a partnership, all partners must sign unless one partner is duly authorized to act in the name of the partnership. In such a case, unless the authorization is provided under local law, the authorization should accompany the power.

If the principal is a corporation or an association, an officer having authority to bind the entity must sign. The Internal Revenue Service does not require the affixing of the corporate seal. Space for affixing the corporate seal is provided as a convenience for corporations required by charter, or by the law of the jurisdiction in which they are incorporated, to affix their corporate seals in the execution of instruments.

Acknowledgment, witnessing, or certification.—A power of attorney must be either acknowledged before a notary public or witnessed by two disinterested individuals, unless it is granted to an attorney or agent enrolled to practice before the Internal Revenue Service who completes the certification at the bottom of the form.

Special cases.—If the principal is deceased, insolvent, or dissolved; or if a trustee, guardian, or other fiduciary is acting for the principal, see section 601.505 of Subpart E of the Conference and Practice Requirements for further instructions regarding the execution of a power of attorney.

FORM NO. 52A

Limited Power of Attorney

[Adopted March 1964]

Form 2848–A
(Mar. 1964)
U. S. Treasury Department—Internal Revenue Service

LIMITED POWER OF ATTORNEY

(IMPORTANT—Please read instructions on reverse before completing this form)

Name and address of principal(s) ....
....
hereby appoint(s) (Name and address of appointee(s)) ....
....
as attorney(s)-in-fact to represent the principal(s) before any office of the Internal Revenue Service with respect to (specify Internal Revenue tax matter(s) and year(s) or period(s)) ....
....
Said attorney(s)-in-fact shall, subject to revocation, have full power to perform on behalf of the principal(s) the following act or acts: ....
....

Copies of correspondence addressed to the taxpayer in proceedings involving the above matter(s) should be sent to: ....
....
....

One or more prior powers of attorney relating to the same matters and same year(s) or period(s) (are) (are not) in effect in the office where this power of attorney is filed. This power of attorney (revokes) (does not revoke) the prior power(s) of attorney. (See Second Paragraph of General Instructions on Reverse as to Requirement Regarding Prior Powers of Attorney.)
Signature if Principal is Individual or Husband and Wife

Signature of Principal   Date
....

Signature of Principal   Date
....

Signature if Principal is Partnership, Estate, Corporation, Etc.

                      CORPORATE SEAL
                       (If applicable)

         Under penalties of perjury, I declare that I have the authority to execute this power of attorney on behalf of the principal.

         Signature for Principal   Title   Date
         ....

         Signature for Principal   Title   Date
         ....

NOTORIZATION

The above-named person(s) signing as or for the principal(s) appeared this day before me and acknowledged this power of attorney as his/her/their voluntary act and deed.
NOTARIAL SEAL
  (If required)

         Signature of Notary
         ....

         Date
         ....

OR
WITNESSING

This power of attorney was signed by or for the principal(s) by a person or persons known to, and in the presence of, the two disinterested witnesses whose signatures appear below:

[Harris Tax Supp]   **121**

Signature of Witness   Date

....

Signature of Witness   Date

....

Certification by Enrolled Attorney or Agent in Lieu of Witnessing
   or Notarization

I certify that I am in good standing and enrolled to practice
before the Internal Revenue Service (the following is applicable
only if the principal is other than an individual or husband and
wife) and that to the best of my knowledge and belief, the
person(s) signing above has/have the authority to execute this
power of attorney on behalf of the pricipal.

Signature of Attorney-In-Fact

....

Enrollment Card Number

....

Expiration Date on Card

....

INSTRUCTIONS

GENERAL

No formal rules govern the preparation of a power of attorney
other than that the instrument should clearly express the scope
of the authority granted the attorney or agent, the tax matters
and taxable years or periods to which it relates, and that it should
follow the instructions set forth in Subpart E, Conference and
Practice Requirements of the Statement of Procedural Rules (Part
601, Title 26 of the Code of Federal Regulations). This form is
made available simply as a convenience. Its use, therefore, is
not mandatory.

This form may be used to confer authority to perform only
expressly stated acts with respect to matters affecting any tax
imposed by the Internal Revenue Code, except alcohol or tobacco
taxes. If alcohol or tobacco taxes are involved, Form 1534 should
be used. A limited power of attorney should state whether or
not any prior power of attorney is in effect in the same office
with respect to the same matters and the same years or periods,
and whether or not the new limited power of attorney revokes
such prior powers of attorney. If a prior limited power of attorney is to remain in effect, the new limited power of attorney
must specifically state that it does not revoke such prior limited
power of attorney, and the new power of attorney must be ac-

122   [Harris Tax Supp]

companied by a copy of such prior limited power of attorney. If the prior power of attorney is a general power of attorney which is to remain in effect, the limited power of attorney will be recognized only if it is accompanied either by a copy of the prior general power of attorney or by a certificate signed by the principal stating the names and addresses of all attorneys and agents authorized under such prior general power of attorney.

A true copy of the power of attorney must be filed with each office of the Service in which the attorney or agent is to represent the principal, together with one additional copy for each taxable year or period in excess of one. However, when a copy of the power is filed with the office of a district director who has the matter under consideration, it shall not be necessary to file another copy of the power with the office of a regional commissioner or regional counsel who subsequently has the matter under consideration, unless an additional copy is specifically requested. Copies reproduced by photographic processes need not be certified as true and correct. Copies reproduced by other methods must be certified either by the attorney or agent (if enrolled), or by a notary public who shall state that he has personally compared the copy with the original and found it to be a true and correct copy.

SPECIFIC INSTRUCTIONS

Name and address of principal(s).—If a joint return is involved, enter the name and address (if different) of both husband and wife.

Example: "John J. Smith, 831 First Ave., Atlanta, Georgia; and Mary M. Smith, 1200 Pine St., Miami, Florida."

If a corporation, partnership, or association is the principal, enter the name and business address.

Example: "The A B C Corporation, (address)"; "A–B Partnership, (address)"; etc.

If an estate or trust is the principal, enter the name, title, and address of the executor, administrator, trustee, etc., and the name of the principal.

Example: "Joseph Jones, (address), Executor of the Estate of Ruth Green."

Specify Internal Revenue tax matter(s) and year(s) or period(s).—The year(s) or period(s) to which the power relates must be clearly identified. Any number of specified years or periods and types of taxes may be listed in the same power, but a mere reference to "all years", "all periods", or "all taxes" will not be acceptable. If the matter relates to estate tax, enter the date of decedent's death instead of the year(s) or period(s).

Authority delegated.—Examples of authority which may be granted by express insertion on this form:

To receive (but not to endorse and collect) checks in payment of any refund of Internal Revenue taxes, penalties, and interest;

To delegate authority or to substitute another attorney or agent;

To execute waivers of restrictions on assessment or collection of deficiencies in tax;

To execute consents extending the statutory period for assessment or collection of taxes;

To execute a closing agreement under section 7121 of the Internal Revenue Code in respect of a tax liability or a specific matter;

To execute a protest to a determination of taxes by a district director;

To submit, withdraw, or enter into agreements, concerning offers in compromise;

To request and receive rulings or determination letters;

To attend conferences in behalf of the principal, and to give or receive information in connection therewith.

Signature of principal(s).—If a joint return is involved, both husband and wife must sign unless one spouse duly authorizes the other in writing to sign for both. In such a case, the authorization should accompany the power.

If the principal is a partnership, all partners must sign unless one partner is duly authorized to act in the name of the partnership. In such a case, unless the authorization is provided under local law, the authorization should accompany the power.

If the principal is a corporation or an association, an officer having authority to bind the entity must sign. The Internal Revenue Service does not require the affixing of the corporate seal. Space for affixing the corporate seal is provided as a convenience for corporations required by charter, or by the law of the jurisdiction in which they are incorporated, to affix their corporate seals in the execution of instruments.

Acknowledgment, witnessing, or certification.—A power of attorney must be either acknowledged before a notary public or witnessed by two disinterested individuals, unless it is granted to an attorney or agent enrolled to practice before the Internal

Revenue Service who completes the certification at the bottom of the form.

Special cases.—If the principal is deceased, insolvent or dissolved; or if a trustee, guardian, or other fiduciary is acting for the principal, see section 601.505 of Subpart E of the Conference and Practice Requirements for further instructions regarding the execution of a power of attorney.

§ 333. Examination of Return.

p. 467, n. 10. The IRS has entered into Tax Administration Agreements with many states providing generally for the exchange of information on a reciprocal basis to secure returns, improve enforcement and collection of taxes and to determine tax liability. There may be provisions for compiling special lists of taxpayers, and for the exploration of possible opportunities for making use of mechanical and electronic equipment. Announcement 64–35, IRB 1965–27, p. 50.

As of April 1965 such agreements were in effect in Arkansas, California, Colorado, District of Columbia, Florida, Idaho, Illinois, Indiana, Iowa, Kansas, Kentucky, Maine, Maryland, Massachusetts, Michigan, Minnesota, Missouri, Montana, Nebraska, New Hampshire, New Mexico, New York, North Carolina, North Dakota, Ohio, Oklahoma, Oregon, South Carolina, South Dakota, Tennessee, Utah, Virginia, Washington, West Virginia, Wisconsin and Wyoming.

The conditions set forth in Rev Proc 64–40, IRB 1964–40, p. 25 for reopening by the Service of an estate or gift tax case, closed by examination in a district director's office, are: evidence of fraud, malfeasance, collusion, concealment, or misrepresentation of material fact; substantial error; or other circumstances indicating serious administrative omission. The case may also be re-opened upon receipt from taxpayer of a claim for refund or request for reopening.

Add new note at end of section:
. . . adopted[11a]

[11a] By Reg. § 601.105(b)(5) added March 25, 1963, a taxpayer may during the course of an audit or conference in connection with a return or claim for refund or credit request that an issue be referred to the National Office on the ground of a lack of uniformity, or that the issue is complex and unusual. If the examining officer or on appeal the Chief, Audit Division, agree, a request for "technical advice" will be made to the National Office; the taxpayer has a right to a conference in that office in connection with the request.

§ 335. Estate Tax Examiner's Report.

Add new note in third line on page 483:
. . . Examining Officers.[14a]

[14a] Form of Instructions as to Preparation of Protests has been revised to provide that the taxpayer, and the agent or attorney, may sign the protest under penalty of perjury, rather than under oath. The opening paragraph now reads as follows:

The protest and any additional statement of facts must be submitted to this office *within 30 days* of the date of the letter with which these instructions [Publication No. 5] are enclosed. Such protest and statement must be submitted in duplicate with a declaration under the penalties of perjury by the taxpayer (in the case of a corporation the declaration must be made by a duly constituted officer). The declaration requirement may be satisfied by adding the following signed statement to the protest:

"I declare under the penalties of perjury that this protest including any accompanying schedules and statements, has been examined by me and to the best of my knowledge and belief is true, correct, and complete."

Paragraphs (e) and (g) were also amended to reflect the change. IRS Publication No. 5, revised Sept., 1961.

If the Audit Division of a District Office finds that the decision on a conference is based on clearly defined error, opportunity for another informal conference may be offered the taxpayer. Reg. § 601.105 (c)(3) added March 25, 1963.

§ 337. Procedure After Report; Protest.

Add new note in sixth from last line on page 485:

. . . under oath.[17a]

[17a] The requirement as to filing protests under oath, as stated in the text, has been changed with respect to protests in unagreed estate and gift tax cases not docketed in the Tax Court, and it is now sufficient that such protests be certified as true under the penalties of perjury. Rev Proc 61–36, IRB 1961–51, p. 12.

§ 339. Extension of Time for Payment; Hardship; Generally.

p. 491, n. 7. By amendment to

Reg. § 20.6161–1(b), approved May 27, 1964, the Commissioner added provisions to the effect that sale of property at a sacrifice price or on a severely depressed market, and the necessity for the sale of an interest in a family business to unrelated parties, even though the interest could be sold at current fair market prices, will be considered undue hardships.

p. 492, n. 10. Reg. 20.6165–1, amended Jan. 18, 1961.

§ 340. Extension of Time for Payment; Where Estate Consists Largely of Interest in Closely Held Business.

p. 494, n. 12e. There is no similar provision in § 6166(a) of the Code, and the community interest of the surviving spouse in closely held businesses cannot be combined with the deceased spouse's interest therein in order to ascertain whether the percentage requirements (in text at page 493) of § 6166(a) are met, so as to entitle the executor to elect to pay part or all of the estate tax in two or more installments. Rev Rul 61–91, IRB 1961–19, p. 22.

Add note in 5th line from bottom of page 495:

". . . qualifies under the statute"[12h.1]

[12h.1] Where a change from a corporate to an unincorporated form does not materially alter the business, or the estate's interest in such business, it does not terminate the privilege of paying the estate tax in installments. Rev Rul 66–62, IRB 1966–11, p. 18.

p. 497, n. 12l. See Reg. 20.6166–1 to 20.6166–4, and amended Reg. 20.6161–1 and 20.6161–2 in Appendix

B, as to installment payment of estate taxes and method of election.

Procedures for processing elections to pay estate taxes in installments have been set up by the IRS Revenue Procedure 60–33, I. R. B. 1960–50 p. 20, and it is suggested that an executor should presume that his election is acceptable if he has not been advised to the contrary.

Ownership, exploration, development, and operation of oil and gas properties constitutes a trade or business, qualifying for installment payment of estate tax. However, mere ownership of royalty interests does not qualify. Rev Rul 61–55, IRB 1961–13, p. 16.

The general instructions, revised Form 706, see § 26, this supplement, were amended to provide for installment payment of tax on closely held businesses as discussed in the text.

§ 342. Payment; How Made; Receipts.

p. 498, n. 16. Form 706, revised Sept 1963, see § 26, this supplement specifies that checks in payment of the tax be made payable to the "Internal Revenue Service".

p. 499, n. 18. A current list of bonds acceptable in payment of estate taxes may be obtained from the Treasury Department, and from the Federal Reserve Bank of New York and of Chicago.

Where an estate has Treasury bonds which can be applied at par in payment of the estate tax, though the bonds are quoted at less than par on the date of decedent's death, their value for estate tax purposes has been held to be at least par, whether or not such bonds are actually applied by the executor in payment of the estate tax. Bankers Trust Co. (Ellis) v United States, (1960) 284 F2d 537 (CA-2).

§ 343. Collection of Unpaid Tax; Remedies.

p. 499, n. 4. Reg. § 301.7404–1.

§ 347. Discharge of Executor.

p. 502, n. 19. Equitable estoppel will prevent a Commissioner from assessing personal liability for a deficiency against the trustee of an inter vivos trust, taxable as part of decedent's gross estate, where a previous Commissioner had concurred with a return excluding the trust corpus (and assessing other deficiencies), and where the trustee, relying on such action had distributed the corpus to one not a "transferee." Schuster v Comm. (1962) 312 F2d 311.

§ 348. Lien of Tax; Generally and Special Lien for Estate Taxes.

p. 503, n. 2. Kaufman v Herter 24 Misc 2d 187, 194 NYS2d 848 (1959).

p. 503, n. 3. In states where the revised Uniform Federal Tax Lien Registration Act is in effect the Internal Revenue Service will file notices affecting personal property with the clerk of the U. S. District Court of taxpayer's domicile, and notices affecting real property in the judicial district where the property is physically located. Technical Information Release No. 595, May 12, 1964, Rev. Rul 64–170. For convenience of title searchers the liens will also be filed with the corresponding county officials in such states. Rev Rul 64–252, 1964 IRB-37 p. 15.

IRC § 6323 and the corresponding Regulations §§ 20.6323 and 25.6323 provide for filing of notice of lien with the office designated by applicable state or territorial law, or with the clerk of the district court, including the District of Columbia district court. An exception to the effectiveness of the lien is provided in case of motor vehicles acquired for adequate or full consideration by a purchaser without notice or knowledge of the lien.

In New York the county clerk has no duty in respect to Federal tax liens other than to see that they are properly filed and indexed in his office and his office only; the Uniform Commercial Code applies only to private commercial instruments and does not affect handling of Federal tax liens. 1964 Op Atty Gen NY (Oct. 28, 1964).

p. 503, n. 4. The lien for estate taxes under IRC 6324 and Reg §§ 20.6324 and 25.6324 is not valid against a purchaser of a motor vehicle for adequate consideration in money or money's worth who at time of purchase and of taking possession is without notice or knowledge of the existence of the lien, unless such purchaser thereafter relinquishes possession to the seller or his agent.

§ 349. Lien of Tax; Liability of Transferees and Others.

p. 505, n. 10. Widow-executrix liable for deficiency as joint tenant transferee, though balance of estate undistributed, where three year period for assessment against the estate had expired (1951 decedent). Schuster v Comm. (1962) 312 F2d 311.

A trust beneficiary is not deemed a transferee liable for decedent-settlor's estate tax deficiency in respect of trust property which should have been included in his gross estate. Englert v Comm, 32 TC 1008, No. 91 (1959). Acquiescence, 1960–1 CB 4.

Where assets of an estate are distributed to a testamentary trust and to residuary legatee without making

provision for possible estate tax deficiency, transferee liability may be asserted both against legatee and a successor trustee of the trust. Where trustee is personally and severally liable under Ohio law for making distributions prior to satisfying estate tax liability, personal liability of such trustee may also be asserted. Hamar v Comm (1964) 42 TC 867.

Trustee and income beneficiary of a trust is not liable as transferee for estate tax deficiency asserted against another estate by reason of the inclusion therein of the value of the remainder, since as such trustee he was not a fiduciary of the future interest (that is, the remainder, taking effect after his death), and his present interest had never been part of decedent remainderman's estate. Grimm v Comm (1965) 43 TC 623, acquiesced in by Comm IRB 65–40, p. 6.

p. 505, n. 11. The Revenue Act of 1964 amended IRC §§ 6323 and 6324 to provide that federal tax liens, though filed, shall not be valid against one who purchases a motor vehicle for full monetary consideration and obtains possession thereof before actual notice or knowledge of the lien, and does not thereafter relinquish possession to the seller or his agent.

§ 351. Lien of Tax; Exception in Case of Securities.

p. 506, n. 17. The exception of securities from the lien for unpaid taxes, and from the special liens for estate taxes, was extended by the Revenue Act of 1964 (§ 238) to motor vehicles other than house trailers, so that the liens, even though notice is filed, will not be valid against rights of mortgagee, pledgee, or purchaser, acquired for full consideration after Feb 26, 1964, without no-

128

tice or knowledge of the existence of such tax lien. IRC Secs 6323(c) (3) and 6324 (c).

§ 359. Limitations; on Assessment and Collection.

p. 513, n. 7. Where estate tax return was received by post office on Saturday and was not delivered to District Director until following Monday, because his office was closed until then, filing of return would not be deemed complete until delivered and received by Director at his office. Phinney v Bank of Southwest National Assn. (1964) 335 F2d 266 (CA 5).

§ 361. Limitations; Collection after Assessment.

p. 514, n. 19. In determining the six-year period "assessment" has the technical meaning spelled out in IRC § 6203, which is one made by recording taxpayer's liability in the office of the Secretary of the Treasury or his delegate. Acceptance by commissioner of an executed "Waiver of Restrictions on Assessment and Collection of Deficiency and Acceptance of Over-assessment" does not constitute such an "assessment." United States v Miller (1963) 318 F2d 637 (CA 7).

§ 366. Interest; Suspension; Waiver of Restrictions.

p. 517, n. 19. An advance payment made after mailing of a statutory notice of deficiency (90-day letter) made as payment of the proposed deficiency, will be assessed as soon as practicable, The Tax Court is not deprived of jurisdiction by such advance payment.

An advance payment made before mailing of notice of deficiency, made

in respect of pending deficiency will also be assessed unless the amount of the deficiency cannot be ascertained, or criminal investigation would be imperilled; if the entire deficiency is satisfied, no statutory notice will be mailed, since this might raise a question as to jurisdiction of Tax Court. If a deficiency is not assessed, the payment made will be treated as a deposit in the nature of a cash bond, bears no interest, and will be returned on request before assessment of deficiency.

In all such cases taxpayer may designate what part of a payment is tax, and what interest; if the entire amount is designated as tax, a plea of hardship will not be accepted as basis for forbearance in collection of interest due on that portion of liability satisfied bp payment. Rev Proc 64–13, IRB 1964–8 p 21, enlarging Rev Proc 63–11, IRB 1963–10 p 16.

§ 367. Penalties; Additions to the Tax.

p. 519, n. 5. Hamar v Comm, 19 TCM 575, TC Memo 1960–107.

p. 519, n. 7. Reg. § 301.6155–1.

Additions to tax for frauds are collectible from transferee of bankrupt decedent taxpayer's assets as a tax, together with interest accruing subsequently to bankruptcy discharge, and are not affected by the discharge. Hamar v Comm (1964) 42 TC 867.

§ 368. Penalties; Civil.

p. 519, n. 9. Reg. § 301.7269–1.

§ 369. Penalties; Criminal.

p. 520, n. 14. Reg. § 301.7207–1.

129

§ 370. Transferred Assets; Method of Collection.

p. 521, n. 1. Administrators who disregarding estate tax liability distribute all estate assets in payment of debts are personally liable for tax, without assessment against them individually, in a proceeding under 31 USC § 192, as alternative remedy to proceeding under IRC § 6901, based on such assessment. United States v Rose (1964) 227 F Supp 259 (DC ED Pa), affd 346 F2d 985.

Additions to tax for frauds are collectible from transferee of bankrupt decedent taxpayer's assets as a tax, together with interest accruing subsequently to bankruptcy discharge, and are not affected by the discharge. Hamar v Comm (1964) 42 TC 867.

§ 371. Transferred Assets; Period of Limitation.

p. 522, n. 2. A transferee's liability for a deficiency is enforceable for four years from filing of estate tax return on Oct. 7, 1951, though three-year period for assessment against estate has expired. Schuster v Comm. (1962) 312 F2d 311.

Assessments against transferees of a decedent may be made within one year after the expiration of the normal period of limitations for assessment against transferor, regardless of whether a request for prompt assessment has been made by the estate. Rev Rul 64–305, IRB 1964–47, p. 75.

§ 376. Credit or Refund; Period of Limitations on Filing Claim.

p. 526, n. 4. Remittance of the tax either with a late estate tax return or in response to a request for payment of a deficiency will constitute "payment" from which date the statutory period for filing a refund claim will commence to run, unless the remittance is accompanied by a statement or letter to the effect that it is solely for the purpose of avoiding penalties and interest pending final determination of the tax liability. Richardson v Smith (1961) 196 F Supp 432 (ED Pa), affd 301 F2d 305 (CA 3), and holding that date stamped on receipt for check was not date of "payment", where check had been received at an earlier date. Hill v United States (1959) 263 F2d 885 (CA 3); Rosenman v United States (1945) 323 US 658, 65 S Ct 536, 89 L ed 535.

Add note in 17th line, page 526: "... made in such last day"[4c]

[4c] Where executor upon being advised that an additional assessment would be made, and without waiting for a formal assessment, forwarded a check therefor, which the government deposited in a suspense account, the date of payment to determine the period of limitation within which a claim for refund can be made is the date of formal assessment when the check was applied in satisfaction thereof. Fox v United States (1965) 248 F Supp 1021 (DC WD Wash).

p. 526, n. 8. Aplington v United States, 169 F Supp 815 (Ct Cl) (1959), cert den 361 US 821, 4 L ed 2d 67, 80 S Ct 69.

Neither the courts nor the Commissioner of Internal Revenue can waive the period of limitations. In one case a claim for refund was filed within the 3-year period based upon the deduction from the decedent's gross estate of expenses, then indefinite as to amount, that would be incurred in connection with winding up decedent's business, and which, as soon as claimant ascertained them, would be made definite. After

130

the expiration of the 3-year period claimant filed a claim asking that additional deductions be allowed based on decedent's federal and state income tax liabilities. This was held not to be an amendment clarifying the original claim, but a new and different claim filed too late, and it was also held immaterial that the original claim was still pending when the expanded claim was filed, or that prior to the expiration of the 3-year period the files of the Internal Revenue Service contained data showing the actual amounts of the tax liabilities sought to be claimed. First Nat. Bank of Montgomery v United States (Blair) (1960) 280 F2d 818 (Ct Cl).

A refund claim can be filed at any time for a restricted Indian, who is a ward of the United States, and the three-year statute of limitation does not apply where estate tax is erroneously assessed on inherited allotted lands. Nash v Wiseman (1963) 227 F Supp 552 (DC WD Okla).

p. 526, n. 9. Where an untimely claim for refund of estate taxes was filed in the estate of a decedent who had died leaving an income tax deficiency, which was promptly paid by his estate representative, the estate tax overpayment was recoverable by making an equitable recoupment against the fully paid income tax deficiency. Bowcut v United States, 175 F Supp 218 (D Mont) (1959), affd 287 F2d 654 (CA 9).

§ 377. Credit or Refund; State Death Taxes; Foreign Death Taxes.

p. 529, n. 16. See § 312, this supplement, regarding claims under new Canadian Death Tax Convention, which is retroactive in effect to Jan. 1, 1959.

p. 529, n. 17. Where state inheritance tax had been paid prior to filing the federal estate tax return, and the executor therein had taken a credit for state inheritance taxes, no part of the refund due and payable could be construed as a credit for state inheritance taxes. Accordingly, interest was due on the entire amount of the refund and not merely on the refund in excess of the credit for paid state inheritance taxes. Morgan Guaranty Trust Co. v United States, (1960) 277 F2d 466 (Ct Cl).

If a refund is based entirely on credit for state inheritance taxes, it will not bear interest; if based partially on state tax credit and partially on other adjustments, only latter portion will bear interest; and if refund is based entirely on adjustments other than state tax credit, the entire refund will bear interest. Rev Rul 61-58, IRB 1961-14, p. 9.

§ 378. Credit or Refund; Limitation on Allowance.

p. 529, n. 19. Taxpayer's claim for refund of gift tax, filed more than three years after the filing of gift tax returns, and more than two years after the payment of the tax, is barred by limitation even though the claim is filed in the same year the state probate court decreed that the gifts were void, and must be returned, because of fraud and undue influence. First National Bank of Miami (Cassidy) v United States (1963) 226 F Supp 166 (DC SD Fla), affd (1965) 341 F2d 737.

§ 379. Credit or Refund; Interest.

p. 530, n. 3. In connection with a refund of estate tax, interest on a deposit made in advance of a possible deficiency assessment is to be computed from date of assessment and not from date of deposit. Colfelt v Comm (1961) 35 TC 769, No. 88.

§ 380. Credit or Refund; Effect of Petition to Tax Court.

p. 531, n. 8. The filing of a petition in the Tax Court is a bar to subsequent action in the District Court, operating in the manner of a statute of limitations, so that although an expense for which deduction or credit is sought was incurred or paid after a decision by the Tax Court, action for refund based on such deduction cannot be brought. Empire Trust Co. (McIntosh) v United States (1963) 214 F Supp 731 (DC D Conn) (the court suggested that Tax Court Rules 50 and 51 discussed in §§ 650 and 651 of text, provide a remedy), affd (1963) 324 F2d 507 (CA 2).

§ 382. Waiver of Restrictions on Assessment; Closing Agreements; Compromises.

p. 533, n. 16. Taxpayer not estopped from prosecuting a claim for refund of additional tax paid, where the claim was filed after the statute of limitations had run against government's right to make further additional assessments, and taxpayer, after audit of the estate tax return had agreed to a settlement of the amount of additional tax, executed a "waiver of restrictions on assessment and collection of deficiency in tax and acceptance of overassessment" and paid the deficiency. Cooney v United States (1963) 218 F Supp 896 (DC D NJ) (the court noted that under decisions in the 3rd circuit the government could have, although it had not, sought addi-

132

tional assessments by recoupment in the district court action.)

p. 533, n. 18. Rev Proc 63–11, IRB 1693–10, p. 16, superseding Rev Proc 58–18, clarifies the effect of an advance payment of taxes to stop running of interest, providing specifically in § 4.01 that such payment made after the mailing of a 90 day letter will be assessed upon receipt or as soon thereafter as is practicable, and will not deprive the tax court of jurisdiction. An advance payment made before the mailing of the notice may also be promptly assessed, if the amount of the deficiency can be ascertained, but if the entire deficiency is satisfied no statutory notice will be mailed, and the tax court has no jurisdiction (§ 4.2). Where the amount of the deficiency cannot be ascertained by the District Director when the advance payment is received, no assessment will be made, and the payment will be treated as a deposit in the nature of a cash bond for payment of taxes thereafter found to be due. In this connection § 4.03 provides as follows: "As such, it will have no effect on the computation of interest or on the running of the period of limitation for filing a claim for refund. The taxpayer will be placed on notice by certified mail as to the status of the payment. At such time as the amount of the deficiency is determined, an assessment will be made and the advance payment will be applied as a payment of tax and/or interest made on the date of the assessment. Upon request by the taxpayer, the deposit will be returned to him, without interest, at any time prior to the assessment of the deficiency. In this event the case will be processed as though no payment had ever been made."

The provisions with respect to interest on advance payments are discussed in the note to § 366, supra, this supplement.

p. 533, n. 19. Administrative Regulation § 301.7121–1 pertaining to closing agreements was adopted February 4, 1960 by TD 6450. See also Administrative Regulation § 301-.7122–1 pertaining to compromises. TD 6450 was promulgated on the aforementioned date.

Rev Proc 62–28, IRB 62–47 p 7, superseding prior rulings, sets forth procedures for the issuance of rulings, determination letters, and closing agreements on specific issues.

p. 533, n. 20. Tax cases closed by a District Director may be reopened (1) upon evidence of fraud, malfeasance, collusion, concealment or misrepresentation of a material fact; (2) if the prior closing involved substantial error, or (3) if circumstances indicate a serious administrative omission. A case may be reopened on additional information originating within or without the service; on regional post review, the approval of the Assistant Regional Commissioner (Audit) is required, except in certain income tax situations, and where taxpayer files a refund claim or requests a reopening. Rev Rul 63–9 IRB 1963–9 p. 38.

p. 534, n. 3. Each Assistant Regional Commissioner, as Chief of the Appellate Division, and each Associate Chief of the Appellate Division is authorized to determine the disposition of any offer in compromise under § 3761 of the 1939 Code or under § 7122 of the 1954 Code, in which (a) the proponent has made a written request for Appellate Division consideration or (b) the liability was previously determined by the Appellate Division and the offer is based in whole or in part on doubt as to liability. Each Assistant to the Chief is authorized to determine the

disposition to be made of any such offer in which the unpaid amount of tax (including any interest, penalty, additional amount or addition to the tax) is less than $100,000.

A determination by the Appellate Division to accept an offer is subject to the Commissioner's approval if the unpaid amount of tax (including interest etc.) is $100,000 or more, Commissioner Delegation Order No. 75 (Rev 2) eff June 14, 1963.

District Directors are delegated authority under § 7122 of the 1954 Code to accept offers in compromise in cases in which the liability subject to be compromised (including interest etc.) is less than $100,000, and in cases involving specific penalties. Commissioner Delegation Order No. 11 (Rev 3), eff June 14, 1963; Rev Proc 64–44, IRB 1964–42 p. 64 superseding Rev Procs 60–22 and 62–19. Tax liability compromise is stated to rest "but one or both of two grounds—(1) doubt as to liability and (2) doubt as to collectibility." These factors must be supported by evidence. Where the liability is substantial or fraud is involved additional consideration is usually required, commonly collateral agreements to pay from future income, or to relinquish present or potential tax benefits. Rev Proc 64–44 Sec 8.

p. 534, n. 5. United States v Saladoff (1964) 233 F Supp 255 (DC ED Pa); compromise procedures outlined by statute and regulations are exclusive and require strict compliance.

§ 383. Reversionary or Remainder Interests; Extension of Time for Payment of Tax.

p. 535, n. 10. Reg. 20.6163–1, amended March 25, 1964.

p. 535, n. 10a. If the time for payment of the tax has not expired on February 26, 1964, the two-year period provided for by IRC § 6163 (b) of 1954 Code, and IRC § 925 of 1939 Code may be extended to three years (as am Rev Act 1964 § 243).

p. 536, n. 14. Reg. 20.6165–1(b) amended May 28, 1962, Appendix B, this supplement.

§ 384. Bonds; Form; Single Bond in Lieu of Multiple Bonds.

p. 536, n. 18. Reg. 20.7101–1, amended May 28, 1962, Appendix B, this supplement.

CHAPTER 6

GENERAL PRINCIPLES OF FEDERAL GIFT TAX

New sections added:

§ 415A. Rulings and Determination Letters Available to Taxpayer or his Representative in Gift Tax Matters.

§ 392. Outline of the Tax.

p. 542, n. 5. Regs. 25.01, 25.2501-1, 25.2511-1, 25.2511-3, amended Jan. 19, 1961, dealing with the taxation of residents of United States possessions.

§ 394. Correlation of Gift Tax, Estate Tax, and Income Tax.

p. 545, n. 10. Where gifts of patent rights are complete when made under gift tax regulations and precedents, and subject to gift tax in year when made, donor is not subject to gift tax thereafter on annual payments of royalties to beneficiaries, though under income tax regulations and precedents a finding of constructive ownership and retention of control might be asserted. Talge v United States (1964) 229 F Supp 836 (DC WD Mo).

§ 396. Domicile; Residence.

p. 547, n. 3. Regs. 25.01, 25.2501-1, 25.2511-1, 25.2511-3, amended Jan. 19, 1961, dealing with the taxation of residents of United States possessions.

§ 398. Applicable Statutes and Regulations.

p. 549, n. 14. The Gift Tax Regulations appearing in the Appendix of the text were adopted by TD 6334

and were published November 15, 1958 in the Federal Register.

§ 399. Definitions; Residents; Nonresidents.

"tangible" at end of third line of section should read "intangible".

Add new text at end of section, page 550:

With respect to gifts made after September 14, 1960, a resident of a United States possession shall for gift tax purposes be considered a nonresident not a citizen of the United States, if he acquired his United States citizenship solely by reason of his being a citizen of such possession or his birth or residence within such possession (Added PL 86-779).[4b]

[4b] Regs. 25.01, 25.2501-1, 25.2511-1, 25.2511-3, amended Jan. 19, 1961.

§ 403. Returns; When Required.

p. 553, n. 20. True v United States (1965) 354 F2d 323 (Ct Cls) (wife does not start running of limitations against assessment of tax by signing husband's gift tax return, and failing to file return).

§ 406. Returns; Nonresident Not a Citizen.

p. 556, n. 18. Where donor is a non-resident British citizen, and donee a British consul here, credits created by deposit in England of English funds in donee's bank account are gifts of intangible property situated outside the US, and not taxable. When donee buys US real property with such funds, subject to a purchase money mortgage, there is a taxable gift of the difference between excess of the fair market value of the real property over the mortgage, but the later gift of a bank credit used to pay off the mortgage is not taxable, as the gift of intangible property situated outside the US. Davies v Comm (1963) 40 TC 525, No. 61.

p. 556, n. 4. Regs. 25.01, 25.2501-1, 25.2511-1, 25.2511-3, amended Jan. 19, 1961, dealing with the taxation of residents of United States possessions.

§ 407. Returns; Contents; Regulations.

p. 558, n. 8. Form 709 may be reproduced. Rev Proc 64-39, IRB 1964-39, 22.

§ 410. Returns; Execution.

p. 562, n. 6. Reg. 25.6061-1 and 25.6065-1, adopted May 28, 1962, Appendix C, this supplement, as to signature and verification of returns.

p. 562, n. 9. Where Int Rev Code and Treas Regulations provide that both spouses shall signify their consent in order to benefit from provisions allowing half of gifts made by one spouse to be attributed to the other, actual signature by consenting spouse on the return, though called for by the return, Form 709, itself,

136

is not necessary. Answers to questions set forth in the return, attached schedules of donated property and other circumstances may reasonably signify unequivocal intention to consent, and the requirement of signature, not supported by official regulations, is not justified. Jones v Comm (1964) 327 F2d 98 (CA 4).

§ 411. Returns; Place of Filing.

p. 563, n. 10. Reg. 25.6091-2, adopted May 28, 1962, Appendix C, this supplement.

§ 413. Returns; Failure to File; Delinquency.

p. 564, n. 16. Wife's reliance upon her husband to furnish their accountant with the necessary information for preparation of their gift tax returns did not constitute reasonable cause excusing penalty assessment. Drybrough v United States (1962) 208 F Supp 279 (WD Ky).

§ 415A (New) Rulings and Determination Letters Available to Taxpayer or his Representative in Gift Tax Matters.

The Internal Revenue Service is authorized to issue rulings and determination letters in response to specific inquiries addressed to it by a taxpayer or his representative. A ruling is a written statement issued by the National Office in Washington, D. C. and is an expression of the official interpretation or policy of the Commissioner of Internal Revenue. It establishes principles and policies in the interpretation and application of substantive tax law to a taxpayer's specific problem or inquiry.[8]

A determination letter is a written statement issued by a district director in response to an inquiry addressed to him which involves the application of clearly established rules as set forth in the statute, Treasury decisions or regulations, or rulings, opinions or court decisions published in the Internal Revenue Bulletin.[9]

The procedure to be followed by a taxpayer seeking a determination letter or a ruling is prescribed by the Rules on Administrative Procedure.[10]

[8] See Rules on Administrative Procedure, § 601.201.

[9] See Rules on Administrative Procedure, § 601.201.

[10] See Rules on Administrative Procedure, § 601.201. Rev Proc 62–28, IRB 62–47, p. 7, superseding prior rulings, sets forth procedures for the issuance of rulings, determination letters, and closing agreements on specific issues. Rulings and determinations ordinarily will not be is-

sued if a gift tax return has been filed and the period of limitation on assessment has not expired; they will not be issued on estate tax matters before death. Rulings will not issue after an estate tax return is filed.

Rulings will not issue on whether a transaction is one in contemplation of death under IRC § 2035. Rev Proc 64–31, Sec 3.01 subd 17; IRB 64–30 p. 14.

Requests for rulings made by an attorney should be accompanied by a copy of a power of attorney to him, and should be addressed to the Commissioner of Internal Revenue Washington, D. C. 20224. If such request is not accompanied by a copy of a power of attorney, and a copy is not furnished on request, the ruling will be mailed to taxpayer. Technical Information Release No. 514, October 8,1963; Reg. §§ 601.503, 601.504.

The CIR has made provision for issuance of advance rulings on the basis of a "two part" request, where in addition to the usual complete statement of facts the taxpayer submits a summary of the facts he believes should control. The ruling may be based on these facts, if they are accepted, but the IRS reserves the right to seek further information or rule on the basis of a more complete statement of facts. Rev Proc 65–8, IRB 1965–12, p. 17.

CHAPTER 7

TRANSFERS SUBJECT TO FEDERAL GIFT TAX

§ 416. Scope of Chapter.

p. 568, n. 1a. Regs. 25.01, 25.2501–1, 25.2511–1, 25.2511–3, amended Jan. 19, 1961, dealing with the taxation of residents of United States possessions.

§ 417. What a Gift is; Generally.

p. 568, n. 3. Payments made to widow of corporation president, equalling his salary for the balance of the year of his death, made in part for public relation purposes, and deducted from income on corporation returns, were not gifts, but taxable income to widow. Gaugler v United States (1963) 312 F2d 681 (CA 2).

Fact finder's determination on issue whether payments made by corporation after executive's death are additional compensation or tax-free gifts will stand unless "clearly erroneous." Cronheim v Comm. (1963) 323 F2d 706 (CA 8).

Monthly payments, spread over two years, made pursuant to corporate resolution by newspaper publishing corporation to widow of publisher of paper who had been majority stockholder, are taxable to widow as income, although payments were stated in resolution to be intended as "gifts", where she was principal beneficiary of decedent's estate, was president of the corporation at date of resolution authorizing the "gift", and her sons also had interests in the company. Evans v Comm (1964) 330 F2d 518 (CA 6).

Payments by corporation to widow of officer and director, made without regard to her financial circumstances and needs, but by reasons of moral obligation to decedent and company morale, were not gifts, but taxable income to her. Fritzel v United States (1964) 339 F2d 995 (CA 7); Meyer v United States (1965) 244 F Supp 103 (DC SD Cal) (payments to widow by 20th Century Fox Film Corp. held not to be gifts).

Where salary of deceased corporate vice-president is continued voluntarily for balance of fiscal year, as the institution of a plan to help widows of high company officials, the payments were at least in part motivated by business and economic reasons, and constituted taxable income to widow, not a gift. McCarthy v United States (1964) 232 F Supp 605 (DC D Mass).

Transfer of remainder interest by surviving tenant by the entireties to stepchildren to compromise claims affecting title to the properties, even though unliquidated, was not a gift, but a transfer made at arm's length, and for adequate consideration. Friedman v Comm (1963) 40 TC 714. The Commissioner has announced acquiescence, IRB 1964–16 p. 7.

Annotation: Income tax: employer's payment to widow of employee as taxable income of widow. 95 ALR2d 520.

Testimony of directors who authorized payment to widow of director, and the absence of evidence of company policy, supported conclusion that payment of $17,500 as a "salary continuation" was motivated by generosity, admiration and respect so as to constitute a gift. Fanning v Conley (1965) 243 F Supp 683 (DC D Conn), affd 357 F2d 37 (CA 2).

p. 568, n. 5. Where patents are assigned to an individual trustee for exploitation and thereafter rights to royalties and other remaining rights are given to bank, in trust for benefit of donor's children, a complete gift results subject to gift tax; donor's controlling interest in corporation that employs the individual trustee and pays the royalties found under all the circumstances not to amount to such retention of control by donor as to make the annual royalty payments subject to gift tax in the years when paid. Talge v United States (1964) 229 F Supp 836 (DC WD Mo).

p. 569, n. 7. A renunciation in 1956 by a widow of part of her interest to income under a will taking effect in 1931, was held not to have been made within a reasonable time after knowledge of the existence of the trust, even though the trust had not been set up as directed until 1956, where no election to take against the will ever had been filed by her, and in addition, she had resided on estate property maintained by funds expended by the executors as directed by the will, which constituted an acceptance of the transfer. Accordingly the renunciation resulted in a taxable gift. Fuller v Comm (1961) 37 TC 147, No. 19.

Waiver of trustees' statutory commissions on principal under NY Surr Ct A § 285-a constitutes taxable gift where waiver is not timely made under Rev Rul 56-472, 1956-2 CB 21, and trustees' services were not intended to be gratuitous. Rev Rul 64-225, IRB 1964-35 p. 7.

[Harris Tax Supp]

§ 420. Delivery and Date of Transfer.

p. 572, n. 15. The fact that a written declaration of trust failed to designate the property transferred when, under local law, a parol declaration of trust is permitted, does not preclude a completed gift if, in fact, property was actually transferred pursuant to the declaration of trust. Causey v Comm, 19 TCM 579, TC Memo 1960–108.

§ 421. Property Interests Subject to the Tax.

p. 573, n. 3. Davies v Comm (1963) 40 TC 525.

§ 422. Transfers by Gift; When Transferred; Generally.

p. 575, n. 12. Where patents are assigned to an individual trustee for exploitation and thereafter rights to royalties and other remaining rights are given to bank, in trust for benefit of donor's children, a complete gift results subject to gift tax; donor's controlling interest in corporation that employs the individual trustee and pays the royalties found under all the circumstances not to amount to such retention of control by donor as to make the annual royalty payments subject to gift tax in the years when paid. Talge v United States (1964) 229 F Supp 836 (DC WD Mo). The court refused to follow income tax rules as to constructive ownership and retained control.

§ 423. Transfers by Gift; When Transferred; Retained Powers.

p. 577, n. 6. Paolozzi, Gramm, and Vander Weele cases, cited in text, have been acquiesced in by Rev Rul 62–13, infra, note 14. Vander Weele case has been affirmed, 254 F2d 895 (CA 6).

p. 579, n. 14. Rev Rul 54–538, CB 1954–2, 316, cited in text, has been modified to remove any implication that a transfer may be considered a completed gift for Federal gift tax purposes where a power to invade income and corpus for the benefit of the grantor is so great that under the circumstances there is no assurance that anything of value will be paid to any beneficiary other than the grantor. Rev Rul 62–13, IRB 1962–5, p. 20.

Holtz (1962) 38 TC 37. Acq. IRB 1963–1, p. 8 (transfer not a taxable gift where trustee could make payments for support or emergency need).

p. 580, n. 1. Transfers of property and cash to an irrevocable trust in 1953 and 1955 were not completed gifts and so not subject to gift tax where trustee had broad powers to distribute principal to settlor for his welfare, comfort and support or emergency needs, since it was "entirely possible" that settlor, though over 80, would receive all the corpus during his life, and thus have made no effective gift. Holtz (1962) 38 TC 37; acq. IRB 1963–1, p. 8.

§ 426. Transfers by Gift; When Transferred; Short Term Trusts.

p. 584, n. 1. State court decree in action instituted by trustees was deemed conclusive as to property rights of parties though trustors did not resist the action, where the federal tax authorities had notice of the state court action, the District Director of Internal Revenue having been originally made a party to the action, and the result was correct

140

under state law (California). Flitcroft v Commissioner of Internal Revenue (1964) 328 F2d 449 (CA 9) (ten-year trust agreement reformed to express irrevocability found to have been intended, resulting in taxation of income to trust, rather than settlor).

§ 428. Transfers by Nonresidents not Citizens.

p. 585, n. 7. Regs 25.01, 25.2501–1, 25.2511–1, 25.2511–3, amended Jan. 19, 1961, dealing with the taxation of residents of United States possessions.

§ 433. Stocks and Bonds; Valuation; Generally.

p. 590, n. 2. Gifts of shares in open-end publicly offered mutual funds, made after October 10, 1963, are valued on the basis of offering price on the date of the gift, less any reduction publicly available in the acquisition of the number of shares being valued. Reg. § 25.2512–6(b); the Commissioner will not disturb valuations made on basis of redemption value, or mean between redemption value and public offering price, in the case of gifts made before October 11, 1963. Rev Proc 64–18, IRB 1964–17, p. 31.

§ 430. Valuation of Gifts; Generally.

p. 588, n. 19. Reg § 25.2512–1 was amended to provide further that the fair market value of an item of property is not to be determined by the sale price of the item in a market other than that in which such item is most commonly sold to the public, taking into account the location of the item wherever appropriate. Thus, in the case of an item which is generally obtained by the public in the retail market, the fair market value of such an item of property is the price at which the item or a comparable item would be sold at retail. For example, the fair market value of an automobile, generally obtained in the retail market, is the price for which a similar automobile can be purchased by the general public, and not the price which a used car dealer would pay. (See Appendix C, this supp.)

§ 434. Stocks and Bonds; Valuation; Closely Held Corporation.

p. 591, n. 11. Rev Rul 54–77, cited in text, has been superseded by Rev Rul 59–60, IRB 1959–9, p. 8, explaining and restating factors to be considered in evaluating closely held stock.

p. 592, n. 12. Where underlying net assets of family holding company had unchallenged value of $11,000 per share of common, with possible future earnings of $400 per share, commissioner's gift tax valuation of $8500 per share will be upheld, as against estate's arguments that market value of stock should reflect facts that such assets included (1) many parcels of real property concentrated in one area, (2) stock holdings in wholly owned subsidiaries, and (3) rental obligations under long term leases; that the gift being appraised was of a minority interest in the closely held corporation, and consisted of stock on which no dividends had ever been paid, and were not payable until arrears on preferred dividends had been paid up. Hamm v Comm (1963) 325 F2d 934 (CA 8).

p. 592, n. 16. Dean v Comm, 19 TCM 281, TC Memo 1960-54.

[Harris Tax Supp]

§ 437. Interest in Business; Valuation.

p. 596, n. 20. Factors considered in evaluating gifts of interests in a limited partnership engaged in the road construction business include: fair market value of tangible assets of the construction company; its good will based on capitalized earnings for a projected 1.8 year period, using an average based on previous years' earnings from private contracts only (since ability to procure public contracts in Louisiana cannot be expected to be transferrable); and anticipated net profits on uncompleted contracts, based on average net profits for prior years, after allowance for indirect costs. Barber v Comm (1963) 22 TCM 1025, TC Memo 1963-206.

§ 440. Annuities, Life Estates, Terms for Years, Remainders and Reversions; Valuation.

p. 597, n. 8. Tables applied to value gift to charity of income of ten-year trust, and commissioner's method, which treated gift as an annuity of the cash dividend paid on the stock forming the trust corpus at the date of the gift, was rejected. Hipp (1962) 215 F Supp 222 (DC SC).

Gift of trust income to charity for 20 year period, consisting of dividends on non-voting stock of family controlled corporation does not qualify for charitable deduction, as not susceptible of valuation, where at time of gift only two dividends had been declared in 11 years despite substantial earnings resulting in increased surplus, trust instrument did not guarantee any income to the charity, and remaindermen were members of family. Morgan v Comm (1964) 42 TC 1080, No. 85, affd 353 F2d 209.

§ 441. Life Insurance and Annuity Contracts; Valuation.

p. 600, n. 4. Reg. 25.2512–6, amended Jan. 19, 1961 to include Example (5), joint and survivor annuity contract.

p. 600, n. 9. Where decedent acquired life insurance with community funds and wife predeceased him, leaving her interest in policies to another, entire proceeds of insurance, less only one half cash surrender value at wife's death, was includible in husband's gross estate. Scott v Comm (1964) 43 TC 2320, No. 72.

§ 442. Annuities, Life Estates, Terms for Years, Remainders, Reversions, Life Insurance and Annuity Contracts; Description.

p. 601, n. 13. Form 938 revised May, 1961.

§ 443. Certain Annuities under Qualified Plans.

Add new note, third line, p. 604 after words:
". . . 401(a)(3), (4), (5), and (6)[14a.1]

[14a.1] For calendar year beginning after December 31, 1962 the words "was a plan described in section 403 (a)" are substituted for "met the requirements of" etc. Sec 7j PL 87–792.

p. 604, n. 14b. Reg. 25.2517–1, adopted Jan. 19, 1961.

Internal Revenue Service procedures for issuing determination letters relating to the initial qualification of pension, annuity, profit sharing and bond purchase plans which include self-employed individuals have been set forth in Rev Proc 63–23, 1963 IRB 41 p. 84, 26 CFR 601.201.

For calendar years beginning after December 31, 1962, contributions made by a donor on his own behalf under a self-employment retirement plan (Section 401(c)(1)) are to be considered to be payments or contributions made by the employee. See 7 j, P.L. 87–792.

§ 444. Miscellaneous Property; Valuation and Description.

p. 605, n. 15. Reg § 25.2512–1 was amended to provide further that the fair market value of an item of property is not to be determined by the sale price of the item in a market other than that in which such item is most commonly sold to the public, taking into account the location of the item wherever appropriate. Thus, in the case of an item which is generally obtained by the public in the retail market, the fair market value of such an item of property is the price at which the item or a comparable item would be sold at retail. For example, the fair market value of an automobile, generally obtained in the retail market, is the price for which a similar automobile can be purchased by the general public, and not the price which a used car dealer would pay. (See Appendix C, this supp.)

§ 450. Tenancies by the Entirety; Generally.

Replace italicized portion of the first line of section with the following: *which is effective only as to gifts made on and after January 1, 1955.*

§ 462. Powers of Appointment; Date of Creation of Power.

Substitute for first ten lines of paragraph on page 629:

Inter vivos instruments create additional questions. Regulation § 25.2514–1(e) has been amended to provide that a power of appointment created by an inter vivos instrument is considered as created on the date the instrument takes effect. Such a power is *not* considered as created at some future date merely because it is not exercisable on the date the instrument takes effect, or because it is *revocable,* or because the identity of its holders is not ascertainable until after the date the instrument takes effect.[20a]

See discussion in § 168, this supplement, in connection with similar amendment made to estate tax regulation.

[20a] Reg § 20.2514–1(e), as amended Dec. 11, 1961 by TD 6582. See App C, this supplement.

§ 472. Gift by Husband or Wife to Third Party; Manner and Time of Signifying Consent.

p. 642, n. 20. Where Int Rev Code and Treas Regulations provide that both spouses shall signify their consent in order to benefit from provisions allowing half of gifts made by one spouse to be attributed to the other, actual signature by consenting spouse on the return, though called for by the return, Form 709, itself, is not necessary. Answers to questions set forth in the return, attached schedules of donated property and other circumstances may reasonably signify unequivocal intention to consent, and the requirement of signature, not supported by official regulations, is not justified. Jones v Comm (1964) 327 F2d 98 (CA 4).

§ 474. Gift by Husband or Wife to Third Party; Return.

p. 645, n. 12. True v United States (1965) 354 F2d 323 (Ct Cls) (wife does not start running of limitations against assessment of tax by signing husband's gift tax return, and failing to file return).

§ 476. Gifts by Nonresidents Not Citizens.

p. 646, n. 18. Regs. 25.01, 25.2501–1, 25.2511–1, 25.2511–3, amended Jan. 19, 1961, dealing with the taxation of residents of United States possessions.

CHAPTER 8

FEDERAL GIFT TAX EXCLUSIONS AND DEDUCTIONS

§ 480. The Annual Exclusion; Generally.

p. 650, n. 12. Where parent deeds rural properties to sons, taking vendor's lien note for full value of properties, payable at the rate of $3,000 a year, and each $3,000 installment secured by a deed of trust on transferred properties, the notes created enforceable indebtedness, though mother intended to, and did, forgive each $3,000 payment as it became due, and upon annual cancellation of a $3,000 indebtedness the annual exclusion applied. Haygood v Comm (1964) 42 TC 936. The Commissioner has acquiesced in this decision in result only. IRB 1965–27, p. 7.

§ 484. The Annual Exclusion; Future Interests; Gifts of Income.

p. 655, n. 10. Payments of income under 1956 trust which in trustee's discretion were to be paid during life beneficiary's minority to its mother, otherwise to be applied for its maintenance, welfare, support, qualified for exclusion under Sec. 2503(b) as present gifts of income, where under reasonable construction of instrument trustee was not vested with discretion to withhold income. Albright v United States (1962), 308 F2d 739 (CA 5).

p. 655, n. 11. Morgan v Comm (1964) 42 TC 1080, No. 85 (where gift of third of trust income for life, to be expended by trustee directly for

144

benefit of mentally retarded institutionalized minor, qualified for annual exclusion), affd 353 F2d 209.

p. 656, n. 1. Fischer v Comm, 19 TCM 327, TC Memo 1960–62, affd 288 F2d 574 (CA 3).

§ 486. The Annual Exclusion; Future Interests; Where Power of Invasion.

p. 658, n. 14. Where the trustee's discretionary power of invasion in favor of the income beneficiaries was broad enough to distribute the trust corpus at any time, thus ending any present right to income, gifts made to the trust did not qualify for the annual gift tax exclusion. Funkhouser v Comm, 275 F2d 245 (CA 4).

p. 658, n. 15. The value of the present right to the income of a trust qualifies for the annual exclusion if the expected annual return and the probable period over which the income will be paid are known or ascertainable; but where the trustee has a discretionary right of termination with corpus payable to the beneficiary the valuation of such a present right of income is uncertain and cannot qualify for the annual exclusion. La Fortune Trust v Comm, 263 F2d 186 (CA 10) (1958).

§ 491. The Annual Exclusion; Gifts to Minors; History of the Statute.

p. 663, n. 13. La Fortune v Comm, 263 F2d 186 (CA 10).

Duffy v United States, 182 F Supp 765 (D Minn) (1960).

p. 663, n. 20. A gift to a minor in trust will not be treated as a gift of a present interest if he has been granted an option upon attaining his majority either to require an immediate distribution of the trust corpus or to extend the trust and receive distribution according to the terms set forth in the trust; to qualify as a present interest the trust instrument must grant to the minor the unequivocal and unconditional right to receive the property without any necessity for affirmative action on his part. Rev Rul 60–218, IRB 1960–23, p. 12, superseding Rev Rul 59–144, CB 1959–1, 249.

§ 492. The Annual Exclusion; Gifts to Minors; Statutory Provision.

Add new note in 6th line from top of page 664:

Both the property itself and its income[1a]

[1a] Where taxpayer in 1959 gave property to a trust for a minor grandchild, the present gift of income (based on grandchild's life expectancy) qualified for the annual exclusion under IRC § 2503(b) on taxpayer's return for 1959, though that part of the gift representing the grandchild's right to receive principal at 21 constituted the gift of a future interest under § 2503(c). Rollman v United States (1965) 342 F2d 62 (Ct Cls), the court finding that Congress did not intend by the enactment of § 2503(c) to change preexisting rules relating to separate qualification of gifts of income and of corpus.

p. 664, n. 2. Provision in trust agreement that should minor beneficiary die before reaching age of 21

property would pass to next of kin, excluding donor, did not satisfy requirement that property in such event should be payable to "estate of donee", and donor was not entitled to take the annual exclusion of $3000 against the value of the gift. Clinard v Comm (1963) 40 TC 878.

§ 493. The Annual Exclusion; Gifts to Minors; Requirements of Power of Appointment.

Add note at end of paragraph (2) on page 665:

. . . term of the trust;[5a]

[5a] A gift to a minor in trust will not be treated as a gift of a present interest if he has been granted an option upon attaining majority either to require an immediate distribution of the trust corpus or to extend the trust and receive distribution according to the terms set forth in the trust; to qualify as a present interest the trust instrument must grant to the minor the unequivocal and unconditional right to receive the property without any necessity for affirmative action on his part. Rev Rul 60–218, IRB 1960–23, p. 12, superseding Rev Rul 59–144, CB 1959–1, 249.

§ 494. The Annual Exclusion; Gifts to Minors; Decisions Prior to 1955.

p. 666, n. 9. Where trusts for benefit of minors provided for payment of income until they became 30, and for distribution of principal at age 30, only the gifts of income interests payable up to majority qualified for the annual exclusion. Herr v Comm (1961) 35 TC 732, No. 81, affd 303 F2d 780 (CA 3); Rollman v United States (1965) 342 F2d 62 (Ct Cls).

p. 666, n. 15. Thorrez v Comm, 272 F2d 945 (1959) (CA 6).

Where a trustee of a gift in trust for a minor is not given uncontrolled discretion, but must use the principal and income for the benefit of the minor as if the trustee were his guardian, then such gift in trust qualifies for the annual exclusion under the 1939 Code, Rev Rul 59–78, IRB 1959–10, p. 44.

Payments of income under 1956 trust which in trustee's discretion were to be paid during life beneficiary's minority to its mother, otherwise to be applied for its maintenance, welfare, support, qualified for exclusion under Sec. 2503(b) as present gifts of income, where under reasonable construction of instrument trustee was not vested with discretion to withhold income. Albright v United States (1962), 308 F2d 739 (CA 5).

§ 495. The Annual Exclusion; Gifts to Minors; Transfers Under "Gifts to Minors" Statutes; Gift, Estate and Income Tax Effect.

p. 667, n. 16. Rev Rul 59–357, IRB 1959–44, p. 18 reaffirms and clarifies earlier rulings as to the gift tax exclusion accorded to gifts made under Model Gifts of Securities to Minors Acts as adopted in some states and the more comprehensive Uniform Gifts to Minors Acts which permit gifts of money and securities. The annual gift tax exclusion applies equally to completed gifts made pursuant to either the model act or the uniform act. No taxable gift occurs for Federal gift tax purposes by reason of a subsequent resignation of the custodian or termination of the custodianship in addition, for Federal tax purposes, the value of the property transferred is includible in the gross estate of the donor if the property is given in contemplation of death within three years of the donor's death, or the donor appoints himself custodian and dies while serving in that capacity. If the custodianship property is includible in the donor's gross estate and a gift tax has been paid on the prior transfer, the donor's estate receives a gift tax credit against any Federal estate tax due pursuant to IRC 2012 (1954 Code).

Although a state law restricting a parent from using the guardianship funds of his child for the support and education of the child unless financially unable so to do, would disqualify for annual exclusion gift to parent-guardian of minor donee, where such parent is willing and able to support donee, since the donee would not have an immediate right to the use and enjoyment of the property, where the gift is accompanied with express authorization to the parent-guardian to use the gift for the support of the child, the state-law destriction on such use was held to be removed, and the gift thereby to be one of present interest which qualified for the annual exclusion. Briggs v Comm (1960) 34 TC 1132. No. 117. Government has indicated its acquiescence. Acq. 1961–11, p. 7.

An outright gift by a donor to the guardian of a minor is considered a gift of a present and not a future interest, and limitations imposed by state law on the guardian's use of the property do not make the gift one of a future interest. Ross v United States (1965) 348 F2d 577 (CA 5).

p. 667, n. 17. Rev Rul 59–357, IRB 1959–44, p. 18; Rev Rul 57–366, CB 1957–2, 618. Lober v U. S., cited in text footnote should be disregarded.

p. 667, n. 18. Where a decedent purchased securities in his own name

146

"as custodian for" a minor daughter under a Gifts to Minors statute permitting the custodian to apply as much income or principal as he may deem advisable to the support, maintenance, education and benefit of the minor, he made a transfer with retained right to discharge his obligation of support under State law, and the value of the securities a⁺ date of death was includible in his gross taxable estate. Chrysler v Comm (1965) 44 TC 2359, No. 4.

§ 496. Deductions; Specific Exemption; Generally.

p. 668, n. 2. Where a taxpayer used her gift tax exemption against gifts of $150,000 made by husband during his life, and on his death $75,000 thereof was included in his estate as a transfer made in contemplation of death, no part of widow's $30,000 exemption may be restored for application to gifts made by her in another year. The subjection of husband's $75,000 gift to estate tax in his estate did not affect the nature of the original transaction, which remained an inter vivos gift, the widow's share of the total gift was likewise unaffected, and she received the benefit of her exemption. The gift tax paid was in effect a down payment on the estate tax, since it was a credit against such tax, and double taxation is thus avoided. Ingalls v Comm (1964) 336 F2d 874 (CA 4).

§ 499. Deductions; Charitable and Similar Gifts; Uses Qualifying.

p. 671, n. 5. Contributions to a political party or to a candidate seeking public office are not deductible charitable contributions for gift tax purposes. Rev Rul 59–57, IRB 1959–8.

p. 672, n. 18. Gifts to the Secretary of Commerce are exempt from Federal estate and gift taxes, and gifts heretofore made to the US Merchant Marine Academy have been transferred to him. Pub L 88–611.

§ 503A. Deductions; Marital Deduction; Life Estate or Other Terminable Interests; Generally.

Add note in seventh line on page 677:

. . . terminable interests.[8a]

[8a] Bequest to wife "if she is living at the time of entry of Order of Final Distribution of my estate" held to be a terminable interest disqualifying bequest for marital deduction. Sbicca v Comm (1960) 35 TC 96, No. 14.

§ 504. Deductions; Marital Deductions; Property Which Another Donee May Possess or Enjoy.

p. 678, n. 14. Where insured assigned insurance policies on his life to spouse with gifts over to his children if spouse predeceased him, and such assigned interest was terminable under state law, it would not qualify for the marital deduction. Berman v Patterson (1959) 171 F Supp 800 (ND Ala).

§ 509. Deductions; Marital Deduction; Life Estate with Power of Appointment in Donee.

p. 681, n. 9. Interest of spouse as transferee and life beneficiary of husband's insurance policies was not terminable where she had absolute right to transfer the policies subject only to insurer's approval, since the requirement of such approval, under applicable state law, was solely for the benefit of the insurer and could be taken advantage of by it alone. For purposes of IRC § 2523(e) spouse's power to dispose of her interest was thus exercisable by her alone. Furthermore, since state law imposed no duty on spouse as life tenant to exercise good faith in respecting rights of remaindermen, her power of disposal was exercisable in all events, and the interest qualifies for the marital deduction. Kidd v Patterson (1964) 230 F Supp 769 (DC ND Ala).

p. 681, n. 11. Reg. 25.2523(e)-1, amended Jan. 19, 1961.

CHAPTER 10

PRACTICE AND PAYMENT OF FEDERAL GIFT TAX

§ 548. Verification of Returns.

p. 722, n. 2. Reg. 25.6061–1 and 25.6065–1, adopted May 28, 1962, Appendix C, this supplement, as to signature and verification of returns.

§ 550. Extension of Time for Payment.

p. 723, n. 15. Reg. 25.6165–1 and 25.7101–1, amended May 28, 1962, Appendix C, this supplement.

§ 555. Lien of Tax; Generally; Donees and Transferees.

p. 725, n. 19. Though ceiling on liability of transferee of inter vivos trust for gift tax is the value of gift received, within that ceiling the liability may be collected from any assets on hand at the time the notice of deficiency is served. Want v Comm (1960) 280 F2d 777 (CA 2).

§ 562. Waiver of Restrictions on Assessments; Closing Agreements; Compromises.

Add text at end of section:

A new form for a gift tax adjustment agreement has been issued by the Treasury Department as Form 2591. If the donor agrees to the increase in net gifts he may avoid paying the resultant deficiency by authorizing an additional specific exemption in the amount of the deficiency. The new Form 2591 is as follows:

FORM NO. 71A

Gift Tax Adjustment Agreement
(Official Form 2591)

U.S. TREASURY DEPARTMENT
INTERNAL REVENUE SERVICE
DISTRICT DIRECTOR

In Reply Refer to

Our recent examination of your gift tax return(s) for the year(s) shown below results in an increase in the amount of the net gifts as shown in the accompanying statement. A deficiency in tax will not be asserted, however, if you agree to the proposed adjustments and claim additional specific exemption.

If you agree to the adjustments please sign below and return the original copy of this letter promptly to this office.

Very truly yours,

District Director

Enclosures:

Statement

Copy of this letter

To: District Director

I agree to the proposed increase in net gifts for the year(s) shown below.

I hereby claim additional specific exemption as shown below.

1. Year(s) ....
2. Total Specific Exemption Used in Prior Years ....
3. Total Specific Exemption Claimed on Return(s) for Year(s) Shown in Item 1 ....
4. Additional Specific Exemption Now Claimed ....
5. Total Specific Exemption Claimed *(Item 2 plus Item 4)* ....

Signature of Donor .... Date ....

CHAPTER 11

PRELIMINARIES TO ESTATE OR GIFT TAX LITIGATION

§ 567. Choice of Forum; Generally.

p. 731, n. 6. The authority of a District Director of Internal Revenue to mail notice of disallowance of claims for refund, as a delegate of the Secretary of the Treasury, is determined by IRC § 6531(a) and Administrative Regulations § 301-.7701(g). Stephens v United States (1963) 216 F Supp 854 (DC ED Ark).

IRC § 6532(a)(1) provides that action on a refund claim may not be brought within six months of date of filing a refund claim unless a decision has been rendered within that period by the Secretary of the Treasury as duly authorized delegate. A "decision" is deemed "rendered" where Internal Revenue agent's report (recommending the disallowance of refund claim and the assessment of a substantial additional deficiency), is transmitted to taxpayer with a 30-day letter giving notice of the deficiency, although the letter does not refer directly to the refund claim. Stephens v United States (1963) 216 F Supp 854 (DC ED Ark) (Government's motion to dismiss action as premature denied, though action brought a week after the 30-day letter and within 3 months of filing claims).

§ 570. Choice of Forum; District Court.

p. 734, n. 17. Filing a petition for refund of estate taxes in the tax court is a bar to subsequent action for refund in the District Court. Empire Trust Co. (McIntosh) v United States (1963) 214 F Supp 731 (DC D Conn), affd (1963) 324 F2d 507 (CA 2).

CHAPTER 12

JURISDICTION OF TAX COURT

§ 575. Jurisdiction; Generally.

p. 739, n. 2. The Tax Court, in determining liability for a deficiency, does not have jurisdiction to provide for the assessment of interest on the deficiency. Schuster v Comm. (1962) 312 F2d 311.

§ 580. Time within Which Petition to Be Filed.

p. 745, n. 19. Administrative Regulation § 301.6213–1 was amended by TD 6425 to include Hawaii and Alaska as states and to coordinate the 90-day and 150-day filing periods with the dates such territories became states.

p. 745, n. 2. Krueger v Comm, 33 TC 667, No. 75 (1960); the Commissioner acquiesced in this decision. IRB 1964–11 p. 5.

p. 745, n. 8. If the mailing is by certified mail, the date of certification is the postmark date. Administrative Reg. § 301.7502–1 as amended by TD 6444.

CHAPTER 13

PLEADINGS AND MOTION PRACTICE IN TAX COURT

§ 607. Appearance, Withdrawal, and Substitution of Counsel.

p. 767, n. 3. There is a presumption that a duly licensed attorney appearing in regular course has authority to act for the litigant he purports to represent, and tax court may not deny jurisdiction over petition for redetermination of income tax deficiency for failure to prove such authority, where duly licensed attorney subscribed petition, together with "acting" treasurer, but officers who originally authorized the appearance and subscription had since died. Communist Party of U. S. A. v Comm (1964) 332 F2d 325 (CA Dist Col).

CHAPTER 14

PROCEEDINGS PREPARATORY TO TRIAL

§ 611. Depositions; Generally.

p. 774, n. 11.   The tax court has no power to grant an order to take depositions before the issuance of the statutory notice of deficiency. Marx (1963) 40 TC 1; (deposition sought of doctor where decedent suffered a heart attack, and preliminary notice of commissioner's proposal to increase estate tax had been issued).

CHAPTER 15

TRIAL IN THE TAX COURT

§ 636. Evidence; Presumptions.

p. 795, n. 4. Reg. § 301.6064–1.

CHAPTER 17

ACTIONS FOR REFUND

§ 656. Prerequisite to Action.

p. 812, n. 5. A proper claim for refund, which is a prerequisite to action in the District Court is one where, if made by one acting for the taxpayer, a power of attorney evidencing his authority to act is filed (Treas Reg §§ 601.502(b)(5) and (c)(1)(2)). This requirement cannot be waived. However, this requirement is satisfied if the power of attorney be filed a reasonable time before the Secretary acts on the claim. Oldham v Campbell (1963) 217 F Supp 819 (DC ND Tex) (filing 47–67 days before disallowance in 1961 of claim held reasonable).

§ 657. United States District Court; Parties and Venue.

p. 813, n. 12. Although the estate taxes are paid by the estate fiduciary, the heirs held proper parties to claim a refund after the estate is closed. Oldham v Campbell (1963) 217 F Supp 819 (DC ND Tex).

§ 658. United States District Court; Complaint.

FORM NO. 80

Complaint in Action for Refund

Delete reference to IRC § 1346 in paragraph 2 of form, p 815 of text.

APPENDIX B

FEDERAL ESTATE TAX REGULATIONS

THE EFFECTIVE DATE OF EACH REGULATION MUST BE COMPARED WITH THE EFFECTIVE DATE OF THE AMENDMENT OF THE GOVERNING CODE PROVISIONS

(UNDER 1954 CODE)

PART 20—ESTATE TAX

PART 301—PROCEDURE AND ADMINISTRATION

TABLE OF CONTENTS

ESTATE TAX REGULATIONS

§ 20.0–1 **Introduction.** (Paragraphs (a) and (b) amended Jan. 20, 1961, to read as follows)

(a) *In general.* (1) The regulations in this part (Part 20, Subchapter B, Chapter I, Title 26, Code of Federal Regulations) are designated "Estate Tax Regulations". These regulations pertain to (i) the Federal estate tax imposed by chapter 11 of subtitle B of the Internal Revenue Code on the transfer of estates of decedents dying after August 16, 1954, and (ii) certain related administrative provisions of subtitle F of the Code. It should be noted that the application of many of the provisions of these regulations may be affected by the provisions of an applicable death tax convention with a foreign country. Unless otherwise indicated, references in the regulations to the "Internal Revenue Code" or the "Code" are references to the Internal Revenue Code of 1954, as amended, and references to a section or other provision of law are references to a section or other provision of the Internal Revenue Code of 1954, as amended. Unless otherwise provided, the Estate Tax Regulations are applicable to the estates of decedents dying after August 16, 1954, and supersede the regulations contained in Part 81, Subchapter B, Chapter I, Title 26, Code of Federal Regulations (1939) (Regulations 105, Estate Tax), as prescribed and made applicable to the Internal Revenue Code of 1954 b Treasury Decision 6091, signed August 16, 1954 (19 F.R. 5167, Aug. 17, 1954).

(2) Section 2208 makes the provisions of chapter 11 of the Code apply to the transfer of the estates of certain decedents dying after September 2, 1958, who were citizens of the United States and residents of a possession thereof at the time of death. Section 2209 makes the provisions of chapter 11 apply to the transfer of the estates of certain other decedents dying after September 14, 1960, who were citizens of the United States and residents of a

possession thereof at the time of death. See §§ 20.2208-1 and 20.2209-1. Except as otherwise provided in §§ 20.2208-1 and 20.2209-1, the provisions of these regulations do not apply to the estates of such decedents.

(b) *Scope of regulations*—(1) *Estates of citizens or residents.* Subchapter A of chapter 11 of the Code pertains to the taxation of the estate of a person who was a citizen or a resident of the United States at the time of his death. The term "resident" means a decedent who, at the time of his death, had his domicile in the United States. The term "United States", as used in the Estate Tax Regulations, includes only the States and the District of Columbia. The term also includes the Territories of Alaska and Hawaii prior to their admission as States. See section 7701(a)(9). A person acquires a domicile in a place by living there, for even a brief period of time, with no definite present intention of later removing therefrom. Residence without the requisite intention to remain indefinitely will not suffice to constitute domicile, nor will intention to change domicile effect such a change unless accompanied by actual removal. For meaning of the term "citizen of the United States" as applied in a case where the decedent was a resident of a possession of the United States, see § 20.2208-1. The regulations pursuant to subchapter A are set forth in §§ 20.2001-1 to 20.2056(e)-3.

(3) *Miscellaneous substantive provisions.* Subchapter C of chapter 11 of the Code contains a number of miscellaneous substantive provisions. The regulations pursuant to subchapter C are set forth in §§ 20.2201-1 to 20.2209-1.

§ 20.0-2 **General description of tax.** (First seven lines of paragraph (b)(2) amended October 23, 1963 to read as follows:)

(2) *Gross estate.* The first step in determining the tax is to ascertain the total value of the decedent's gross estate. The value of the gross estate includes the value of all property to the extent of the interest therein of the decedent at the time of his death. (For certain exceptions in the case of real property situated outside of the United States, see paragraphs (a) and (c) of § 20.2031-1.) In addition, the gross estate may include property in which the decedent did not have an interest at the time of his death. A decedent's gross estate for Federal estate

§ 20.2011-1 **Credit for State death taxes.** (Paragraph (a) amended Jan. 18, 1961, to read as follows)

(a) *In general.* A credit is allowed under section 2011 against the Federal estate tax for estate, inheritance, legacy or succession taxes actually paid to any State, Territory, or the District of Columbia, or, in the case of decedents dying before September 3, 1958, any possession of the United States (hereafter referred to as "State death taxes"). The credit, however, is allowed only for State death taxes paid (1) with respect to property included in the decedent's gross estate, and (2) with respect to the decedent's estate. The amount of the credit is subject to the limitation described in paragraph (b) of this section. It is subject to further limitations described in § 20.2011-2 if a deduction is allowed under section 2053(d) for State death taxes paid with respect to a charitable gift. See paragraph (a) of § 20.2014-1 as to the allowance of a credit for death taxes paid to a possession of the United States in a case where the decedent died after September 2, 1958.

(Paragraph (c) amended to insert the following sentence after ". . . is last to expire" in fourth from last line on page 881) If a claim for refund or credit of an overpayment of the Federal estate tax is filed within the time prescribed in section 6511, the credit for State death taxes is limited to such taxes as were actually paid and credit therefor claimed within four years after the filing of the return or before the expiration of 60 days from the date of mailing by certified or registered mail by the district director to the taxpayer of a notice of disallowance of any part of the claim, or before the expiration of 60 days after a decision by any court of competent jurisdiction becomes final with respect to a timely suit instituted upon the claim, whichever period is the last to expire.

§ 20.2011–2 **Limitation on credit if a deduction for State death taxes is allowed under section 2053(d).** (Amended May 28, 1962, as follows)

(Heading amended to include phrase "for State death taxes")

(Paragraph (c) amended to insert new sentence in eighth line of Example, after word "charity":)

No death taxes were imposed by a foreign country with respect to any property in the gross estate.

§ 20.2014–1 **Credit for foreign death taxes.** (Paragraph (a)(1) amended to insert following after ". . . of foreign states," in eighteenth line on page 898) With respect to the estate of a decedent dying after September 2, 1958, the term "foreign country", as used in this section and §§ 20.2014–2 to 20.2014–6, includes a possession of the United States. See §§ 20.2011–1 and 20.2011–2 for the allowance of a credit for death taxes paid to a possession of the United States in the case of a decedent dying before September 3, 1958.

§ 20.2014–1 **Credit for foreign death taxes.** (Paragraph (a) amended May 28, 1962 to insert new paragraph (4) as follows)

(4) Where a deduction is allowed under section 2053(d) for foreign death taxes paid with respect to a charitable gift, the credit for foreign death taxes is subject to further limitations as explained in § 20.2014–7.

§ 20.2014–2 **"First limitation".** (Paragraph (a) amended May 28, 1962, as follows)

(a) The amount of a particular foreign death tax attributable to property situated in the country imposing the tax and included in the decedent's gross estate for Federal estate tax purposes is the "first limitaion." Thus, the credit for any foreign death tax is limited to an amount, A, which bears the same ratio to B (the amount of the foreign death tax without allowance of credit, if any, for Federal estate tax) as C (the value of the property situated in the country imposing the foreign death tax, subjected to the foreign death tax, included in the gross estate and for which a deduction is not allowed under section 2053(d)) bears to D (the value of all property subjected to the foreign death tax). Stated algebraically, the "first limitation" (A) equals—

$$\frac{\text{Value of property in foreign country subjected to foreign death tax, included in gross estate and for which a deduction is not allowed under section 2053(d)(C)}}{\text{Value of all property subjected to foreign death tax (D)}} \times \text{Amount of foreign death tax (B)}$$

(and continuing as in original)

(*Example* in paragraph (a) amended October 23, 1963 to read as follows:)
Example. At the time of his death, the decedent, a citizen of the United States, owned stock in X Corporation (a corporation organized under the laws of Country Y) valued at $80,000. In addition he owned bonds issued by X Corporation valued at $80,000. The stock and bond certificates were in the United States. Decedent left by will $20,000 of the stock and $50,000 of the bonds in X Corporation to his surviving spouse. He left the rest of the stock and bonds to his son. Under the situs rules referred to in paragraph (a)(3) of § 20.2014–1 the stock is deemed situated in Country Y while the bonds are deemed to have their situs in the United States. There is no death tax convention in existence between the United States and Country Y. The laws of Country Y provide for inheritance taxes computed as follows:

Inheritance tax of surviving spouse:

Value of stock	$20,000
Value of bonds	$50,000
Total value	70,000
Tax (16 percent rate)	11,200

Inheritance tax of son:

Value of stocks	60,000
Value of bonds	30,000
Total value	90,000
Tax (16 percent rate)	14,400

The "first limitation" on the credit for foreign death taxes is:

$$\frac{\$20,000+\$60,000 \text{ (factor C of the ratio stated at § 20.2014–1(a))}}{\$70,000+\$90,000 \text{ (factor D of the ratio stated at § 20.2014–2(a))}} \times (\$11,200+\$14,000) \text{ (factor B of the ratio stated at § 20.2014–2(a))} = \$12,800$$

§ 20.2014–3 "Second limitation". (Paragraph (b) amended May 28, 1962, as follows)

(b) Adjustment is required to factor "G" of the ratio stated in paragraph (a) of this section if a deduction for foreign death taxes under section 2053(d), a charitable deduction under section 2055, or a marital deduction under section 2056 is allowed with respect to the foreign property. If a deduction for foreign death taxes is allowed, the value of the property situated in the foreign country, subjected to foreign death tax, and included in the gross estate does not include the value of any property in respect of which the deduction for foreign death taxes is allowed. See § 20.2014–7. If a charitable deduction or a marital deduction is allowed, the value of such foreign property (after exclusion of the value of any property in respect of which the deduction for foreign death taxes is allowed) is reduced as follows:

(1) If a charitable deduction or a marital deduction is allowed to a decedent's estate with respect to any part of the foreign property, except foreign property in respect of which a deduction for foreign death taxes

is allowed, specifically bequeathed, devised, or otherwise specifically passing to a charitable organization or to the decedent's spouse, the value of the foreign property is reduced by the amount of the charitable deduction or marital deduction allowed with respect to such specific transfer. See example (1) of paragraph (c) of this section.

(2) If a charitable deduction or a marital deduction is allowed to a decedent's estate with respect to a bequest, devise or other transfer of an interest in a group of assets including both the foreign property and other property, the value of the foreign property is reduced by an amount, I, which bears the same ratio to J (the amount of the charitable deduction or marital deduction allowed with respect to such transfer of an interest in a group of assets) as K (the value of the foreign property, except foreign property in respect of which a deduction for foreign death taxes is allowed, included in the group of assets) bears to L (the value of the entire group of assets). As used in this subparagraph, the term "group of assets" has reference to those assets which, under applicable law, are chargeable with the charitable or marital transfer. See example (2) of paragraph (c) of this section.

Any reduction described in subparagraph (1) or (2) of this paragraph on account of the marital deduction must proportionately take into account the 50-percent limitation on the aggregate amount of the marital deduction contained in section 2056(c), if applicable. See example (3) of paragraph (c) of this section.

§ 20.2014-4 "Application of credit in cases involving a death tax convention". (Paragraphs (a)(1) and (b) amended June 15, 1964, as follows)

(a) *In general.*—(1) If credit for a particular foreign death tax is authorized by a death tax convention, there is allowed either the credit provided for by the convention or the credit provided for by section 2014, whichever is the more beneficial to the estate. For cases where credit may be taken under both the death tax convention and section 2014, see paragraph (b) of this section. The application of this paragraph may be illustrated by the following example:

*   *   *   *   *   *   *

(b) *Taxes imposed by both a foreign country and a political subdivision thereof.*—If death taxes are imposed by both a foreign country with which the United States has entered into a death tax convention and one or more of its possessions or political subdivisions, there is allowed, against the tax imposed by section 2001—

(1) A credit for the combined death taxes paid to the foreign country and its political subdivisions or possessions as provided for by the convention, or

(2) A credit for the combined death taxes paid to the foreign country and its political subdivisions or possessions as determined under section 2014, or

(3)(i) A credit for that amount of the combined death taxes paid to the foreign country and its political subdivisions or possessions as is allowable under the convention, and

(ii) A credit under section 2014 for the death taxes paid to each political subdivision or possession, but only to the extent such death taxes are not directly or indirectly creditable under the convention,

162   [Harris Tax Supp]

whichever is the most beneficial to the estate. The application of this paragraph may be illustrated by the following example:

Example. (1) Decedent, a citizen of the United States and a domiciliary of Country X at the time of his death, left a gross estate of $250,000 which includes: bonds issued by Country X physically located in Y, a province of Country X, valued at $75,000; bonds issued by a Country X corporation physically located in the United States, valued at $50,000; and shares of stock issued by a United States corporation, valued at $125,000. Decedent left his entire estate to his son. Expenses, indebtedness, etc., amounted to $26,000. The Federal estate tax after allowance of the credit for state death taxes is $38,124. Province Y imposed a death tax of 8 percent on the Country X bonds located therein which amounted to $6,000. Country X imposed a death tax of 15 percent on the Country X bonds and Country X corporation bonds which amounted to $18,750 before allowance of any credit for provincial death tax. Country X allows against its death taxes a credit for death taxes paid to any of its provinces on property which it also taxes but only to the extent of one-half of the Country X death tax attributable to such property, or the amount of death taxes paid to its province, whichever is less. Country X, therefore, allowed a credit of $5,625 for the death taxes paid to Province Y. There is in effect a death tax convention between the United States and Country X which provides for allowance of credit by the United States for death taxes imposed by the national government of Country X. The death tax convention provides that in computing the "first limitation" for the credit under the convention, the tax of Country X is not to be reduced by the amount of the credit allowed for taxes of Province Y. Under the situs rule described in paragraph (a)(3) of § 20.2014-1, only the Country X bonds located in Province Y are deemed situated in Country X. Under the convention, both the Country X bonds and the Country X corporation bonds are deemed to be situated in Country X. In this example all figures are rounded to the nearest dollar.

(2)(i) The credit authorized by section 2014 for death taxes imposed by Country X (which includes death taxes imposed by Province Y according to § 20.2014-1(a)(1)) is computed as follows:

(*a*) "First limitation" with respect to tax imposed by national government of Country X (computed under paragraph (b) of § 20.2014-2)

(*1*) Gross Country X death tax attributable to Country X bonds (before allowance of provincial death taxes)

$$\frac{\$\ 75,000}{(\$125,000} \times \$18,750) \dots\dots\dots\dots\dots\dots\dots\dots\dots\dots\dots\dots\dots \$11,250$$

(*2*) Less credit for Province Y death taxes on such bonds 5,625

(*3*) Net Country X death tax attributable to such bonds 5,625

(*b*) "First limitation" with respect to tax imposed by Province Y (computed under paragraph (b) of § 20.2014-2)

$$\frac{(\$75,000}{(\$75,000} \times \$6,000) \dots\dots\dots\dots\dots\dots\dots\dots\dots\dots\dots\dots\dots 6,000$$

(*c*) Total "first limitation" 11,625

(*d*) "Second limitation" (computed under paragraph (d) of
§ 20.2014–3)

$$\frac{(\$\,75{,}000}{(\$250{,}000} \times \$38{,}124) \dots\dots\dots\dots\dots\dots\dots\dots\dots\dots\dots\dots\dots\dots \quad 11{,}437$$

(*e*) Credit (subdivision (*c*) or (*d*), whichever is less) 11,437

(ii) The credit authorized under the death tax convention between the United States and Country X is computed as follows:

(*a*) Country X tax attributable to property situated in Country X and subject to tax by both countries

$$\frac{(\$125{,}000}{(\$125{,}000} \times \$18{,}750) \dots\dots\dots\dots\dots\dots\dots\dots\dots\dots\dots\dots\dots\dots \quad 18{,}750$$

(*b*) Federal estate tax attributable to property situated in Country X and subjected to tax by both countries:

$$\frac{(\$125{,}000}{(\$250{,}000} \times \$38{,}124) \dots\dots\dots\dots\dots\dots\dots\dots\dots\dots\dots\dots\dots\dots \quad 19{,}062$$

(*c*) Credit (subdivision (*a*) or (*b*), whichever is less) 18,750

(3) If the estate takes a credit for death taxes under the convention, it would receive a credit of $18,750 which would include an indirect credit of $5,625 for death taxes paid to Province Y. The death tax of Province Y which was not directly or indirectly creditable under the convention is $375 ($6,000–$5,625). A credit for this tax would also be allowed under section 2014 but only to the extent of $187, as the amount of credit for the combined foreign death taxes is limited to the amount of Federal estate tax attributable to the property, determined in accordance with the rules prescribed for computing the "second limitation" under section 2014. In this case, the "second limitation" under section 2014 on the taxes attributable to the Country X bonds is $11,437 (see computation set forth in (2)(i)(*d*) of this example). The amount of credit under the convention for taxes attributable to Country X bonds is $11,250

$$\frac{(\$\,75{,}000}{(\$125{,}000} \times \$18{,}750).$$ Inasmuch as the "second limitation" under section

2014 in respect of the Country X bonds ($11,437) exceeds the amount of the credit allowed under the convention in respect of the Country X bonds ($11,250) by $187, the additional credit allowable under section 2014 for the death taxes paid to Province Y not directly or indirectly creditable under the convention is limited to $187.

§ 20.2014–7 Limitation on credit if a deduction for foreign death taxes is allowed under section 2053(d). (Adopted May 28, 1962)

If a deduction is allowed under section 2053(d) for foreign death taxes paid with respect to a charitable gift, the credit for foreign death taxes is subject to special limitations. In such a case the property described in subparagraphs (A), (B), and (C) of paragraphs (1) and (2) of section 2014(b) shall not include any property with respect to which a deduction is allowed under section 2053(d). The application of this section may be illustrated by the following example:

Example. The decedent, a citizen of the United States, died July 1, 1955, leaving a gross estate of $1,200,000 consisting of: Shares of stock issued by United States corporations, valued at $600,000; bonds issued by the United States Government physically located in the United States, valued at $300,000; and shares of stock issued by a Country X corporation, valued at $300,000. Expenses, indebtedness, etc., amounted to $40,000. The decedent made specific bequests of $400,000 of the United States corporation stock to a niece and $100,000 of the Country X corporation stock to a nephew. The residue of his estate was left to charity. There is no death tax convention in existence between the United States and Country X. The Country X tax imposed was at a 50-percent rate on all beneficiaries. A State inheritance tax of $20,000 was imposed on the niece and nephew. The decedent did not provide in his will for the payment of the death taxes, and under local law the Federal estate tax is payable from the general estate, the same as administration expenses.

DISTRIBUTION OF THE ESTATE

Gross estate		$1,200,000.00
Debts and charges	$40,000.00	
Bequest of U.S. corporation stock to niece	400,000.00	
Bequest of country X corporation stock to nephew	100,000.00	
Net Federal estate tax	136,917.88	
		676,917.88
Residue before country X tax		523,082.12
Country X succession tax on charity		100,000.00
Charitable deduction		423,082.12

TAXABLE ESTATE AND FEDERAL ESTATE TAX

Gross estate		$1,200,000.00
Debts and charges	$40,000.00	
Deduction of foreign death tax under section 2053(d)	100,000.00	
Charitable deduction	423,082.12	
Exemption	60,000.00	
		623,082.12
Taxable estate		576,917.88
Gross estate tax		172,621.26
Credit for State death taxes		15,476.72
Gross estate tax less credit for State death taxes		157,144.54
Credit for foreign death taxes		20,226.66
Net Federal estate tax		136,917.88

CREDIT FOR FOREIGN DEATH TAXES
COUNTRY X TAX

Succession tax on nephew:	
Value of stock of country X corporation	$100,000
Tax (50% rate)	50,000
Succession tax on charity:	
Value of stock of country X corporation	200,000
Tax (50% rate)	100,000

COMPUTATION OF EXCLUSION UNDER SECTION 2014(b)

Value of property situated in country X $300,000

Value of property in respect of which a deduction is allowed under
§ section 2053(d) 200,000

Value of property situated within country X, subjected to tax,
and included in gross estate as limited by section 2014(f) . 100,000

FIRST LIMITATION, § 20.2014-2(a)

$$\frac{\$100,000 \text{ (factor C of the ratio stated at § 20.2014-2(a))}}{\$100,000 + \$200,000 \text{ (factor D of the ratio stated at § 20.2014-2(a))}} \times \begin{array}{c}(\$50,000 + \$100,000) \text{ (factor B of}\\ \text{the ratio stated at}\\ \text{§ 20.2014-2(a))}\end{array}$$

=$50,000.00

SECOND LIMITATION, § 20.2014-3(a)

$$\frac{\$100,000 \text{ (factor G of the ratio stated at § 20.2014-3(a)) (as limited by section 2014(f))}}{\$1,200,000 - \$423,082.12 \text{ (factor H of the ratio stated at § 20.2014-3(a))}} \times (\$172,621.26 - \$15,476.72) \text{ (factor F of the ratio stated at § 20.2014-3(a))}$$

=$20,226.66

§ 20.2015-1 **Credit for death taxes on remainders.** (Paragraph (a) and examples (1) and (2) of paragraph (c) amended Jan. 18, 1961 to read as follows)

(a) * * *

(2) Within the time for payment of the tax imposed by section 2001 or 2101 as postponed under section 6163(a) and as extended under section 6163 (b) (on account of undue hardship) or, if the precedent interest terminated before July 5, 1958, within 60 days after the termination of the preceding interest or interests in the property.

The allowance of credit, however, is subject to the other limitations contained in sections 2011 and 2014.

* * * * * *

(c) * * *

Example (1). One-third of the Federal estate tax was attributable to a remainder interest in real property located in State Y, and two-thirds of the Federal estate tax was attributable to other property located in State X. The payment of the tax attributable to the remainder interest was postponed under the provisions of section 6163(a). The maximum credit allowable for State death taxes under the provisions of section 2011 is $12,000. Therefore, of the maximum credit allowable, $4,000 is attributable to the remainder interest and $8,000 is attributable to the other property. Within the 4-year period provided for in section 2011, inheritance tax in the amount of $9,000 was paid to State X in connection with the other property. With respect to this $9,000, $8,000 (the maximum amount allowable) is allowed as a credit

[Harris Tax Supp]

against the Federal estate tax attributable to the other property, and $1,000 is allowed as a credit against the postponed tax. The life estate or other precedent interest expired after July 4, 1958. After the expiration of the 4-year period but before the expiration of the period of postponement elected under section 6168(a) and of the period of extension granted under section 6163(b) for payment of the tax, inheritance tax in the amount of $5,000 was paid to State Y in connection with the remainder interest. As the maximum credit allowable with respect to the remainder interest is $4,000 and $1,000 has already been allowed as a credit, an additional $3,000 will be credited against the Federal estate tax attributable to the remainder interest. It should be noted that if the life estate or other precedent interest had expired after the expiration of the 4-year period but before July 5, 1958, the same result would be reached only if the inheritance tax had been paid to State Y before the expiration of 60 days after the termination of the life estate or other precedent interest.

Example (2). The facts are the same as in example (1), except that withni the 4-year period inheritance tax in the amount of $2,500 was paid to State Y with respect to the remainder interest and inheritance tax in the amount of $7,500 was paid to State X with respect to the other property. The amount of $8,000 is allowed as a credit against the Federal estate tax attributable to the other property and the amount of $2,000 is allowed as a credit against the postponed tax. The life estate or other precedent interest expired after July 4, 1958. After the expiration of the 4-year period but before the expiration of the period of postponement elected under section 6163(a) and of the period of extension granted under section 6163(b) for payment of the tax, inheritance tax in the amount of $5,000 was paid to State Y in connection with the remainder interest. As the maximum credit allowable with respect to the remainder interest is $4,000 and $2,000 already has been allowed as a credit, an additional $2,000 will be credited against the Federal estate tax attributable to the remainder interest. It should be noted that if the life estate or other precedent interest had expired after the expiration of the 4-year period but before July 5, 1958, the same result would be reached only if the inheritance tax had been paid to State Y before the expiration of 60 days after the termination of the life estate or other precedent interest.

§ 20.2031–1 **Definition of gross estate; valuation of property.** (Paragraph (a) amended October 23, 1963 to read as follows:)

(a) *Definition of gross estate.* Except as otherwise provided in this paragraph the value of the gross estate of a decedent who was a citizen or resident of the United States at the time of his death is the total value of the interests described in sections 2033 through 2044. The gross estate of a decedent who dies before October 17, 1962, does not include real property situated outside the United States (as defined in paragraph (b)(1) of § 20.0–1). Except as provided in paragraph (c) of this section (relating to the estates of decedents dying after October 16, 1962, and before July 1, 1964), in the case of a decedent dying after October 16, 1962, real property situated outside the United States which comes within the scope of sections 2033 through 2044 is included in the gross estate to the same extent as any other property coming within the scope of those sections. In arriving at the value of the gross estate the interests described in sections 2033 through 2044 are valued as described in this section, §§ 20.2031–2 through 20.2031–9 and § 20.2032–1. The contents of sections 2033 through 2044 are, in general, as follows:

(b) *Valuation of property in general.* The value of every item of property includible in a decedent's gross estate under sections 2031 through 2044 is its fair market value at the time of the decedent's death, except that if the executor elects the alternative valuation method under section 2032, it is the fair market value thereof at the date, and with the adjustments, prescribed in that section. The fair market value is the price at which the property would change hands between a willing buyer and a willing seller, neither being under any compulsion to buy or to sell and both having reasonable knowledge of relevant facts. The fair market value of a particular item of property includible in the decedent's gross estate is not to be determined by a forced sale price. Nor is the fair market value of an item of property to be determined by the sale price of the item in a market other than that in which such item is most commonly sold to the public, taking in to account the location of the item wherever appropriate. Thus, in the case of an item of property includible in the decedent's gross estate, which is generally obtained by the public in the retail market, the fair market value of such an item of property is the price at which the item or a comparable item would be sold at retail. For example, the fair market value of an automobile (an article generally obtained by the public in the retail market) includible in the decedent's gross estate is the price for which an automobile of the same or approximately the same description, make, model, age, condition, etc., could be purchased by a member of the general public and not the price for which the particular automobile of the decedent would be purchased by a dealer in used automobiles. Examples of items of property which are generally sold to the public at retail may be found in §§ 20.2031–6 and 20.2031–8. The value is generally to be determined by ascertaining as a basis the fair market value as of the applicable valuation date of each unit of property. For example, in the case of shares of stock or bonds, such unit of property is generally a share of stock or a bond. Livestock, farm machinery, harvested and growing crops must generally be itemized and the value of each item separately returned. Property shall not be returned at the value at which it is assessed for local tax purposes unless that value represents the fair market value as of the applicable valuation date. All relevant facts and elements of value as of the applicable valuation date shall be considered in every case. The value of items of property which were held by the decedent for sale in the course of a business generally should be reflected in the values of the business. For valuation of interests in businesses, see § 20.2031–3. See § 20.2031–2 and §§ 20.2031–4 through 20.2031–8 for further information concerning the valuation of other particular kinds of property. For certain circumstances under which the sale of an item of property at a price below its fair market value may result in a deduction for the estate, see paragraph (d)(2) of § 20.2053–3. (As am June 14, 1965 in TD 6826.)

(Paragraph (c) adopted October 23, 1963, reading as follows:)

(c) *Real property situated outside the United States; gross estate of decedent dying after October 16, 1962, and before July 1, 1964.* (1) *In general.* In the case of a decedent dying after October 16, 1962, and before July

1, 1964, the value of real property situated outside the United States (as defined in paragraph (b)(1) of § 20.0–1) is not included in the gross estate of the decedent—

(i) Under section 2033, 2034, 2035(a), 2036(a), 2037(a), or 2038(a) to the extent the real property, or the decedent's interest in it, was acquired by the decedent before February 1, 1962;

(ii) Under section 2040 to the extent such property or interest was acquired by the decedent before February 1, 1962, or was held by the decedent and the survivor in a joint tenancy or tenancy by the entirety before February 1, 1962; or

(iii) Under section 2041(a) to the extent that before February 1, 1962, such property or interest was subject to a general power of appointment (as defined in section 2041) possessed by the decedent.

(2) *Certain property treated as acquired before February 1, 1962.* For purposes of this paragraph real property situated outside the United States (including property held by the decedent and the survivor in a joint tenancy or tenancy by the entirety), or an interest in such property or a general power of appointment in respect of such property, which was acquired by the decedent after January 31, 1962, is treated as acquired by the decedent before February 1, 1962, if

(i) Such property, interest, or power was acquired by the decedent by gift within the meaning of section 2511 or from a prior decedent by devise or inheritance, or by reason of death, form of ownership, or other conditions (including the exercise or non-exercise of a power of appointment); and

(ii) Before February 1, 1962, the donor of prior decedent had acquired the property or his interest therein or had possessed a power of appointment in respect thereof.

(3) *Certain property treated as acquired after January 31, 1962.* For purposes of this paragraph that portion of capital additions or improvements made after January 31, 1962, to real property situated outside the United States is, to the extent that it materially increases the value of the property, treated as real property acquired after January 31, 1962. Accordingly, the gross estate may include the value of improvements on unimproved real property, such as office buildings, factories, houses, fences, drainage ditches, and other capital items, and the value of capital additions and improvements to existing improvements, placed on real property after January 31, 1962, whether or not the value of such real property or existing improvements is included in the gross estate.

§ 20.2031–2 **Valuation of stocks and bonds.**

(i) Stock sold "ex-dividend." In any case where a dividend is declared on a share of stock before the decedent's death but payable to stockholders of record on a date after his death and the stock is selling "ex-dividend" on the date of the decedent's death, the amount of the dividend is added to the ex-dividend quotation in determining the fair market value of the stock as of the date of the decedent's death. (Subparagraph (j) was redesignated as subparagraph (i), June 14, 1965, TD 6826.)

§ 20.2031–8 **Valuation of certain life insurance and annuity contracts.** (Section designated as Paragraph (a) and new Paragraph (b) added October 9, 1963, as follows) "(b) *Valuation of shares in an open-end investment company.* (1) The fair market value of a share in an open-end investment company (commonly known as a 'mutual fund') is the public offering price of a share, adjusted for any reduction in price available to the public in acquiring the number of shares being valued. In the absence of an affirmative showing of the public offering price in effect at the time of death, the last public offering price quoted by the company for the date of death shall be presumed to be the applicable public offering price. If the alternate valuation under section 2032 is elected, the last public offering price quoted by the company for the alternate valuation date shall be the applicable public offering price. If there is no public offering price quoted by the company for the applicable valuation date (e. g., the valuation date is a Saturday, Sunday, or holiday), the fair market value of the mutual fund share is the last public offering price quoted by the company for the first day preceding the applicable valuation date for which there is a quotation, adjusted for any reduction in price available to the public in acquiring the number of shares being valued. In any case where a dividend is declared on a share in an open-end investment company before the decedent's death but payable to shareholders of record on a date after his death and the share is selling 'ex-dividend' on the date of the decedent's death, the amount of the dividend is added to the ex-dividend quotation in determining the fair market value of the share as of the date of the decedent's death. As used in this paragraph, the term 'open-end investment company' includes only a company which on the applicable valuation date was engaged in offering its shares to the public in the capacity of an open-end investment company.

"(2) The provisions of this paragraph shall apply with respect to estates of decedents dying after October 10, 1963."

§ 20.2033-1 **Property in which decedent had an interest.** (Paragraph (a) amended October 23, 1963, by deleting the words "except real property situated outside of the United States" at the end of the first sentence, sixth line of section, and inserting parenthetical matter changing second sentence as follows:)

(For certain exceptions in the case of real property situated outside the United States, see paragraphs (a) and (c) of § 20.2031–1.) Real property is included whether it came into the possession and control of the executor or administrator or passed directly to heirs or devisees.

§ 20.2036-1 **Transfers with retained life estate.** (Paragraph (a)(3)(ii) amended Nov 15, 1960, by adding the following at end thereof)

, except that, if the transfer was made before June 7, 1932, the right to designate must be retained by or reserved to the decedent alone.

§ 20.2038-1 **Revocable transfers.** (Paragraph (f) added May 28, 1962, as follows)

(f) *Effect of disability to relinquish power in certain cases.* Notwithstanding anything to the contrary in paragraphs (a) through (e) of this section the provisions of this section do not apply to a transfer if—

(1) The relinquishment on or after January 1, 1940, and on or before December 31, 1947, of the power would, by reason of section 1000(e), of

170   [Harris Tax Supp]

the Internal Revenue Code of 1939, be deemed not a transfer of property for the purpose of the gift tax under chapter 4 of the Internal Revenue Code of 1939, and

(2) The decedent was, for a continuous period beginning on or before September 30, 1947, and ending with his death, after August 16, 1954, under a mental disability to relinquish a power.

For the purpose of the foregoing provision, the term "mental disability" means mental incompetence, in fact, to release the power whether or not there was an adjudication of incompetence. Such provision shall apply even though a guardian could have released the power for the decedent. No interest shall be allowed or paid on any overpayment allowable under section 2038(c) with respect to amounts paid before August 7, 1959.

§ 20.2039–2 **Annuities under "qualified plans" and section 403(b) annuity contracts.** (Paragraphs (a) (b) and (c) amended Jan. 18, 1961, as follows; paragraphs (b)(2) and (c)(1) amended July 15, 1963)

(a) *In general.* Section 2039(c) excludes from a decedent's gross estate the value of an annuity or other payment receivable under certain "qualified plans" and under certain annuity contracts to the extent provided in paragraph (c) of this section. Section 2039(c), other than paragraph (3) thereof, applies to estates of all persons dying after December 31, 1953.

(b) *Plans and annuity contracts to which section 2039(c) applies.* Section 2039(c) excludes from a decedent's gross estate, to the extent provided in paragraph (c) of this section, the value of an annuity or other payment receivable by any beneficiary (except the value of an annuity or other payment receivable by or for the benefit of the decedent's estate) under—

(1) An employees' trust (or under a contract purchased by an employees' trust) forming part of a pension, stock bonus, or profit-sharing plan which, at the time of the decedent's separation from employment (whether by death or otherwise), or at the time of the earlier termination of the plan, met the requirements of section 401(a);

(2) A retirement annuity contract purchased by an employer (and not by an employees' trust) pursuant to a plan which, at the time of decedent's separation from employment (by death or otherwise), or at the time of the earlier termination of the plan, met the requirements of section 403(a); or [am July 16, 1963]

(3) In the case of a decedent dying after December 31, 1957, a retirement annuity contract purchased for an employee by an employer which, for its taxable year in which the purchase occurred, is an organization referred to in section 503(b)(1), (2), or (3), and is exempt from tax under section 501(a). For the meaning of the term "annuity or other payment", see paragraph (b) of § 20.2039–1. For the meaning of the phrase "receivable by or for the benefit of the decedent's estate", see paragraph (b) of § 20.2042–1. The application of this paragraph may be illustrated by the following examples in each of which it is assumed that the amount stated to be excludable from the decedent's gross estate is determined in accordance with paragraph (c) of this section:

Example (5). An employer purchased a retirement annuity contract for an employee which was to provide the employee, upon his retirement at age 60, with an annuity for life and which was to provide his wife, upon the employee's death after retirement, with a similar annuity for life. The employer, for its taxable year in which the annuity contract was purchased, was an organization referred to in section 503(b)(1), (2), or (3), and was exempt from tax under section 501(a). The entire amount of the purchase price of the annuity contract was excluded from the employee's gross income under section 403(b). No part of the value of the survivor annuity payable after the employee's death is includible in the decedent's gross estate by reason of the provisions of section 2039(c).

(c) *Amount excludable from the gross estate.* (1) The amount to be excluded from a decedent's gross estate under section 2039(c) is an amount which bears the same ratio to the value at the decedent's death of the annuity or other payment receivable by the beneficiary as the employer's contribution (or a contribution made on his behalf) on the employee's account to the plan or towards the purchase of the annuity contract bears to the total contributions on the employee's account to the plan or towards the purchase of the annuity contract. In applying the ratio set forth in the preceding sentence, payments or contributions made by the employer (or on its behalf) toward the purchase of an annuity contract described in paragraph (b)(3) of this section shall be considered to include only such payments or contributions as are, or were, excludable from the employee's gross income under section 403(b). For purposes of this ratio, contributions or payments made under a plan described in subparagraph (1) or (2) of paragraph (b) of this section on behalf of the decedent while he was an employee within the meaning of section 401(c)(1) with respect to such plan shall be considered to be contributions or payments made by decedent and not by employer. Furthermore, in applying this ratio, the value at the decedent's death of the annuity or other payment is determined in accordance with the rules set forth in §§ 20.2031-1, 20.2031-7, 20.2031-8, and 20.2031-9.

(2) In certain cases, the employer's contribution (or a contribution made on his behalf) to a plan on the employee's account and thus the total contributions to the plan on the employee's account cannot be readily ascertained. In order to apply the ratio stated in subparagraph (1) of this paragraph in such a case, the method outlined in the following two sentences must be used unless a more precise method is presented. In such a case, the total contributions to the plan on the employee's account is the value of any annuity or other payment payable to the decedent and his survivor computed as of the time the decedent's rights first mature (or as of the time the survivor's rights first mature if the decedent's rights never mature) and computed in accordance with the rules set forth in §§ 20.2031-1, 20.2031-7, 20.2031-8, and 20.2031-9. By subtracting from such value the amount of the employee's contribution to the plan, the amount of the employer's contribution to the plan on the employee's account may be obtained. The application of this paragraph may be illustrated by the following example:

Example. Pursuant to a pension plan, the employer and the employee contributed to a trust which was to provide the employee, upon his retirement at age 60, with an annuity for life, and which was to provide his wife, upon the employee's death after retirement, with a similar annuity for life. At the time of the employee's retirement, the pension trust formed part of a plan meeting the requirements of section 401(a). Assume the following: (i) That the employer's contributions to the fund were not credited to the accounts of individual employees; (ii) that the value of the employee's annuity and his wife's annuity, computed as of the time of the decedent's retirement, was $40,000; (iii) that the employee contributed $10,000 to the plan; and (iv) that the value at the decedent's death of the wife's annuity was $16,000. On the basis of these facts, the total contributions to the fund on the employee's account are presumed to be $40,000 and the employer's contribution to the plan on the employee's account is presumed to be $30,000 ($40,000 less $10,000). Since the wife's annuity was receivable under a qualified pension plan, that part of the value of such annuity which is

attributable to the employer's contributions $\left[\dfrac{\$30,000}{\$40,000} \times \$16,000, \text{ or } \$12,000 \right]$

is excludable from the decedent's gross estate by reason of the provisions of section 2039(c). Compare this result with the results reached in the examples set forth in paragraph (b) of this section in which all contributions to the plans were made by the employer.

§ 20.2041–1 **Powers of appointment; in general.** (Paragraph (e) amended Dec. 11, 1961 to read as follows)

(e) *Time of creation of power.* A power of appointment created by will is, in general, considered as created on the date of the testator's death. However, section 2041(b)(3) provides that a power of appointment created by a will executed on or before October 21, 1942, is considered a power created on or before that date if the testator dies before July 1, 1949, without having republished the will, by codicil or otherwise, after October 21, 1942. A power of appointment created by an inter vivos instrument is considered as created on the date the instrument takes effect. Such a power is not considered as created at some future date merely because it is not exercisable on the date the instrument takes effect, or because it is revocable, or because the identity of its holders is not ascertainable until after the date the instrument takes effect. However, if the holder of a power exercises it by creating a second power, the second power is considered as created at the time of the exercise of the first. The application of this paragraph may be illustrated by the following examples:

Example (1). A created a revocable trust before October 22, 1942, providing for payment of income to B for life with remainder as B shall appoint by will. Even though A dies after October 21, 1942, without having exercised his power of revocation, B's power of appointment is considered a power created before October 22, 1942.

Example (2). C created an irrevocable inter vivos trust before October 22, 1942, naming T as trustee and providing for payment of income to D for life with remainder to E. T was given the power to pay corpus to D and the power to appoint a successor trustee. If T resigns after October 21, 1942, and appoints D as successor trustee, D is considered to have a power of appointment created before October 22, 1942.

Example (3). F created an irrevocable inter vivos trust before October 22, 1942, providing for payment of income to G for life with remainder as G shall appoint by will, but in default of appointment income to H for life with remainder as H shall appoint by will. If G died after October 21, 1942, without having exercised his power of appointment, H's power of appointment is considered a power created before October 22, 1942, even though it was only a contingent interest until G's death.

Example (4). If in example (3) above G had exercised his power of appointment by creating a similar power in J, J's power of appointment would be considered a power created after October 21, 1942.

§ 20.2053–3 **Deduction for expenses of administering estate.**

* * *

(d) *Miscellaneous administration expenses.* (1) Miscellaneous administration expenses include such expenses as court costs, surrogates' fees, accountants' fees, appraisers' fees, clerk hire, etc. Expenses necessarily incurred in preserving and distributing the estate are deductible, including the cost of storing or maintaining property of the estate, if it is impossible to effect immediate distribution to the beneficiaries. Expenses for preserving and caring for the property may not include outlays for additions or improvements; nor will such expenses be allowed for a longer period than the executor is reasonably required to retain the property.

(2) Expenses for selling property of the estate are deductible if the sale is necessary in order to pay the decedent's debts, expenses of administration, or taxes, to preserve the estate, or to effect distribution. The phrase "expenses for selling property" includes brokerage fees and other expenses attending the sale, such as the fees of an auctioneer if it is reasonably necessary to employ one. Where an item included in the gross estate is disposed of in a bona fide sale (including a redemption) to a dealer in such items at a price below its fair market value, for purposes of this paragraph there shall be treated as an expense for selling the item whichever of the following amounts is the lesser: (i) the amount by which the fair market value of the property on the applicable valuation date exceeds the proceeds of the sale, or (ii) the amount by which the fair market value of the property on the date of the sale exceeds the proceeds of the sale. The principles used in determining the value at which an item of property is included in the gross estate shall be followed in arriving at the fair market value of the property for purposes of this paragraph. See §§ 20.2031–1 through 20.2031–9. (Am June 14, 1965, TD 6826.)

§ 20.2053–7 **Deduction for unpaid mortgages.** (Last sentence of paragraph amended October 23, 1963 to read as follows:)

In any case where real property situated outside the United States does not form a part of the gross estate, no deduction may be taken of any mortgage thereon or any other indebtedness in respect thereof.

§ 20.2053–9 **Deduction for certain State death taxes.** Paragraph (a) amended Jan. 18, 1961, to read as follows:

(a) *General rule.* A deduction is allowed a decedent's estate under section 2053(d) for the amount of any estate, succession, legacy, or inheritance tax imposed by a State, Territory, or the District of Columbia, or, in the case of a decedent dying before September 3, 1958, a possession of the United States upon a transfer by the decedent for charitable, etc., uses described in section 2055 or 2106(a)(2) (relating to the estates of nonresidents not citizens), but only if (1) the conditions stated in paragraph (b) of this section are met, and (2) an election is made in accordance with the provisions

174   [Harris Tax Supp]

of paragraph (c) of this section. See section 2011(e) and § 20.2011–2 for the effect which the allowance of this deduction has upon the credit for State death taxes.

(Paragraph (b)(2) amended July 16, 1963 to read as follows)

(b)(2) For purposes of this paragraph, the Federal estate tax is considered to be equitably apportioned among all the transferees (including the decedent's surviving spouse and the charitable, etc., transferees) of property included in the decedent's gross estate only if each transferee's share of the tax is based upon the net amount of his transfer subjected to the tax (taking into account any exemptions, credits, or deductions allowed by chapter 11). See examples (2) through (5) of paragraph (e) of this section.

§ 20.2053–10 **Deduction for certain foreign death taxes.** (Adopted May 28, 1962)

(a) *General rule.* A deduction is allowed the estate of a decedent dying on or after July 1, 1955, under section 2053(d) for the amount of any estate, succession, legacy, or inheritance tax imposed by and actually paid to any foreign country, in respect of any property situated within such foreign country and included in the gross estate of a citizen or resident of the United States, upon a transfer by the decedent for charitable, etc., uses described in section 2055, but only if (1) the conditions stated in paragraph (b) of this section are met, and (2) an election is made in accordance with the provisions of paragraph (c) of this section. The determination of the country within which property is situated is made in accordance with the rules contained in §§ 20.2104 and 20.2105 in determining whether property is situated within or without the United States. See section 2014(f) and § 20.2014–7 for the effect which the allowance of this deduction has upon the credit for foreign death taxes.

(b) *Condition for allowance of deduction.* (1) The deduction is not allowed unless either—

(i) The entire decrease in the Federal estate tax resulting from the allowance of the deduction inures solely to the benefit of a charitable, etc., transferee described in section 2055, or

(ii) The Federal estate tax is equitably apportioned among all the transferees (including the decedent's surviving spouse and the charitable, etc., transferees) of property included in the decedent's gross estate.

For allowance of the deduction, it is sufficient if either of these conditions is satisfied. Thus, in a case where the entire decrease in Federal estate tax inures to the benefit of a charitable transferee, the deduction is allowable even though the Federal estate tax is not equitably apportioned among all the transferees of property included in the decedent's gross estate. Similarly, if the Federal estate tax is equitably apportioned among all the transferees of property included in the decedent's gross estate, the deduction is allowable even though a noncharitable transferee receives some benefit from the allowance of the deduction.

(2) For purposes of this paragraph, the Federal estate tax is considered to be equitably apportioned among all the transferees (including the decedent's surviving spouse and the charitable, etc., transferees) of property included in the decedent's gross estate only if each transferee's share of the tax is based upon the net amount of his transfer subjected to the tax (taking

into account any exemptions, credits, or deductions allowed by chapter 11). See examples (2) through (5) of paragraph (e) of § 20.2053–9.

(c) *Exercise of election.* The election to take a deduction for a foreign death tax imposed upon a transfer for charitable, etc. uses shall be exercised by the executor by the filing of a written notification to that effect with the district director of internal revenue in whose district the estate tax return for the decedent's estate was filed. An election to take the deduction for foreign death taxes is deemed to be a waiver of the right to claim a credit under a treaty with any foreign country for any tax or portion thereof claimed as a deduction under this section. The notification shall be filed before the expiration of the period of limitation for assessment provided in section 6501 (usually 3 years from the last day for filing the return). The election may be revoked by the executor by the filing of a written notification to that effect with the district director at any time before the expiration of such period.

(d) *Amount of foreign death tax imposed upon a transfer.* If a foreign death tax is imposed upon the transfer of the entire part of the decedent's estate subject to such tax and not upon the transfer of a particular share thereof, the foreign death tax imposed upon a transfer for charitable, etc., uses is deemed to be an amount, J, which bears the same ratio to K (the amount of the foreign death tax imposed with respect to the transfer of the entire part of the decedent's estate subject to such tax) as M (the value of the charitable, etc., transfer, reduced as provided in the next sentence) bears to N (the total value of the properties, interests, and benefits subjected to the foreign death tax received by all persons interested in the estate, reduced as provided in the last sentence of this paragraph). In arriving at amount M of the ratio, the value of the charitable, etc., transfer is reduced by the amount of any deduction or exclusion allowed with respect to such property in determining the amount of the foreign death tax. In arriving at amount N of the ratio, the total value of the properties, interests, and benefits subjected to foreign death tax received by all persons interested in the estate is reduced by the amount of all deductions and exclusions allowed in determining the amount of the foreign death tax on account of the nature of a beneficiary or a beneficiary's relationship to the decedent.

§ 20.2103–1 Estates of nonresidents not citizens; "entire gross estate." (Third sentence, lines six and part of seven of section, amended October 23, 1963 to read as follows:)

See paragraphs (a) and (c) of § 20.2031–1 for the circumstances under which real property situated outside the United States is excluded from the gross estate of a citizen or resident of the United States.

§ 20.2105–1 Estates of nonresidents not citizens; property without the United States. (Paragraph (a) amended October 23, 1963 to read as follows:)

(a)(1) Real property located outside the United States, except to the extent excludable from the entire gross estate wherever situated under § 20.2103–1.

(2) Tangible personal property located outside the United States.

§ 20.2106–1 Estates of nonresidents not citizens; taxable estate, deductions in general. (Paragraphs (a)(3) and (c) amended Jan. 18, 1961, to read as follows)

(a) * * *

(3)(i) In the case of a decedent who is considered to be a "nonresident not a citizen of the United States" under the provisions of section 2209, an exemption which is the greater of (a) $2,000 or (b) that proportion of $60,000 (the exemption authorized by section 2052) which the value of that part of the decedent's gross estate which is situated in the United States at the time of his death bears to the value of the decedent's entire gross estate wherever situated.

(ii) In the case of every other decedent who was a nonresident not a citizen of the United States at the time of his death, an exemption of $2,000, unless a death tax convention provides for another amount, such as a pro-rated exemption similar to that described in subdivision (i)(b) of this subparagraph.

(c)(i) The exemption described in paragraph (a)(3)(i) of this section may be illustrated by the following example:

Example. The decedent, who died on October 1, 1960, is considered to be a nonresident not a citizen of the United States by reason of the provisions of section 2209. He was a resident of the Virgin Islands and his entire gross estate wherever situated included bonds valued at $45,000, which were situated in the Virgin Islands, and shares of United States corporations valued at $30,000 (property situated in the United States under section 2104). The amount described in paragraph (a)(3)(i)(b) of this section is $24,000, computed as follows:

$$\frac{\$30,000 \text{ (value of property in United States)}}{\$75,000 \text{ (value of entire gross estate wherever situated)}} \times \$60,000 = \$24,000$$

Since the amount so computed exceeds $2,000, the exemption to be allowed the decedent's estate is $24,000.

(ii) In connection with the provisions of section 2106(c), see paragraph (a)(3) of § 20.2104–1 and paragraph (d) or § 20.2105–1.

§ 20.2208–1 Certain residents of possessions considered citizens of the United States. (Adopted Jan. 18, 1961)

As used in this part, the term "citizen of the United States" is considered to include a decedent dying after September 2, 1958, who, at the time of his death, was domiciled in a possession of the United States and was a United States citizen, and who did not acquire his United States citizenship solely by reason of his being a citizen of such possession or by reason of his birth or residence within such possession. The estate of such a decedent is, therefore, subject to the tax imposed by section 2001. See paragraph (a)(2) of § 20.0–1 and § 20.2209–1 for further information relating to the application of the Federal estate tax to the estates of decedents who were residents of possessions of the United States. The application of this section may be illustrated by the following example and the examples set forth in § 20-.2209-1:

Example. A, a citizen of the United States by reason of his birth in the United States at San Francisco, established residence in Puerto Rico and acquired a Puerto Rican citizenship. A died on September 4, 1958, while a citizen and domiciliary of Puerto Rico. A's estate is, by reason of the provisions of section 2208, subject to the tax imposed by section 2001 inasmuch as his United States citizenship is based on birth in the United States and is not based solely on being a citizen of a possession or solely on birth or residence in a possession.

§ 20.2209-1 **Certain residents of possessions considered nonresidents not citizens of the United States.** (Adopted Jan. 18, 1961)

As used in this part, the term "nonresident not a citizen of the United States" is considered to include a decedent dying after September 14, 1960, who, at the time of his death, was domiciled in a possession of the United States and was a United States citizen, and who acquired his United States citizenship solely by reason of his being a citizen of such possession or by reason of his birth or residence within such possession. The estate of such a decedent is, therefore, subject to the tax imposed by section 2101 which is the tax applicable in the case of a "nonresident not a citizen of the United States." See paragraph (a)(2) of § 20.0-1 and § 20.2208-1 for further information relating to the application of the Federal estate tax to the estates of decedents who were residents of possessions of the United States. The application of this section may be illustrated by the following examples and the example set forth in § 20.2208-1. In each of the following examples the decedent is deemed a "nonresident not a citizen of the United States" and his estate is subject to the tax imposed by section 2101 since the decedent died after September 14, 1960, but would not have been so deemed and subject to such tax if the decedent had died on or before September 14, 1960.

Example (1). C, who acquired his United States citizenship under section 5 of the Act of March 2, 1917 (39 Stat. 953), by reason of being a citizen of Puerto Rico, died in Puerto Rico on October 1, 1960, while domiciled therein. C is considered to have acquired his United States citizenship solely by reason of his being a citizen of Puerto Rico.

Example (2). E, whose parents were United States citizens by reason of their birth in Boston, was born in the Virgin Islands on March 1, 1927. On September 30, 1960, he died in the Virgin Islands while domiciled therein. E is considered to have acquired his United States citizenship solely by reason of his birth in the Virgin Islands (section 306 of the Immigration and Nationality Act (66 Stat. 237, 8 U.S.C. 1406)).

Example (3). N, who acquired United States citizenship by reason of being a native of the Virgin Islands and a resident thereof on June 28, 1932 (section 306 of the Immigration and Nationality Act (66 Stat. 237, 8 U.S.C. 1406)), died on October 1, 1960, while domiciled in the Virgin Islands. N is considered to have acquired his United States citizenship solely by reason of his birth or residence in the Virgin Islands.

Example (4). P, a former Danish citizen, who on January 17, 1917, resided in the Virgin Islands, made the declaration to preserve his Danish citizenship required by Article 6 of the treaty entered into on August 4, 1916, between the United States and Denmark. Subsequently P acquired United States citizenship when he renounced such declaration before a court of record (section 306 of the Immigration and Nationality Act (66 Stat. 237, 8 U.S.C. 1406)). P died on October 1, 1960, while domiciled in the Virgin Islands. P is considered to have acquired his United States citizenship solely by reason of his birth or residence in the Virgin Islands.

Example (5). R, a former French citizen, acquired his United States citizenship through naturalization proceedings in a court located in the Virgin Islands after having qualified for citizenship by residing in the Virgin Islands for 5 years. R died on October 1, 1960, while domiciled in the Virgin Islands. R is considered to have acquired his United States citizenship solely by reason of his birth or residence within the Virgin Islands.

§ 20.6061–1 **Signing of returns and other documents.** (Adopted May 28, 1962)

Any return, statement, or other document required to be made under any provision of chapter 11 or subtitle F of the Code or regulations prescribed thereunder with respect to any tax imposed by chapter 11 of the Code shall be signed by the executor, administrator or other person required or duly authorized to sign in accordance with the regulations, forms or instructions prescribed with respect to such return, statement, or other document. See § 20.2203 for definition of executor, administrator, etc. The person required or duly authorized to make the return may incur liability for the penalties provided for erroneous, false, or fraudulent returns. For criminal penalties see sections 7201, 7203, 7206, 7207, and 7269.

§ 20.6065–1 **Verification of returns.** (Adopted May 28, 1962)

(a) *Penalties of perjury.* If a return, statement, or other document made under the provisions of chapter 11 or subtitle F of the Code or the regulations thereunder with respect to any tax imposed by chapter 11 of the Code, or the form and instructions issued with respect to such return, statement, or other document, requires that it shall contain or be verified by a written declaration that it is made under the penalties of perjury, it must be so verified by the person or persons required to sign such return, statement or other document. In addition, any other statement or document submitted under any provision of chapter 11 or subtitle F of the Code or regulations thereunder with respect to any tax imposed by chapter 11 of the Code may be required to contain or be verified by a written declaration that it is made under the penalties of perjury.

(b) *Oath.* Any return, statement, or other document required to be submitted under chapter 11 or subtitle F of the Code or regulations prescribed thereunder with respect to any tax imposed by chapter 11 of the Code may be required to be verified by an oath.

§ 20.6081–1 **Extension of time for filing return.** (Paragraph (b) amended March 23, 1964 to read as follows)

(b) The application for an extension of time for filing the return shall be addressed to the district director for the district in which the return is to be filed, and must contain a full recital of the causes for the delay. It should be made before the expiration of the time within which the return otherwise must be filed and failure to do so may indicate negligence and constitute sufficient cause for denial. It should, where possible, be made sufficiently early to permit the district director to consider the matter and reply before what otherwise would be the due date of the return.

§ 20.6091–1 Place for filing returns or other documents. (Amended May 28, 1962, to read as follows)

If the decedent was a resident of the United States, the preliminary notice required by § 20.6036–1 and the estate tax return required by § 20.6018–1 shall be filed with the district director in whose district the decedent had his domicile at the time of death. If the decedent was a nonresident (whether a citizen or not a citizen), the notice and the return shall be filed with the Director of International Operations, Internal Revenue Service, Washington 25, D. C.

§ 20.6091–2 Exceptional cases. (Adopted May 28, 1962)

Notwithstanding the provisions of § 20.6091–1 the Commissioner may permit the filing of the preliminary notice required by § 20.6036–1 and the estate tax return required by § 20.6018–1 in any internal revenue district.

§ 20.6151–1 Time and place for paying tax shown on the return. (Paragraph (b) amended Dec. 28, 1960 by inserting new subparagraph (3) to read as follows)

(b) *Extension of time for paying.* * * *

(3) *Interest in a closely held business.* For provisions relating to payment in installments of the estate tax attributable to inclusion in the gross estate of an interest in a closely held business, see §§ 20.6166–1 through 20.6166–4.

§ 20.6161–1 Extension of time for paying tax shown on the return. (Paragraphs (a) and (c) amended Dec. 28, 1960, to read as follows)

(a) In any case where the district director finds that payment on the due date of any part of the tax shown on the return, or payment of any part of an installment under section 6166 (including any part of a deficiency prorated to an installment the date for payment of which had not arrived) on the date fixed for payment thereof, would impose undue hardship upon the estate, he may extend the time for payment for a period or periods not to exceed one year for any one period and for all periods not to exceed more than 10 years from the date prescribed in section 6151(a) for payment of the tax. See paragraph (a) of § 20.6151–1. In addition, if the district director finds that payment upon notice and demand of any part of a deficiency prorated under the provisions of section 6166 to installments the date for payment of which had arrived would impose undue hardship upon the estate, he may extend the time for payment for a similar period or periods.

(Paragraph (b) amended May 27, 1964 to read)

(b) The extension will not be granted upon a general statement of hardship. The term "undue hardship" means more than an inconvenience to the estate. A sale of property at a price equal to its current fair market value, where a market exists, is not ordinarily considered as resulting in an undue hardship. However, a sale of property at a sacrifice price or on a severely depressed market would constitute an undue hardship. Furthermore, the necessity for selling an interest in a family business, which is included in the gross estate, to unrelated persons will be considered to be an undue hardship even though the interest could be sold at a price equal to its current fair market value.

(c) An application for such an extension must be in writing and must contain, or be supported by, information in a written statement declaring that it is made under penalties of perjury, showing the undue hardship that would result to the estate if the requested extension were refused. The application, with the supporting information, must be filed with the district director. When received, it will be examined, and, if possible, within 30 days will be denied, granted, or tentatively granted subject to certain conditions of which the executor will be notified. The district director will not consider an application for such an extension of time for payment of the tax or of an installment under section 6166 (including any part of a deficiency prorated to an installment the date for payment of which had not arrived) unless the extension is applied for on or before the date fixed for payment of the tax or the installment. Similarly, the district director will not consider an application for such an extension of time for payment of any part of a deficiency prorated under the provisions of section 6166 to installments the date for payment of which had arrived, unless the extension is applied for on or before the date prescribed for payment of the deficiency as shown by the notice and demand from the district director. If the executor desires to obtain an additional extension of time for payment of any part of the tax shown on the return, or any part of an installment under section 6166 (including any part of a deficiency prorated to an installment), it must be applied for on or before the date of the expiration of the previous extension. The granting of the extension of time for paying the tax is discretionary with the district director and his authority will be exercised under such conditions as he may deem advisable. If, in the mistaken belief that an estate satisfies the requirements of section 6166, the executor, within the time prescribed in paragraph (e) of § 20.6166–1, files a notification of election to pay estate tax in installments, the notification of election to pay tax in installments will be treated as a timely filed application for an extension, under section 6161, of time for payment of the tax if the executor so requests, in writing, within a reasonable time after being notified by the district director that the estate does not satisfy the requirements of section 6166. A request that the election under section 6166 be treated as a timely filed application for an extension under section 6161 must contain, or be supported by, information in a written statement declaring that it is made under penalties of perjury, setting forth the period of the extension requested, and showing the undue hardship that would result if the requested extension were refused.

§ 20.6161–2 **Extension of time for paying deficiency in tax.** (Paragraph (a) amended Dec. 28, 1960, to read as follows)

(a) In any case in which the district director finds that payment, on the date prescribed therefor, of any part of a deficiency would impose undue hardship upon the estate, he may extend the time for payment for a period or periods not to exceed one year for any one period and for all periods not to exceed four years from the date prescribed for payment thereof. However, see § 20.6161–1 for extensions of time for payment of the part of a

[Harris Tax Supp]   **181** deficiency which is prorated to installments under the provisions of section 6166.

§ 20.6163–1 **Extension of time for payment of estate tax on value of reversionary or remainder interest in property.** (Paragraph (a) amended March 25, 1964 to read as follows)

(a)(1) In case there is included in the gross estate a reversionary or remainder interest in property, the payment of the part of the tax attributable to that interest may, at the election of the executor, be postponed until six months after the termination of the precedent interest or interests in the property. The provisions of this section are limited to cases in which the reversionary or remainder interest is included in the decedent's gross estate as such and do not extend to cases in which the decedent creates future interests by his own testamentary act.

(2) If the district director finds that the payment of the tax at the expiration of the period of postponement described in subparagraph (1) of this paragraph would result in undue hardship to the estate, he may—

(i) After September 2, 1958, and before February 27, 1964, extend the time for payment for a reasonable period or periods not to exceed in all 2 years from the expiration of the period of postponement, but only if the precedent interest or interests in the property terminated after March 2, 1958, or

(ii) After February 26, 1964, extend the time for payment for a reasonable period or periods not to exceed in all 3 years from the expiration of the period of postponement, but only if the time for payment of the tax, including any extensions thereof, did not expire before February 26, 1964.

See paragraph (b) of § 20.6161–1 for the meaning of the term "undue hardship." An example of undue hardship is a case where, by reason of the time required to settle the complex issues involved in a trust, the decedent's heirs or beneficiaries cannot reasonably expect to receive the decedent's remainder interest in the trust before the expiration of the period of postponement. The extension will be granted only in the manner provided in paragraph (c) of § 20.6161–1, and the amount of the tax for which the extension is granted, with the additions thereto, shall be paid on or before the expiration of the period of extension without the necessity of notice and demand from the district director.

§ 20.6165–1 **Bonds where time to pay tax or deficiency has been extended.** (Paragraph (a) amended Jan. 18, 1961, to read as follows)

(a) *Extensions under sections 6161 and 6163(b) of time to pay tax or deficiency.* If an extension of time for payment of tax or deficiency is granted under section 6161 or 6163(b), the district director may, if he deems it necessary, require the executor to furnish a bond for the payment of the amount in respect of which the extension is granted in accordance with the terms of the extension. However, such bond shall not exceed double the amount with respect to which the extension is granted. For other provisions relating to bonds required where extensions of time to pay estate taxes or deficiencies are granted under sections 6161 or 6163(b), see the regulations under section 7101 contained in Part 301 of this chapter (Regulations on Procedure and Administration).

§ 20.6165–1 Bonds where time to pay tax or deficiency has been extended.
(Paragraph (b) amended May 28, 1962, as follows)

(b) *Extensions under section 6163 of time to pay estate tax attributable to reversionary or remainder interests.* As a prerequisite to the postponement of the payment of the tax attributable to a reversionary or remainder interest as provided in § 20.6163–1, a bond equal to double the amount of the tax and interest for the estimated duration of the precedent interest must be furnished conditioned upon the payment of the tax and interest accrued thereon within six months after the termination of the precedent interest. If after the acceptance of a bond it is determined that the amount of the tax attributable to the reversionary or remainder interest was understated in the bond, a new bond or a supplemental bond may be required, or the tax, to the extent of the understatement, may be collected. The bond must be conditioned upon the principal or surety promptly notifying the district director when the precedent interest terminates and upon the principal or surety notifying the district director during the month of September of each year as to the continuance of the precedent interest, if the duration of the precedent interest is dependent upon the life or lives of any person or persons, or is otherwise indefinite. For other provisions relating to bonds where an extension of time has been granted for paying the tax, see the regulations under section 7101 contained in Part 301 of this chapter (Regulations on Procedure and Administration).

§ 20.6166–1 Extension of time for payment of estate tax where estate consists largely of interest in closely held business. (Adopted Dec 28, 1960)

(a) *In general.* Section 6166 provides that where the value of an interest in a closely held business, which is included in the gross estate of a decedent who was a citizen or resident of the United States at the time of his death, exceeds either (1) 35 per cent of the value of the gross estate, or (2) 50 per cent of the taxable estate, the executor may elect to pay part or all of the Federal estate tax in installments. The election to pay the tax in installments applies to deficiencies in tax as well as to the tax shown on the return, unless the deficiency is due to negligence, to intentional disregard of rules and regulations, or to fraud with intent to evade tax. Except as otherwise provided in section 6166(i) and § 20.6166–4, the provisions of section 6166 and this section apply only if the due date of the return is after September 2, 1958. See § 20.6166–4 for special rules applicable where the decedent died after August 16, 1954, and the due date of the return was on or before September 2, 1958. See also § 20.6075–1 for the due date of the return, and § 20.6166–2 for definition of the term "interest in a closely held business". Since the election must be made on or before the due date of the return, the provisions of section 6166 will not apply to a deficiency in a case where, for whatever reason, no election was made to pay in installments the tax shown on the return. However, see paragraph (e)(3) of this section concerning a protective election. The general administrative provisions of subtitle F of the Code are applicable in connection with an election by the executor to pay the estate tax in installment in the same manner in which they are applied in a case where an extension of time under section 6161 is granted for payment of the tax. See paragraph (a) of § 20.6165–1 for provisions requiring the furnishing of security for the payment of the tax in cases where an extension is granted under section 6161.

(b) *Limitation on amount of tax payable in installments.* The amount of estate tax which the executor may elect to pay in installments is limited to an amount A, which bears the same ratio to B (the gross Federal estate tax, reduced by the credits authorized by sections 2011 through 2014 and any death tax convention) as C (the value of the interest in a closely held business which is included in the gross estate) bears to D (the value of the gross estate). Stated algebraically, the limitation (A) equals

$$\frac{\text{Value of interest in a closely held business which is included in the gross estate (C)}}{\text{Value of gross estate (D).}} \times \begin{array}{l}\text{Gross Federal estate tax reduced by the credits authorized by sections 2011 through 2014 and any death tax convention (B).}\end{array}$$

The executor may elect to pay in installments an amount less than the amount computed under the limitation in this paragraph. For example, if the total estate tax payable is $100,000 and the amount computed under the limitation in this paragraph is $60,000, the executor may elect to pay in installments some lesser sum such as $30,000, in which event the executor must pay $73,000 to the district director on or before the date prescribed by section 6151(a) for payment of the tax. Of such payment, $70,000 represents tax which the executor either could not elect to pay in installments or did not choose to so elect, and $3,000 represents a payment of the first installment of the tax which the executor elected to pay in installments.

(c) *Number of installments and dates for payment.* The executor may elect to pay part or all of the tax (determined after application of the limitation contained in paragraph (b) of this section) in two or more, but not exceeding 10, equal annual installments. The first installment shall be paid on or before the date prescribed by section 6151(a) for payment of the tax (see paragraph (a) of § 20.6151–1), and each succeeding installment shall be paid on or before the date which is one year after the date prescribed for the payment of the preceding installment. See § 20.6166–3 for the circumstances under which the privilege of paying the tax in installments will terminate.

(d) *Deficiencies.* The amount of a deficiency which may be paid in installments shall not exceed the difference between the amount of tax which the executor elected to pay in installments and the maximum amount of tax (determined under paragraph (b) of this section) which the executor could have elected to pay in installments on the basis of a return which reflects the adjustments which resulted in the deficiency. This amount is then prorated to the installments in which the executor elected to pay the tax. The part of the deficiency prorated to installments not yet due shall be paid at the same time as, and as a part of, such installments. The part of the deficiency prorated to installments already paid or due shall be paid upon notice and demand from the district director. At the time the executor receives such notice and demand he may, of course, prepay the portions of the deficiency which have been prorated to installments not yet due. See paragraph (h) of this section.

184

(e) *Notice of election*—(1) *Filing of notice.* The notice of election to pay the estate tax in installments shall be filed with the district director on or before the due date of the return. However, if the due date of the return is after September 2, 1958, but before November 3, 1958, the election will be considered as timely made if the notice is filed with the district director on or before November 3, 1958. See § 20.6075–1 for the due date of the return.

(2) *Form of notice.* The notice of election to pay the estate tax in installments may be in the form of a letter addressed to the district director. The executor shall state in the notice the amount of tax which he elects to pay in installments, and the total number of installments (including the installment due 15 months after the date of the decedent's death) in which he elects to pay the tax. The properties in the gross estate which constitute the decedent's interest in a closely held business should be listed in the notice, and identified by the schedule and item number at which they appear on the estate tax return. The notice should be set forth the facts which formed the basis for the executor's conclusion that the estate qualifies for the payment of the estate tax in installments.

(3) *Protective election.* In a case where the estate does not qualify under section 6166(a) on the basis of the values as returned, or where the return shows no tax as due, an election may be made, contingent upon the values as finally determined meeting the percentage requirements set forth in section 6166(a), to pay in installments any portion of the estate tax, including a deficiency, which may be unpaid at the time of such final determination and which does not exceed the limitation provided in section 6166(b). The protective election must be made on or before the due date of the return and should state that it is a protective election. In the absence of a statement in the protective election as to the amount of tax to be paid in installments and the number of installments, the election will be presumed to be made for the maximum amount so payable and for the payment thereof in 10 equal annual installments, the first of which would have been due on the date prescribed in section 6151(a) for payment of the tax. The unpaid portion of the tax which may be paid in installments is prorated to the installments which would have been due if the provisions of section 6166(a) had applied to the tax, if any, shown on the return. The part of the unpaid portion of the tax so prorated to installments the date for payment of which would not have arrived before the deficiency is assessed shall be paid at the time such installments would have been due. The part of the unpaid portion of the tax so prorated to any installment the date for payment of which would have arrived before the deficiency is assessed shall be paid upon receipt of notice and demand from the district director. At the time the executor receives such notice and demand he may, of course, prepay the unpaid portions of the tax which have been prorated to installments not yet due. See paragraph (h) of this section.

(f) *Time for paying interest.* Under the provisions of section 6601, interest at the rate of 4 per cent per annum shall be paid on the unpaid balance of the estate tax which the executor has elected to pay in installments, and on the unpaid balance of any deficiency prorated to the installments. Interest on such unpaid balance of estate tax shall be paid annually at the same time as, and as a part of, each installment of the tax. Accordingly, interest is computed on the entire unpaid balance for the period from the preceding installment date to the current installment date, and is paid with the current installment. In making such a computation, proper adjustment shall be made for any advance payments made during the period, whether the advance payments are voluntary or are brought about by the operation of section 6166(h)(2). In computing the annual interest payment, the portion of any deficiency which is prorated to installments the date for payment of which has not arrived shall be added to the unpaid balance at the beginning of the annual period during which the assessment of the deficiency occurs. Interest on such portion of the deficiency for the period from the original due date of the tax to the date fixed for the payment of the last installment preceding the date of assessment of a deficiency shall be paid upon notice and demand from the district director. Any extension of time under section 6161(a)(2) (on account of undue hardship to the estate) for payment of an installment will not extend the time for payment of the interest which is due on the installment date.

(g) *Extensions of time for payment in hardship cases.* The provisions of section 6161, under which extensions of time may be granted for payment of estate tax in cases involving undue hardship, apply to both the portion of the tax which may be paid in installments under section 6166 and the portion of the tax which is not so payable. Therefore, in a case involving undue hardship, the executor may elect under section 6166 to pay in installments the portion of the tax which is attributable to the interest in the closely held business and, in addition, may file an application under section 6161 for an extension of time to pay both the portion of the tax which is not attributable to the interest in the closely held business and such of the installments as are payable within the period of the requested extension. If an executor files a notice of election to pay the tax in installments and thereafter it is determined that the estate does not qualify for the privilege of paying the tax in installments, the executor is not deprived of the right to request an extension under section 6161 of time for payment of the tax to which the purported election applied. See § 20.6161–1 for the circumstances under which a timely filed election to pay the tax in installments will be treated as a timely filed application for an extension of time to pay the tax on account of undue hardship to the estate.

(h) *Prepayments.* Voluntary prepayment may be made at any time of all, or of any part, of the unpaid portion of the tax (including deficiences) payable in installments. Voluntary prepayments shall be applied in payment of such installments, installment, or part of an installment as the person making the prepayment shall designate. For purposes of this paragraph a payment described in paragraph (d)(2) of § 20.6166–3 of tax in an amount not less than the amount of money or other property distributed in a section 303 redemption is considered to be a voluntary prepayment to the extent paid before the date prescribed for payment of the first installment after the redemption or, if paid on the date prescribed for payment of such installment, to the extent it exceeds the amount due on the installment. See paragraph (b)(3) of § 20.6166–3 for the application to be made of the prepayment required by section 6166(h)(2).

§ 20.6166–2 Definition of an interest in a closely held business. (Adopted Dec 28, 1960)

(a) *In general.* For purposes of §§ 20.6166–1, 20.6166–3, and 20.6166–4, the term "interest in a closely held business" means

(1) An interest as a proprietor in a trade or business carried on as a proprietorship.

(2) An interest as a partner in a partnership carrying on a trade or business if 20 per cent or more of the total capital interest in the partnership is included in determining the decedent's gross estate or if the partnership had 10 or less partners.

(3) Stock in a corporation carrying on a trade or business if 20 per cent or more in value of the voting stock of the corporation is included in determining the decedent's gross estate or if the corporation had 10 or less shareholders.

(b) *Number of partners or shareholders.* The number of partners of the partnership, or stock in a corporation, is the community property of husband time immediately before the decedent's death. Where an interest in a partnership, or stock in a corporation, is the community property of husband and wife, both the husband and the wife are counted as partners or shareholders in arriving at the number of partners or shareholders. Similarly, if stock is held by co-owners, tenants in common, tenants by the entirety, or joint tenants, each co-owner, tenant in common, tenant by the entirety, or joint tenant is counted as a shareholder.

(c) *Carrying on a trade or business.* (1) In order for the interest in a partnership or the stock of a corporation to qualify as an interest in a closely held business it is necessary that the partnership or the corporation be engaged in carrying on a trade or business at the time of the decedent's death. However, it is not necessary that all the assets of the partnership or the corporation be utilized in the carrying on of the trade or business.

(2) In the case of a trade or business carried on as a proprietorship, the interest in the closely held businesss includes only those assets of the decedent which were actually utilized by him in the trade or business. Thus, if a building was used by the decedent in part as a personal residence and in part for the carrying on of a mercantile business, the part of the building used as a residence does not form any part of the interest in the closely held business. Whether an asset will be considered as used in the trade or business will depend on the facts and circumstances of the particular case. For example, if a bank account was held by the decedent in his individual name (as distinguished from the trade or business name) and it can be clearly shown that the amount on deposit represents working capital of the business as well as nonbusiness funds (e.g., receipts from investments, such as dividends and interest), then that part of the amount on deposit which represents working capital of the business will constitute a part of the interest in the closely held business. On the other hand, if a bank account is held by the decedent in the trade or business name and it can be shown that the amount represents nonbusiness funds as well as working capital, then only that part of the amount on deposit

which represents working capital of the business will constitute a part of the interest in the closely held business. In a case where an interest in a partnership or stock of a corporation qualifies as an interest in a closely held business, the decedent's entire interest in the partnership, or the decedent's entire holding of stock in the corporation, constitutes an interest in a closely held business even though a portion of the partnership or corporate assets is used for a purpose other than the carrying on of a trade or business.

(d) *Interests in two or more closely held businesses.* For purposes of paragraphs (a) and (b) of § 20.6166–1 and paragraphs (d) and (e) of § 20.6166–3, interests in two or more closely held businesses shall be treated as an interest in a single closely held business if more than 50 per cent of the total value of each such business is included in determining the value of the decedent's gross estate. For the purpose of the 50 per cent requirement set forth in the preceding sentence, an interest in a closely held business which represents the surviving spouse's interest in community property shall be considered as having been included in determining the value of the decedent's gross estate.

§ 20.6166–3 **Acceleration of payment.** (Adopted Dec 28, 1960)

(a) *In general.* Under the circumstances described in this section all or a part of the tax which the executor has elected to pay in installments shall be paid before the date fixed for payment of the installments. Upon an estate's having undistributed net income described in paragraph (b) of this section for any taxable year after its fourth taxable year, the executor shall pay an amount equal to such undistributed net income in liquidation of the unpaid portion of the tax payable in installments. Upon the happening of any of the events described in paragraphs (c), (d), and (e) of this section, any unpaid portion of the tax payable in installments shall be paid upon notice and demand from the district director.

(b) *Undistributed net income of estate.* (1) If an estate has undistributed net income for any taxable year after its fourth taxable year, the executor shall pay an amount equal to such undistributed net income in liquidation of the unpaid portion of the tax payable in installments. The amount shall be paid to the district director on or before the time prescribed for the filing of the estate's income tax return for such taxable year. For this purpose extensions of time granted for the filing of the income tax return are taken into consideration in determining the time prescribed for filing the return and making such payment. In determining the number of taxable years, a short taxable year is counted as if it were a full taxable year.

(2) The term "undistributed net income" of the estate for any taxable year for purposes of this section is the amount by which the distributable net income of the estate, as defined in section 643, exceeds the sum of—

(i) The amount for such year specified in section 661(a)(1) and (2),

(ii) The amount of the Federal income tax imposed on the estate for such taxable year under chapter 1 of the Code, and

(iii) The amount of the Federal estate tax, including interest thereon, paid for the estate during such taxable year (other than any amount paid by reason of the application of this acceleration rule).

(3) The payment described in subparagraph (1) of this paragraph shall

188

be applied against the total unpaid portion of the tax which the executor elected to pay in installments, and shall be divided equally among the installments due after the date of such payment. The application of this subparagraph may be illustrated by the following example:

Example. The decedent died on January 1, 1959. The executor elects under section 6166 to pay tax in the amount of $100,000 in 10 installments of $10,000. The first installment is due on April 1, 1960. The estate files its income tax returns on a calendar year basis. For its fifth taxable year (calendar year 1963) it has undistributed net income of $6,000. If the prepayment of $6,000 required by section 6166(h)(2)(A), and due on or before April 15, 1964, is paid before the fifth installment (due April 1, 1964), the $6,000 is apportioned equally among installments 5 through 10, leaving $9,000 as the amount due on each of such installments. However, if the prepayment of $6,000 is paid after the fifth installment, it is apportioned equally among installments 6 through 10, leaving $8,800 as the amount due on each of such installments.

(c) *Failure to pay installment on or before due date.* If any installment of tax is not paid on or before the date fixed for its payment (including any extension of time for the payment thereof), the whole of the unpaid portion of the tax which is payable in installments becomes due and shall be paid upon notice and demand from the district director. See paragraph (c) of § 20.6166–1 for the dates fixed for the payment of installments. See also § 20.6161–1 for the circumstances under which an extension of time for the payment of an installment will be granted.

(d) *Withdrawal of funds from business.* (1) In any case where money or other property is withdrawn from the trade or business and the aggregate withdrawals of money or other property equal or exceed 50 per cent of the value of the trade or business, the privilege of paying the tax in installments terminates and the whole of the unpaid portion of the tax which is payable in installments becomes due and shall be paid upon notice and demand from the district director. The withdrawals of money or other property from the trade or business must be in connection with the interest therein included in the gross estate, and must equal or exceed 50 percent of the value of the entire trade or business (and not just 50 percent of the value of the interest therein included in the gross estate). The withdrawal must be a withdrawal of money or other property which constitutes "included property" within the meaning of that term as used in paragraph (d) of § 20.2032–1. The provisions of this section do not apply to the withdrawal of money or other property which constitutes "excluded property" within the meaning of that term as used in such paragraph (d)

(2) If a distribution in redemption of stock is (by reason of the provisions of section 303 or so much of section 304 as relates to section 303) treated for income tax purposes as a distribution in full payment in exchange for the stock so redeemed, the amount of such distribution is not counted as a withdrawal of money or other property made with respect to the decedent's interest in the trade or business for purposes of determining whether the withdrawals of money or other property made with respect to the decedent's interest in the trade or business equal or exceed 50 percent of the value of the trade or business. However, in the case described in the preceding sentence the value of the trade or business

for purposes of applying the rule set forth in subparagraph (1) of this paragraph is the value thereof reduced by the proportionate part thereof which such distribution represents. The proportionate part of the value of the trade or business which the distribution represents is determined at the time of the distribution, but the reduction in the value of the trade or business represented by it relates back to the time of the decedent's death, or the alternate valuation date if an election is made under section 2032, for purposes of determining whether other withdrawals with respect to the decedent's interest in the trade or business constitute withdrawals equaling or exceeding 50 percent of the value of the trade or business. See example (3) of paragraph (e)(6) of this section for illustration of this principle. The rule stated in the first sentence of this subparagraph does not apply unless after the redemption, but on or before the date prescribed for payment of the first installment which becomes due after the redemption, there is paid an amount of estate tax not less than the amount of money or other property distributed. Where there are a series of section 303 redemptions, each redemption is treated separately and the failure of one redemption to qualify under the rule stated in the first sentence of this subparagraph does not necessarily mean that another redemption will not qualify.

(3) The application of this paragraph may be illustrated by the following examples, in each of which the executor elected to pay the estate tax in installments:

Example (1). A, who died on July 1, 1957, owned an 80 percent interest in a partnership which qualified as an interest in a closely held business. B owned the other 20 percent interest in the partnership. On the date of A's death the value of the business was $200,000 and the value of A's interest therein was included in his gross estate at $160,000. On October 1, 1958, when the value of the business was the same as at A's death, the executor withdrew $80,000 from the business. On December 1, 1958, when the value of the remaining portion of the business was $160,000, the executor withdrew $20,000 from the business and B withdrew $10,000. On February 1, 1959, when the value of the then remaining portion of the business was $150,000 the executor withdrew $15,000. The withdrawals of money or other property from the trade or business with respect to the interest therein included in the gross estate are considered as not having equaled or exceeded 50 percent of the value of the trade or business until February 1, 1959. The executor is considered as having withdrawn 40 percent of the value of the trade or business on October 1, 1958, computed as follows:

$$\frac{\$80,000 \text{ (withdrawal)}}{\$200,000 \text{ (value of trade or business at time of withdrawal)}} \times 100 \text{ percent} = 40 \text{ percent}$$

Immediately following the October withdrawal the remaining portion of the business represents 60 percent of the value of the trade or business in existence at the time of A's death (100 percent less than 40 percent withdrawn). The executor is considered as having withdrawn 7.5 percent of the value of the trade or business on December 1, 1958, and B as having withdrawn 3.75 percent of the value thereof at that time, computed as follows:

Executor's withdrawal—

$$\frac{\$20{,}000 \text{ (withdrawal)}}{\$160{,}000 \text{ (value of trade or business at time of withdrawal)}} \times 60 \text{ percent} = 7.5 \text{ percent}$$

B's withdrawal—

$$\frac{\$10{,}000 \text{ (withdrawal)}}{\$160{,}000 \text{ (value of trade or business at time of withdrawal)}} \times 60 \text{ percent} = 3.75 \text{ percent}$$

Immediately following the December withdrawal the then remaining portion of the business represented 48.75 percent of the value of the trade or business in existence at the time of A's death (100 percent less 40 percent withdrawn by executor in October, 7.5 percent withdrawn by executor in December, and 3.75 percent withdrawn by B in December). It should be noted that while at this point the total withdrawals by the executor and B from the trade or business exceed 50 percent of the value thereof, the aggregate of the withdrawals by the executor were less than 50 percent of the value of the trade or business. Also it should be noted that while the total withdrawals by the executor exceeded 50 percent of the value of A's interest in the trade or business, they did not exceed 50 percent of the value of the entire trade or business. The executor is considered as having withdrawn 4.875 percent of the value of the trade or business on February 1, 1959, computed as follows:

$$\frac{\$15{,}000 \text{ (withdrawal)}}{\$150{,}000 \text{ (value of trade or business at time of withdrawal)}} \times 48.75 \text{ percent} = 4.875 \text{ percent}$$

As of February 1, 1959, the total withdrawals from the trade or business made with respect to A's interest therein was 52.375 percent of the value of the trade or business.

Example (2). The decedent's 40-percent interest in the XYZ partnership constituted an interest in a closely held business. Since the decedent's interest in the closely held business amounted to less than 50 percent of the value of the business, money or other property equaling or exceeding 50 percent of the value of the business could not be withdrawn from the decedent's interest in the business. Therefore, withdrawals of money or other property from this trade or business never would accelerate the payment of the tax under the provisions of this paragraph.

Example (3). The decedent died on September 1, 1957. He owned 100 shares of B Corporation (the total number of shares outstanding at the time of his death) and a 75 percent interest in a partnership of which C was the other partner. The B Corporation stock and the interest in the partnership together make up the interest in the closely held business which was included in the decedent's gross estate. The B Corporation stock was included in the gross estate at a value of $400,000 and the interest in the partnership was included at a value of $300,000. On November 1, 1957, at which time the value of the corporation's assets had not changed, in a section 303 redemption the executor surrendered 26 shares of B Corporation stock for $104,000. On December 1, 1957, at which time the value of the partnership's assets had not changed, the partners withdrew 90 percent of the assets of the partnership, with the executor receiving $270,000 and C receiving $90,000. The estate tax amounts to $240,000, of which the executor elected under section 6166 to pay $140,000 in 10 installments of $14,000 each. On December 1, 1958, the due date for paying the estate tax which was not payable in installments and for paying the first installment under section 6166, the executor paid estate tax of $114,000, of which $100,000 represented the tax not payable in installments and $14,000 represented the first installment. Inasmuch as after the section 303 distribution and on or before the due date of the first installment (December 1, 1958) after the section 303 distribution the executor paid as estate tax an amount not less than the amount of the distribution, the section 303 distribution does not constitute a withdrawal of money or other property from the business for purposes of section 6166(h)(1). Therefore, the value of the trade or business is reduced by the amount of the section 303 distribution. Accordingly, the value of the entire trade or business is $696,000, of which $400,000 represents the value of the partnership and $296,000 represents the value of the B Corporation stock. Since the executor is considered as having withdrawn only $270,000 (the withdrawal from the partnership) from the trade or business, the withdrawal of money or other property from the trade or business made with respect to the decedent's interest therein was 270,000/696,000 of the value of the entire trade or business, or less than 50 percent thereof.

(e) *Disposition of interest in business.* (1) In any case where in the aggregate 50 percent or more of the decedent's interest in a closely held business has been distributed, sold, exchanged, or otherwise disposed of, the privilege of paying the tax in installments terminates and the whole of the unpaid portion of the tax which is payable in installments becomes due and shall be paid upon notice and demand from the district director. A transfer by the executor of an interest in the closely held business to a beneficiary or trustee named in the decedent's will or to an heir who is entitled to receive it under the applicable intestacy law does not constitute a distribution thereof for purposes of determining whether 50 percent or more of an interest in a closely held business has been distributed, sold, exchanged, or otherwise disposed of. However, a subsequent transfer of the interest by the beneficiary, trustee, or heir will constitute a distribution, sale, exchange, or other disposition thereof for such purposes. The disposition must be a disposition of an interest which constitutes "included property" within the meaning of that term as used in paragraph (d) of § 20.2032–1. The provisions of this section do not apply to the disposition of an interest which constitutes "excluded property" within the meaning of that term as used in such paragraph (d).

(2) The phrase "distributed, sold, exchanged, or otherwise disposed of" comprehends all possible ways by which an interest in a closely held business ceases to form a part of the gross estate. The term includes the surrender of a stock certificate for corporate assets in complete or partial liquidation of a corporation pursuant to section 331. The term also includes the surrender of stock

for stock pursuant to a transaction described in subparagraphs (A), (B), or (C) of section 368(a)(1). In general the term does not, however, extend to transactions which are mere changes in form. It does not include a transfer of assets to a corporation in exchange for its stock in a transaction with respect to which no gain or loss would be recognizable for income tax purposes under section 351. It does not include an exchange of stock in a corporation for stock in the same corporation or another corporation pursuant to a plan of reorganization described in subparagraphs (D), (E), or (F) of section 368 (a)(1), nor to an exchange to which section 355 (or so much of section 356 as relates to section 355) applies. However, any stock received in an exchange to which the two preceding sentences apply shall for purposes of this paragraph be treated as an interest in a closely held business.

(3) An interest in a closely held business may be "distributed" by either a trustee who received it from the executor, or a trustee of an interest which is included in the gross estate under sections 2035 through 2038 or section 2041. See subparagraph (1) of this paragraph relative to the distribution of an interest by the executor to the person entitled to receive it under the decedent's will or an intestacy law.

(4) An interest in a closely held business may be "sold, exchanged, or otherwise disposed of" by (i) the executor; (ii) a trustee or other donee to whom the decedent in his lifetime transferred the interest included in his gross estate under section 2035 through 2038, or section 2041; (iii) a beneficiary, trustee, or heir entitled to receive the property from the executor under the decedent's will or under the applicable law of descent and distribution, or to whom title to the interest passed directly under local law; (iv) a surviving joint tenant or tenant by the entirety; or (v) any other person.

(5) If a distribution in redemption of stock is (by reason of the provisions of section 303 or so much of section 304 as relates to section 303) treated for income tax purposes as a distribution in full payment in exchange for the stock redeemed, the stock so redeemed is not counted as distributed, sold, exchanged, or otherwise disposed of for purposes of determining whether 50 percent or more of the decedent's interest in a closely held business has been distributed, sold, exchanged, or otherwise disposed of. However, in the case described in the preceding sentence the interest in the closely held business for purposes of applying the rule set forth in subparagraph (1) of this paragraph is such interest reduced by the proportionate part thereof which the redeemed stock represents. The proportionate part of the interest which the redeemed stock represents is determined at the time of the redemption, but the reduction in the interest represented by it relates back to the time of the decedent's death, or the alternate valuation date if an election is made under section 2032, for purposes of determining whether other distributions, sales, exchanges, and dispositions of the decedent's interest in the closely held business equal or exceed in the aggregate 50 percent of such interest. See example (3) of subparagraph (6) of this paragraph for illustration of this principle. The rule stated in the first sentence of this subparagraph does not apply unless after the redemption, but on or before the date prescribed for payment of the first installment which becomes due after the redemption, there is paid an amount of estate tax not less than the amount of money or other property distributed. Where there are a series of section 303 redemptions, each redemption is treated

separately and the failure of one redemption to qualify under the rule stated in the first sentence of this subparagraph does not necessarily mean that another redemption will not qualify.

(6) The application of this paragraph may be illustrated by the following examples, in each of which the executor elected to pay the tax in installments:

Example (1). The decedent died on October 1, 1957. He owned 8,000 of the 12,000 shares of D Corporation outstanding at the time of his death and 3,000 of the 5,000 shares of E Corporation outstanding at that time. The D Corporation stock was included in the gross estate at $50 per share, or a total of $400,000. The E Corporation stock was included in the gross estate at $100 per share, or a total of $300,000. On November 1, 1958, the executor sold the 3,000 shares of E Corporation and on February 1, 1959, he sold 1,000 shares of D Corporation. Since the decedent's shares of D Corporation and E Corporation together constituted the interest in a closely held business, the value of such interest was $700,000 ($400,000 plus $300,000) and the D Corporation stock represented 400,000/700,000 thereof and the E Corporation stock represented 300,000/700,000 thereof. While the sale of 3,000 shares of E Corporation on November 1, 1958, was a sale of the decedent's entire interest in E Corporation and a sale of more than 50 percent of the outstanding stock of E Corporation, nevertheless it constituted a sale of only 300,000/700,000 of the interest in the closely held business. The sale of 1,000 shares of D Corporation stock on February 1, 1959, represented a sale of 50,000/700,000 of the interest in the closely held business. The numerator of $50,000 is determined as follows:

$$\frac{1,000 \text{ (shares sold)}}{8,000 \text{ (shares owned)}} \times \$400,000 \text{ (value of shares owned, as included in gross estate)}$$

Taken together the two sales represented a sale of 50 percent $\left[\dfrac{350,000}{700,000} \right]$

of the interest in the closely held business. Therefore, as of February 1, 1959 (the date of the sale of 1,000 shares of E Corporation), 50 percent or more in value of the interest in the closely held business is considered as distributed, sold, exchanged, or otherwise disposed of.

Example (2). The decedent died on September 1, 1958. The interest owned by him in a closely held business consisted of 100 shares of the M Corporation. On February 1, 1959, in a section 303 redemption, 20 shares were redeemed for cash and an amount equivalent to the proceeds was paid on the Federal estate tax before that date of the next installment. On July 1, 1959, the executor sold 40 of the remaining shares of the stock. The section 303 redemption is not considered to be a distribution, sale, exchange, or other disposition of the portion of the interest represented by the 20 shares redeemed. As a result of the section 303 redemption the remaining 80 shares represent the decedent's entire interest in the closely held business for purposes of determining whether in the aggregate 50 percent or more of the interest in the closely held business has been distributed, sold, exchanged, or otherwise disposed of. The sale on July 1, 1959, of the 40 shares represents a sale of 50 percent of the interest in the closely held business.

Example (3). The facts are the same as in example (2) except that the 40 shares were sold on December 1, 1958 (before the section 303 redemption was made) instead of on July 1, 1959 (after the section 303 redemption was made). The sale of the 40 shares in December represents, as of that date, a sale of 40 percent of the interest in the closely held business. However, the section 303 redemption of 20 shares does not count as a distribution, sale, exchange, or other disposition of the interest, but it does reduce the interest to 80 shares (100 shares less 20 shares redeemed) for purposes of determining whether other distributions, sales, exchanges, and dispositions in the aggregate equal or exceed 50 percent of the interest in the closely held business. Since the reduction of the interest to 80 shares relates back to the time of the decedent's death, or the alternate valuation date if an election is made under section 2032, the sale of the 40 shares, as recomputed represents a sale of 50 percent of the interest. However, since the sale of the 40 shares did not represent a sale of 50 percent of the interest until the section 303 distribution was made, February 1, 1959 (the date of the section 303 distribution) is considered the date on which 50 percent of the interest was distributed, sold, exchanged, or otherwise disposed of.

(f) *Information to be furnished by executor.* (1) If the executor acquires knowledge of the happening of any transaction described in paragraph (d) or (e) of this section which, in his opinion, standing alone or when taken together with other transactions of which he has knowledge, would result in

(i) Aggregate withdrawals of money or other property from the trade or business equal to or exceeding 50 percent of the value of the entire trade or business, or

(ii) Aggregate distributions, sales, exchanges, and other dispositions equal to or exceeding 50 percent of the interest in the closely held business which was included in the gross estate,
the executor shall so notify the district director, in writing, within 30 days of acquiring such knowledge.

(2) On the date fixed for payment of each installment of tax (determined without regard to any extension of time for the payment thereof), other than the final installment, the executor shall furnish the district director, in writing, with either

(i) A complete disclosure of all transactions described in paragraphs (d) and (e) of this section of which he has knowledge and which have not previously been made known by him to the district director, or

(ii) A statement that to the best knowledge of the executor all transactions described in paragraphs (d) and (e) of this section which have occurred have not produced a result described in subparagraph (1)(i) or (ii) of this paragraph.

(3) The district director may require the submission of such additional information as is deemed necessary to establish the estate's right to continue payment of the tax in installments.

§ 20.6166–4 Special rules applicable where due date of return was before September 3, 1958. (Adopted Dec 28, 1960)

(a) *In general.* Section 206(f) of the Small Business Tax Revision Act of 1958 (72 Stat. 1685) provides that section 6166(i) of the Code shall apply in cases where the decedent died after August 16, 1954, but only if the date for filing the estate tax return (including extensions thereof) expired before September 3, 1958. Therefore, the privilege of paying the estate tax in installments as described in §§ 20.6166–1 through 20.6166–3 is available also in cases where the due date of the return is before September 3, 1958, but under somewhat different circumstances. These differences are explained in paragraphs (b) through (e) of this section. Therefore, except as otherwise provided in paragraphs (b) through (e) of this section, the regulations contained in §§ 20.6166–1 through 20.6166–3 apply also in cases where the due date of the return is before September 3, 1958. See § 20.6075–1 for the due date of the return. The value of the gross estate as determined for purposes of a deficiency in tax assessed after September 2, 1958, and the value at which the interest in the closely held business, to which the election applies, is included in such value of the gross estate are used in ascertaining whether an estate coming within the purview of section 6166(i) and this section satisfies the percentage requirements as to qualification set forth in section 6166(a).

(b) *Tax to which election applies.* In a case where the due date of the return was before September 3, 1958, an election to pay estate tax in installments does not apply to the tax shown on the return nor to a deficiency in tax assessed before that date. It does apply to a deficiency in tax assessed after September 2, 1958, unless the deficiency is due to negligence, to intentional disregard of rules and regulations, or to fraud with intent to evade tax. The amount of the deficiency which may be paid in installments shall not exceed that proportion of the total tax (including the deficiency) which is determined by applying thereto the ratio set forth in paragraph (b) of § 20.6166–1. See paragraph (c) of this section for the method of prorating the deficiency to the installments.

(c) *Proration of deficiency to installments.* The deficiency in tax which may be paid in installments is prorated to the installments which would have been due if the provisions of section 6166(a) had applied to the tax shown on the return and if an election had been timely made at the time the estate tax return was filed. The part of the deficiency so prorated to any installment the date for payment of which would have arrived before the election is made shall be paid at the time the election is made. The portion of the deficiency so prorated to installments the date for payment of which would not have arrived before the election is made shall be paid at the time such installments would have been due if such an election had been made.

(d) *Notice of election.* The notice of election to pay the deficiency in installments shall be filed with the district director not later than 60 days after issuance of notice and demand by the district director for payment of the deficiency. The number of installments in which the executor elects to pay the deficiency includes those installments the dates for payment of which would have arrived within the meaning of paragraph (c) of this section. See paragraph (c)(2) of § 20.6166–1 for further information relative to the notice of election.

(e) *Undistributed income of estate.* In any case where the due date of the estate tax return was before September 3, 1958, the provisions of paragraph (b) of § 20.6166–3 (providing for acceleration of payment of estate tax by amount of estate's undistributed net income for any taxable year after its fourth taxable year) shall not apply with respect to the estate's undistributed net income for any taxable year ending before January 1, 1960.

§ 20.7101–1 **Form of** bonds. (Amended May 28, 1962, as follows)

See paragraph (b) of § 20.6165–1 for provisions relating to the bond required in any case in which the payment of the tax attributable to a reversionary or remainder interest has been postponed under the provisions of § 20.6163–1. For further provisions relating to bonds, see § 20.6165–1 of these regulations and the regulations under section 7101 contained in Part 301 of this chapter (Regulations on Procedure and Administration).

ADMINISTRATIVE REGULATIONS

§ 301.6021–1 **Listing by district directors of taxable objects owned by nonresidents of internal revenue districts.** (Adopted Oct. 24, 1960)

Whenever there are in any internal revenue district any articles subject to tax, which are not owned or possessed by or under the care or control of any person within such district, and of which no list has been transmitted to the district director, as required by law or by regulations prescribed pursuant to law, the district director, or other authorized internal revenue officer or employee, shall enter the premises where such articles are situated, shall make such inspection of the articles as may be necessary, and shall make lists of the same according to the forms prescribed. Such lists, being subscribed by the district director or other authorized internal revenue officer or employee, shall be sufficient lists of such articles for all purposes.

§ 301.6064–1 **Signature presumed authentic.** (Adopted Oct. 24, 1960)

An individual's name signed to a return, statement, or other document shall be prima facie evidence for all purposes that the return, statement, or other document was actually signed by him.

§ 301.6155–1 **Payment on notice and demand.** (Adopted Oct. 24, 1960, amended Dec. 27, 1961).

Upon receipt of notice and demand from the district director (including the Director of International Operations), or the director of the regional service center, there shall be paid at the place and time stated in such notice the amount of any tax (including any interest, additional amounts, additions to the tax, and assessable penalties) stated in such notice and demand.

§ 301.7207–1 **Fraudulent returns, statements, or other documents.** (Adopted Oct. 24, 1960)

Any person who willfully delivers or discloses to any officer or employee of the Internal Revenue Service any list, return, account, statement, or other document, known by him to be fraudulent or to be false as to any material matter, shall be fined not more than $1,000, or imprisoned not more than 1 year, or both.

§ 301.7269–1 **Failure to produce records.** (Adopted Oct. 24, 1960)

Whoever fails to comply with any duty imposed upon him by section 6018, 6036 (in the case of an executor), or 6075(a), or, having in his possession or control any record, file, or paper, containing or supposed to contain any information concerning the estate of the decedent, or having in his possession or control any property comprised in the gross estate of the decedent, fails to exhibit the same upon request of any officer or employee of the Internal Revenue Service who desires to examine the same in the performance of his duties under chapter 11 of the Code (relating to estate taxes) shall be liable to a penalty of not exceeding $500, to be recovered with costs of suit, in a civil action in the name of the United States.

§ 301.7404–1 **Authority to bring civil action for estate taxes.** (Adopted Oct. 24, 1960)

(a) If the estate tax imposed by chapter 11 of the Code is not paid on or before the last date prescribed for payment, the district director shall proceed to collect the tax under the provisions of general law; or appropriate proceedings in the name of the United States may be commenced in any court having jurisdiction to subject the property of the decedent to be sold under the judgment or decree of the court.

(b) The remedy by action provided in section 7404 is not exclusive. The district director may proceed to collect the tax by levy, as provided in section 6331, on any or all property or rights to property of the estate, or collection may be enforced by an appropriate action against the executor, certain transferees, trustees, and beneficiaries for their personal liability. See § 20.2002–1 of this chapter (Estate Tax Regulations).

APPENDIX C

FEDERAL GIFT TAX REGULATIONS

(UNDER 1954 CODE)

THE EFFECTIVE DATE OF EACH REGULATION MUST BE COMPARED WITH THE EFFECTIVE DATE OF THE. AMENDMENT OF THE GOVERNING CODE PROVISIONS

PART 25—GIFT TAX

TABLE OF CONTENTS

§ 25.01 **Introduction.** (Paragraph (a) amended Jan. 19, 1961, to read as follows)

(a) *In general.* (1) The regulations in this part are designated "Gift Tax Regulations." These regulations pertain to (i) the gift tax imposed by chapter 12 of subtitle B of the Internal Revenue Code, on the transfer of property by gift by individuals in the calendar year 1955 and subsequent calendar years, and (ii) certain related administrative provisions of subtitle F of the Code. It should be noted that the application of some of the provisions of these regulations may be affected by the provisions of an applicable gift tax convention with a foreign country. Unless otherwise indicated, references in these regulations to the "Internal Revenue Code" or the "Code" are references to the Internal Revenue Code of 1954, as amended, and references to a section or other provision of law are references to a section or other provision of the Internal Revenue Code of 1954, as amended.

The Gift Tax Regulations are applicable to the transfer of property by gift by individuals in the calendar year 1955 and subsequent calendar years, and supersede the regulations contained in Part 86, Subchapter B, Chapter I, Title 26, Code of Federal Regulations (1939) (Regulations 108, Gift Tax), as prescribed and made applicable to the Internal Revenue Code of 1954 by Treasury Decision 6091, signed August 16, 1954 (19 F.R. 5167, Aug. 17, 1954).

(2) Section 2501(b) makes the provisions of chapter 12 of the Code apply in the case of gifts made after September 2, 1958, by certain citizens of the United States who were residents of a possession thereof at the time the gifts were made. Section 2501(c) makes the provisions of chapter 12 apply in the case of gifts made after September 14, 1960, by certain other citizens of the United States who were residents of a possession thereof at the time the gifts were made. See paragraphs (c) and (d) of § 25.2501–1. Except as otherwise provided in paragraphs (c) and (d) of § 25.2501–1, the provisions of these regulations do not apply to the making of gifts by such citizens.

§ 25.2501–1 **Imposition of tax.** (Paragraph (b) stricken Jan. 19, 1961, and following inserted in lieu thereof)

(b) *Resident.* A resident is an individual who has his domicile in the United States at the time of the gift. For this purpose the United States includes the States and the District of Columbia. The term also includes the Territories of Alaska and Hawaii prior to admission as a State. See section 7701(a)(9). All other individuals are nonresidents. A person acquires a domicile in a place by living there, for even a brief period of time, with no definite present intention of moving therefrom. Residence without the requisite intention to remain indefinitely will not constitute domicile, nor will intention to change domicile effect such a change unless accompanied by actual removal.

(c) *Certain residents of possessions considered citizens of the United States.* As used in this part, the term "citizen of the United States" includes a person who makes a gift after September 2, 1958 and who at the time of making the gift, was domiciled in a possession of the United States and was a United States citizen, and who did not acquire his United States citizenship solely by reason of his being a citizen of such possession or by reason of his birth or residence within such possession. The gift of such a person is, therefore, subject to the tax imposed by section 2501 in the same manner in which a gift made by a resident of the United States is subject to the tax. See paragraph (a) of § 25.01 and paragraph (d) of this section for further information relating to the application of the Federal gift tax to gifts made by persons who were residents of possessions of the United States. The application of this paragraph may be illustrated by the following example and the examples set forth in paragraph (d) of this section:

Example. A, a citizen of the United States by reason of his birth in the United States at San Francisco, established residence in Puerto Rico and acquired Puerto Rican citizenship. A makes a gift of stock of a Spanish corporation on September 4, 1958, while a citizen and domiciliary of Puerto Rico. A's gift is, by reason of the provisions of section 2501(b) subject to the tax imposed by section 2501 inasmuch as his United States citizenship is based on birth in the United States and is not based solely on being a citizen of a possession or solely on birth or residence in a possession.

(d) *Certain residents of possessions considered nonresidents not citizens of*

202

the United States. As used in this part, the term "nonresident not a citizen of the United States" includes a person who makes a gift after September 14, 1960, and who at the time of making the gift, was domiciled in a possession of the United States and was a United States citizen, and who acquired his United States citizenship solely by reason of his being a citizen of such possession or by reason of his birth or residence within such possession. The gift of such a person is, therefore, subject to the tax imposed by section 2501 in the same manner in which a gift is subject to the tax when made by a donor who is a "nonresident not a citizen of the United States." See paragraph (a) of § 25.01 and paragraph (c) of this section for further information relating to the application of the Federal gift tax to gifts made by persons who were residents of possessions of the United States. The application of this paragraph may be illustrated by the following examples and the example set forth in paragraph (c) of this section. In each of the following examples the person who makes the gift is deemed a "nonresident not a citizen of the United States" and his gift is subject to the tax imposed by section 2501 in the same manner in which a gift is subject to the tax when made by a donor who is a nonresident not a citizen of the United States, since he made the gift after September 14, 1960, but would not have been so deemed and subject to such tax if the person who made the gift had made it on or before September 14, 1960.

Example (1). C, who acquired his United States citizenship under section 5 of the Act of March 2, 1917 (39 Stat. 953), by reason of being a citizen of Puerto Rico, while domiciled in Puerto Rico makes a gift on October 1, 1960, of real estate located in New York. C is considered to have acquired his United States citizenship solely by reason of his being a citizen of Puerto Rico.

Example (2). E, whose parents were United States citizens by reason of their birth in Boston, was born in the Virgin Islands on March 1, 1927. On September 30, 1960, while domiciled in the Virgin Islands, he made a gift of tangible personal property situated in Kansas. B is considered to have acquired his United States citizenship solely by reason of his birth in the Virgin Islands (section 306 of the Immigration and Nationality Act (66 Stat. 237, 8 U.S.C. 1406)).

Example (3). N, who acquired United States citizenship by reason of being a native of the Virgin Islands and a resident thereof on June 28, 1932 (section 306 of the Immigration and Nationality Act (66 Stat. 237, 8 U.S.C. 1406)), made a gift on October 1, 1960, at which time he was domiciled in the Virgin Islands, of tangible personal property situated in Wisconsin. N is considered to have acquired his United States citizenship solely by reason of his birth or residence in the Virgin Islands.

Example (4). P, a former Danish citizen, who on January 17, 1917, resided in the Virgin Islands, made the declaration to preserve his Danish citizenship required by Article 6 of the treaty entered into on August 4, 1916, between the United States and Denmark. Subsequently P acquired United States citizenship when he renounced such declaration before a court of record (section 306 of the Immigration and Nationality Act (66 Stat. 237, 8 U.S.C. 1406)). P, while domiciled in the Virgin Islands, made a gift on October 1, 1960, of tangible personal property situated in California. P is considered to have acquired his United States citizenship solely by reason of his birth or residence in the Virgin Islands.

Example (5). R, a former French citizen, acquired his United States citizenship through naturalization proceedings in a court located in the Virgin Islands after having qualified for citizenship by residing in the Virgin Islands for 5 years. R, while domiciled in the Virgin Islands, made a gift of tangible personal property situated in Hawaii on October 1, 1960. R is considered to have acquired his United States citizenship solely by reason of his birth or residence within the Virgin Islands.

§ 25.2511-1 **Transfers in general.** (Paragraph (b) amended Jan. 19, 1961, to read as follows)

(b) In the case of a nonresident not a citizen who was not engaged in business in the United States (see § 25.2501-1) during the calendar year, the tax is imposed only if the gift consisted of real estate or tangible personal property situated within the United States at the time of transfer. See §§ 25.2501-1 and 25.2511-3.

§ 25.2511-3 **Transfers by nonresidents not citizens.** (Amended Jan. 19, 1961 to substitute "nonresident not a citizen of the United States" for "nonresident alien donor," wherever the latter appears in this regulation.)

§ 25.2512.1 **Valuation of property; in general.**

Section 2512 provides that if a gift is made in property, its value at the date of the gift shall be considered the amount of the gift. The value of the property is the price at which such property would change hands between a willing buyer and a willing seller, neither being under any compulsion to buy or to sell, and both having reasonable knowledge of relevant facts. The value of a particular kind of property is not the price that a forced sale of the property would produce. Nor is the fair market value of an item of property the sale price in a market other than that in which such item is most commonly sold to the public, taking into account the location of the item wherever appropriate. Thus, in the case of an item of property made the subject of a gift, which is generally obtained by the public in the retail market, the fair market value of such an item of property is the price at which the item or a comparable item would be sold at retail. For example, the value of an automobile (an article generally obtained by the public in the retail market) which is the subject of a gift, is the price for which an automobile of the same or approximately the same description, make, model, age, condition, etc., could be purchased by a member of the general public and not the price for which the particular automobile of the donor would be purchased by a dealer in used automobiles. Examples of items of property which are generally sold to the public at retail may be found in § 25.2512-6. The value is generally to be determined by ascertaining as a basis the fair market value at the time of the gift of each unit of the property. For example, in the case of shares of stocks or bonds, such unit of property is generally a share or a bond. Property shall not be returned at the value at which it is assessed for local tax purposes unless that value represents the fair market value thereof on the date of the gift. All relevant facts and elements of value as of the gift shall be considered. Where the subject of a gift is an interest in a business, the value of items of property in the inventory of the business generally should be reflected in the value of the business. For valuation of interests in businesses, see § 25.2512–3. See § 25.2512–2 and §§ 25.2512–4 through 25.2512–6 for further information concerning the valuation of other particular kinds of property. (Am June 14, 1965, TD 6826.)

§ 25.2512–6 Valuation of certain life insurance and annuity contracts. (Amended Jan. 19, 1961, by adding Example (5) at the end of the regulation)

Example (5). A donor purchases from a life insurance company for $15,198 a joint and survivor annuity contract which provides for the payment of $60 a month to the donor during his lifetime, and then to his sister for such time as she may survive him. The premium which would have been charged by the company for an annuity of $60 monthly payable during the life of the donor alone is $10,690. The value of the gift is $4,508 ($15,198 less $10,690).

(§ 25.2512–6 amended Oct 9, 1963 by designating it as paragraph (a), and by adding new paragraph (b) as follows)

"(b) *Valuation of shares in an open-end investment company.* (1) The fair market value of a share in an open-end investment company (commonly known as a 'mutual fund') is the public offering price of a share, adjusted for any reduction in price available to the public in acquiring the number of shares included in the particular gift. In the absence of an affirmative showing of the public offering price in effect at the time of the gift, the last public offering price quoted by the company for the date of the gift shall be presumed to be the applicable public offering price. If there is no public offering price quoted by the company for the date of the gift (e.g., the date of the gift is a Saturday, Sunday, or holiday), the fair market value of the mutual fund share is the last public offering price quoted by the company for the first day preceding the date of the gift for which there is a quotation, adjusted for any reduction in price available to the public in acquiring the number of shares included in the particular gift. As used in this paragraph, the term 'open-end investment company' includes only a company which on the date of the gift was engaged in offering its shares to the public in the capacity of an open-end investment company.

"(2) The provisions of this paragraph shall apply with respect to gifts made after October 10, 1963."

§ 25.2514–1 Transfers under power of appointment. (Paragraph (e) amended Dec. 11, 1961 to read as follows)

(e) *Time of creation of power.* A power of appointment created by will is, in general, considered as created on the date of the testator's death. However, section 2514(f) provides that a power of appointment created by a will executed on or before October 21, 1942, is considered a power created on or before that date if the testator dies before July 1, 1949, without having republished the will, by codicil or otherwise, after October 21, 1942. A power of appointment created by an inter vivos instrument is considered as created on the date the instrument takes effect. Such a power is not considered as created at some future date merely because it is not exercisable on the date the instrument takes effect, or because it is revocable, or because the identity of its holders is not ascertainable until after the date the instrument takes effect. However, if the holder of a power exercises it by creating a second power, the second power is considered as created at the time of the exercise of the first. The application of this paragraph may be illustrated by the following examples:

Example (1). A created a revocable trust before October 22, 1942, providing for payment of income to B for life with remainder as B shall appoint by deed or will. Even though A dies after October 21, 1942, without having exercised his power of revocation, B's power of appointment is considered a power created before October 22, 1942.

Example (2). C created an irrevocable inter vivos trust before October 22, 1942, naming T as trustee and providing for payment of income to D for life with remainder to E. T was given the power to pay corpus to D and the power to appoint a successor trustee. If T resigns after October 21, 1942, and appoints D as successor trustee, D is considered to have a power of appointment created before October 22, 1942.

Example (3). F created an irrevocable inter vivos trust before October 22, 1942, providing for payment of income to G for life with remainder as G shall appoint by deed or will, but in default of appointment income to H for life with remainder as H shall appoint by deed or will. If G died after October 21, 1942, without having exercised his power of appointment, H's power of appointment is considered a power created before October 22, 1942, even though it was only a contingent interest until G's death.

Example (4). If in example (3) above G had exercised by will his power of appointment, by creating a similar power in J, J's power of appointment would be considered a power created after October 21, 1942.

§ 25.2517–1 Employees' annuities. (Adopted Jan. 19, 1961)

(a) *In General.* (1) Section 2517 provides an exception to the general rule of section 2511 by exempting from gift tax all or part of the value of certain annuities or other payments for the benefit of employees' surviving beneficiaries. Under the general rule in section 2511, where an employee has an unqualified right to an annuity but takes a lesser annuity with the provision that upon his death a survivor annuity or other payment will be paid to his designated beneficiary, the employee has made a gift to the beneficiary at the time he gives up his power to deprive the beneficiary of the survivor annuity or other payment. See especially § 25.2511–1(h)(10). The making of such a gift by the employee may be accomplished in three principal ways:

(i) By irrevocably electing to take the reduced annuity and designating the individual who is to receive the survivor annuity or other payment. In this case the gift is made at the time the election and designation are irrevocably made.

(ii) By permitting a prior revocable election of a reduced annuity and designation of beneficiary to become irrevocable through failure to revoke during the period during which revocation could be made. In this case the gift is made at the time the prior election and designation become irrevocable.

(iii) By permitting an option to expire under which the employee could, by exercising the option, have defeated the beneficiary's interest in the survivor annuity or other payment, and thereby regain for himself the right

206

to a full annuity. In this case the gift is made at the time the employee permits the option to expire.

The value of the gift is the value, on the date of the gift, of the survivor annuity or other payment, computed in accordance with the principles set forth in §§ 25.2512–1, 25.2512–5, and 25.2512–6. It should be noted that such a gift is a gift of a future interest within the contemplation of § 25.2503–3 and no part thereof may be excluded in determining the total amount of gifts made during the calendar year.

(2) Section 2517 exempts from gift tax all or a portion of the value of the annuities or other payments described in subparagraph (1) of this paragraph which otherwise would be considered as gifts by employees to their beneficiaries. See paragraph (b) of this section for a complete description of the annuities and other payments to which the exemption applies. Also see paragraph (c) of this section for the portion of the annuity or other payment which is to be excluded in those cases where the annuity or other payment is attributable to payments or contributions made by both the employee and the employer. In the case of an annuity or other payment payable under an employees' trust or under a retirement annuity contract described in paragraph (b)(1)(i) or (ii) of this section, the exemption applies if the gift would otherwise be considered as having been made on or after January 1, 1955. In the case of an annuity or other payment payable under a retirement annuity contract described in paragraph (b)(1) (iii) of this section, the exclusion applies if the gift would otherwise be considered as having been made on or after January 1, 1958.

(b) *Annuities or other payments to which section 2517 applies.* (1) Except to the extent provided otherwise in paragraph (c) of this section, section 2517 exempts from transfers subject to the gift tax the value of an annuity or other payment which, upon the death of an employee, will become payable to the employee's beneficiary under:

(i) An employees' trust (or under a contract purchased by an employees' trust) forming part of a pension, stock bonus or profit-sharing plan which, at the time of such exercise or nonexercise, or at the time of termination of the plan if earlier, met the requirements of section 401(a);

(ii) A retirement annuity contract purchased by an employer (and not by an employees' trust) pursuant to a plan which, at the time of such exercise or non-exercise, or at the time of termination of the plan if earlier, was a plan described in section 403(a); or [am July 16, 1963]

(iii) A retirement annuity contract purchased for an employee by an employer which is an organization referred to in section 503(b)(1), (2), or (3), and which is exempt from tax under section 501(a).

(2) The term "annuity or other payment" as used in this section, has reference to one or more payments extending over any period of time. The payments may be equal or unequal, conditional or unconditional, periodic or sporadic. For purposes of this section, the term "employee" includes a former employee. The application of this paragraph may be illustrated by the following example:

Example. Pursuant to a pension plan, the employer made contributions to a trust which was to provide each employee, upon his retirement at age 60, with an annuity for life, and which contained a provision for designating either before or after retirement, a surviving beneficiary. No contributions under the plan were made by the employee. At the time of designating the surviving beneficiary (January 20, 1955), the pension trust formed part of a plan meeting the requirements of section 401(a). Assume that an employee made an irrevocable election whereby he would receive a lesser annuity, and after his death, annuity payments would be continued to his wife. Since the wife was designated annuitant under a qualified pension plan, no part of the value of such annuity is includible in the total amount of gifts for the calendar year by reason of the provisions of section 2517.

(c) *Amount excludable from gift.* (1) If an annuity or other payment described in paragraph (a)(1) of this section is attributable to payments or contributions made by both the employee and the employer, the exclusion is limited to that proportion of the value on the date of the gift (see paragraph (a)(1) of this section) of the annuity or other payment which the employer's contribution (or a contribution made on the employer's behalf) to the plan on the employee's account bears to the total contributions to the plan on the employee's account. In applying the ratio set forth in the preceding sentence, payments or contributions made by the employer toward the purchase of an annuity contract described in paragraph (b)(1)(iii) of this section are considered to be contributions made by the employee (and not by the employer) to the extent that such contributions are, or were, not excludable from the employee's gross income under section 403(b). For purposes of this ratio, payments or contributions made to a plan described in subdivision (i) or (ii) of paragraph (b)(1) of this section on behalf of an individual while he was an employee within the meaning of section 401(c)(1) with respect to such plan shall be considered to be payments or contributions made by the employee. The application of this paragraph may be illustrated by the following examples, none of which involves employees within the meaning of section 401(c)(1): [am July 16, 1963]

Example (1). Pursuant to a pension plan, contributions were made by employer and employee to a trust which was to provide the employee, upon his retirement at age 60, with an annuity for life, and which contained a provision for designating either before or after retirement, a surviving beneficiary upon the employee's death. Assume that the employee made an irrevocable election on January 20, 1955, whereby he would receive a lesser annuity and that after his death annuity payments would be continued to his wife. At the time of making the election, the pension trust formed part of a plan meeting the requirements of section 401(a); contributions to the plan on the employee's account amounted to $20,000 of which $15,000 was contributed by the employer and $5,000 was contributed by the employee; and the value of the survivor annuity was $8,000. Since the wife's annuity was receivable under a qualified pension plan, that part of the value of such

annuity which is attributable to the employer's contributions $\left[\dfrac{\$15,000}{\$20,000} \right]$

$\times$ $8,000 or $6,000 is excludable from gifts by reason of the provisions of section 2517(b).

Example (2). An employer purchased a retirement annuity contract for an employee which was to provide the employee, upon his retirement at age 60, with an annuity for life and which in accordance with the employee's irrevocable election, under which he agreed to accept reduced annuity payments, provided that annuity payments would be continued to his wife after his death. At the time of making the election (January 20, 1955), the plan under which the retirement annuity contract was purchased met the requirements of section 401(a)(3), (4), (5), and (6). The retirement annuity contract was purchased from a life insurance company at a cost of $15,198 of which $3,039.60 was contributed by the employee. The premium which would have been charged by the life insurance company for the reduced retirement annuity payments for the life of the employee alone is $10,690. The value, at the time of the election, of the survivor annuity which will become payable to the wife if she survives the employee is $4,508 ($15,198—$10.690). Of such amount, only $901.60 is includible in the employee's gifts, computed as follows:

$$\frac{\$3,039.60 \text{ (employee's contribution)}}{\$15,198.00 \text{ (total contribution)}} \times \$4,508 = \$901.60.$$

Example (3). An employer purchased a retirement annuity contract for an employee which was to provide the employee, upon his retirement at age 60, with an annuity for life and which contained a provision for designating a surviving beneficiary. Assume that the employee made an irrevocable election whereby he would receive a lesser annuity, and after his death, annuity payments would be continued to his wife. At the time of making the election (January 20, 1959), the employer was an organization referred to in section 503(b)(1), (2), or (3) and exempt from tax under section 501 (a). As of the date of the election the total contributions toward the cost of the annuity, all by the employer, amounted to $25,000. Of this amount $5,000 was includible in the employee's income under the requirements of section 403(b) and is, therefore, considered as the employee's contributions for the purpose of applying section 2517(b).

(2) In certain cases, the employer's contribution (or a contribution made on his behalf) to a plan on the employee's account and thus the total contributions to the plan on the employee's account cannot be readily ascertained. In order to apply the ratio stated in subparagraph (1) of this paragraph in such a case, the method outlined in the following two sentences must be used unless a more precise method is presented. In such a case, the total contributions to the plan on the employee's account is the value of the annuities or other payments payable to the employee and his beneficiary computed in accordance with the rules set forth in § 25.2512-5. By subtracting from such value the amount of the employee's contribution to the plan, the amount of the employer's contribution to the plan on the employee's account may be obtained. The application of this subparagraph may be illustrated by the following example:

Example. Pursuant to a pension plan, the employer and the employee contributed to a trust which was to provide the employee, upon his retirement at age 60, with an annuity for life, and which contained a provision for designating either before or after retirement, a surviving beneficiary to receive an annuity upon the employee's death. At the time of the employee's retirement on January 20, 1955, he made an irrevocable election designating his wife as beneficiary. Also, at that time, the pension trust formed part of a plan meeting the requirements of section 401(a). Assume the following: (i) That the employer's contributions to the fund were not credited to the accounts of individual employees; (ii) that the value of the employee's annuity and his wife's annuity, computed as of the time of the employee's retirement, was $40,000; (iii) that the employee contributed $10,000 to the plan; and (iv) that the value at the time of the employee's retirement of the wife's annuity was $16,000. On the basis of these facts, the total contributions to the fund on the employee's account are presumed to be $40,000 and the employer's contribution to the plan on the employee's account is presumed to be $30,000 ($40,000 less $10,000). Since the election and the wife's annuity were provided for under a qualified pension plan, that part of the value of such annuity which is attributable to the employer's con-

$$\text{tributions} \left[\frac{\$30,000}{\$40,000} \times \$16,000, \text{ or } \$12,000 \right] \text{ is excludable in determining}$$

the total amount of gifts for the calendar year by reason of the provisions of section 2517. Since the wife's right to a deferred annuity is a gift of a future interest the $3,000 exclusion provided in section 2503 is not allowable.

§ 25.2523(e)–1 **Marital deduction; life estate with power of appointment in donee spouse.** (Paragraph (1)(f)(4) amended Jan. 19, 1961, to substitute word "disqualify" for "qualify" in last sentence, in next to last line of subparagraph (4) on page 1117)

§ 25.6061–1 **Signing of returns and other documents.** (Adopted May 28, 1962)

Any return, statement, or other document required to be made under any provision of chapter 12 or subtitle F of the Code or regulations prescribed thereunder with respect to any tax imposed by chapter 12 of the Code shall be signed by the donor or other person required or duly authorized to sign in accordance with the regulations, forms or instructions prescribed with respect to such return, statement, or other document. The person required or duly authorized to make the return may incur liability for the penalties provided for erroneous, false, or fraudulent returns. For criminal penalties see sections 7201, 7203, 7206, 7207, and 7269.

§ 25.6065–1 **Verification of returns.** (Adopted May 28, 1962)

(a) *Penalties of perjury.* If a return, statement, or other document made under the provisions of chapter 12 or subtitle F of the Code or the regulations thereunder with respect to any tax imposed by chapter 12 of the Code, or the form and instructions issued with respect to such return, statement, or other document, requires that it shall contain or be verified by a written declaration that it is made under the penalties of perjury, it must be so verified by the person or persons required to sign such return, statement, or other document. In addition, any other statement or document submitted under any provision of chapter 12 or subtitle F of the Code or regulations thereunder with respect to any tax imposed by chapter 12 of the Code may be required to contain or be verified by a written declaration that it is made under the penalties of perjury.

(b) *Oath.* Any return, statement, or other document required to be submitted under chapter 12 or subtitle F of the Code or regulations prescribed thereunder with respect to any tax imposed by chapter 12 of the Code may be required to be verified by an oath.

§ 25.6091-2 **Exceptional cases.** (Adopted May 28, 1962)

Notwithstanding the provisions of § 25.6091-1 the Commissioner may permit the filing of the gift tax return required by section 6019 in any internal revenue district.

§ 25.6165-1 **Bonds where time to pay tax or deficiency has been extended.** (Amended May 28, 1962, as follows)

If an extension of time for payment of tax or deficiency is granted under section 6161, the district director may, if he deems it necessary, require a bond for the payment of the amount in respect of which the extension is granted in accordance with the terms of the extension. However, such bond shall not exceed double the amount with respect to which the extension is granted. For provisions relating to form of bonds, see the regulations under section 7101 contained in Part 301 of this chapter (Regulations on Procedure and Administration).

§ 25.7101-1 **Form of bonds.** (Amended May 28, 1962, as follows)

For provisions relating to form of bonds, see the regulations under section 7101 contained in Part 301 of this chapter (Regulations on Procedure and Administration).

INDEX TO FORMS

(Numbers refer to sections)

*

INDEX

(References are to sections)